THE
CROSSING

THE
CROSSING

SIR VIVIEN FUCHS, SIR EDMUND HILLARY AND THE TRANS-ANTARCTIC EXPEDITION 1955–58

JOHN KNIGHT

AMBERLEY

Front of jacket: Sno-cat A for Able about to be rescued from a perilous position above a deep crevasse. The driver was David Pratt and such incidents would be repeated on the journey. David told the author he remembered extricating Sno-cat Able half a dozen times from such situations. No doubt his experience in charge of a tank on Juno Beach, 6 June 1944, stood him in good stead.

First published 2018

Amberley Publishing
The Hill, Stroud
Gloucestershire, GL5 4EP

www.amberley-books.com

British Library Cataloguing in Publication Data.
A catalogue record for this book is available from the British Library.

ISBN 978 1 4456 8629 5 (hardback)
ISBN 978 1 4456 8630 1 (ebook)

Typesetting and Origination by Amberley Publishing.
Printed in the UK.

Contents

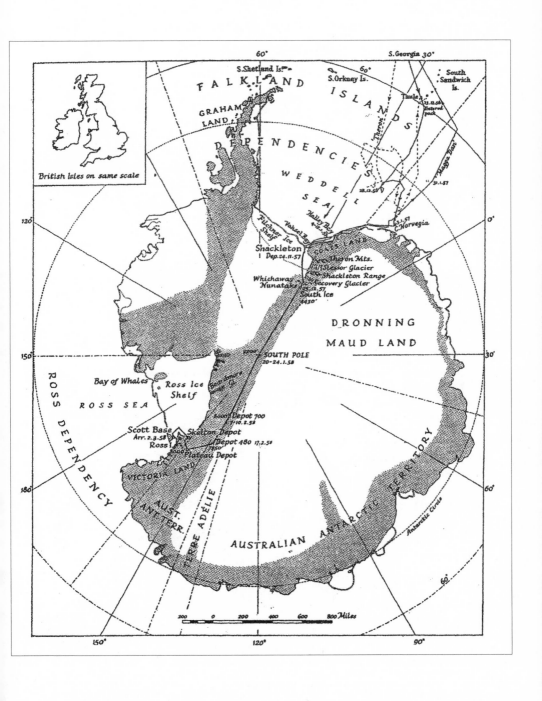

British Isles on same scale

S. Shetland Is.
FALKLAND
GRAHAM
LAND
S. Georgia 30°
S. Orkney Is.
South Sandwich Is.
Thule
13.12.56
Entered pack
ISLANDS
DEPENDENCIES
Theron
Magga Dan
31.1.57
WEDDELL
SEA
28.12.55
C. Norvegia
5.1.57
COATS LAND
Vahsel Bay
8.1.56
Halley Bay
Filchner Ice Shelf
Shackleton
1 Dep. 24.11.57
Theron Mts.
Slessor Glacier
Shackleton Range
Recovery Glacier
25.12.57
South Ice
4430'
DRONNING
MAUD LAND
Whichaway Nunataks
120°
0°
Bay of Whales
Ross Ice Shelf
ROSS SEA
ROSS DEPENDENCY
1200
SOUTH POLE
20-24.1.58
30°
150°
8600 Depot 700
1.10.2.58
Skelton Depot
Depot 480 17.2.58
7850'
9000 Plateau Depot
Scott Base
Arr. 2.3.58
Ross I.
VICTORIA LAND
AUST.
ANT.TERR.
TERRE ADÉLIE
AUSTRALIAN ANTARCTIC TERRITORY
60°
Antarctic Circle
60°
180°
150°
120°
90°

200   0   200   400   600   800 Miles

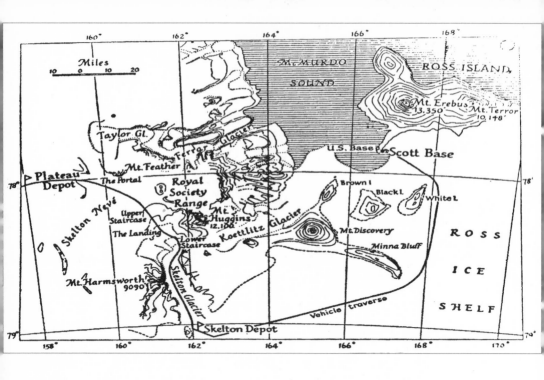

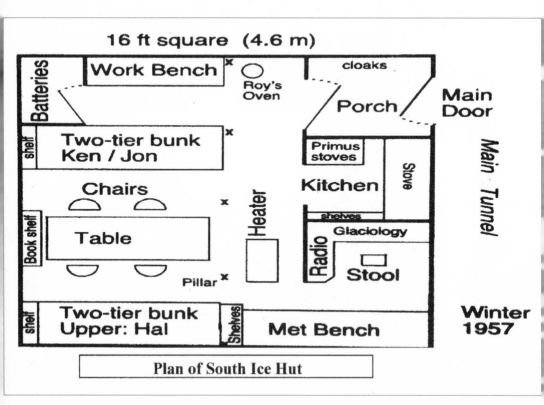

16 ft square (4.6 m)

| Batteries | Work Bench | x | Roy's Oven | cloaks | | Main Door |

Plan of South Ice Hut

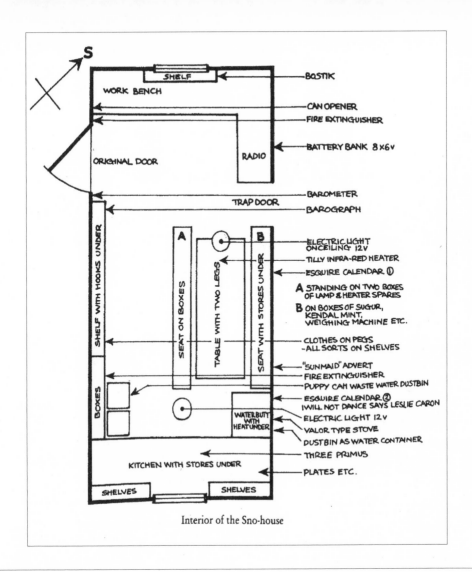

S

SHELF

WORK BENCH

ORIGINAL DOOR

RADIO

TRAP DOOR

SHELF WITH HOOKS UNDER

A

B

TABLE WITH TWO LEGS

SEAT ON BOXES

SEAT WITH STORES UNDER

BOXES

WATERBUTT WITH HEAT UNDER

KITCHEN WITH STORES UNDER

SHELVES

SHELVES

BOSTIK

CAN OPENER

FIRE EXTINGUISHER

BATTERY BANK 8 x 6v

BAROMETER

BAROGRAPH

ELECTRIC LIGHT ON CEILING 12V

TILLY INFRA-RED HEATER

ESQUIRE CALENDAR ①

A STANDING ON TWO BOXES OF LAMP & HEATER SPARES

B ON BOXES OF SUGAR, KENDAL MINT, WEIGHING MACHINE ETC.

CLOTHES ON PEGS – ALL SORTS ON SHELVES

"SUNMAID" ADVERT

FIRE EXTINGUISHER

PUPPY CAN WASTE WATER DUSTBIN

ESQUIRE CALENDAR ②
I WILL NOT DANCE SAYS LESLIE CARON

ELECTRIC LIGHT 12V

VALOR TYPE STOVE

DUSTBIN AS WATER CONTAINER

THREE PRIMUS

PLATES ETC.

Interior of the Sno-house

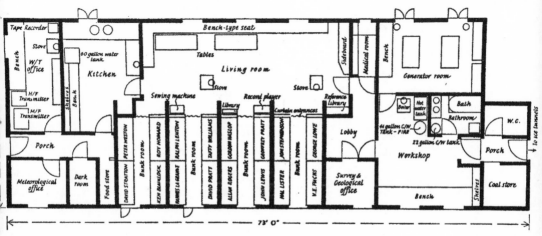

SHACKLETON BASE HUT PLAN

TAE Personnel

UK Party

Fuchs, Dr Vivian 'Bunny'	Expedition Leader
Stratton, David G	Deputy leader, main party and surveyor
Blaiklock, Ken V	Advance party leader and surveyor
Goldsmith, Dr Rainer	Medical officer, advance party only
Homard, Major David E L	Engineer, advance party
Jeffries, Peter H	Meteorologist, advance party only
La Grange, J J Hannes	Meteorologist, advance party
Lenton, Ralph A	Deputy leader, radio operator, advance party
Stewart, R H A Tony	Meteorologist, advance party only
Williams, Sergeant E, 'Taffy'	Radio operator, advance party
Lewis, Sq Leader John H	Senior pilot
Haslop, Fl Lt Gordon M	Second pilot
Weston, Fl Sgt Peter	Aircraft mechanic
Lister, Dr Hal	Glaciologist
Lowe, George	Photographer
Pratt, David L	Engineer
Pratt, J George D	Geophysicist
Rogers, Dr Allan F	Medical officer
Stephenson, Dr P Jon	Geologist
Williams, Derek	BP photographer

New Zealand Party

Hillary, Sir Edmund	Leader
Miller, J H (Bob)	Deputy leader and surveyor, Beardmore Glacier
Ayres, Harry H	Mountaineer, Darwin Glacier
Brooke, Lt Com F Richard	Surveyor, climbed Mt Huggins
Carlyon, Roy A	Surveyor, Darwin Glacier
Claydon, Sq Leader John R	Senior pilot
Cranfield, Fly Officer W J (Bill)	Second pilot
Tarr, Sgt L Wally	Aircraft mechanic
Gawn, J E (Ted)	Radio operator and temporary driver
Mulgrew, Peter D	Radio operator, tractor driver
Sandford, H Neil	Radio mechanic
Balham, Dr Ron W	Meteorologist and biologist
Bates, Jim G	Mechanic, tractor driver
Ellis, Murray R	Engineer, tractor driver
Mckenzie, Douglas	Official journalist
Wright, Derek	Cameraman and stand-in driver
Douglas, Murray H	Mechanic
Marsh, Dr George W	Medical officer, Beardmore Glacier
Hatherton, Dr Trevor	Geophysicist
Gerard, V B	Geophysicist
Gunn, Bernie M	Geologist, Climbed Mt Huggins
Warren, Guyon	Geologist, Northern Journey
Smith, Lt Commander W	Hydrographer, advance party
Bucknell, E Selwyn	Cook
Macdonald, W J P	Technician
Orr, R H	Technician
Tate, Pete	At fuel depot on ice shelf and aircraft mechanic
Breese, Taffy	At fuel depot on ice shelf

Acknowledgements

Garnering information relevant to the writing of a book is one of the most difficult and time-consuming operations to carry out. It is crucial to a book that is full of facts about an historical event that the data contained in it is as correct as can be. The starting point for me lay in the fortunate circumstance that I already had a substantial collection of books on polar exploration. Included amongst them were quite a number that related directly to the Commonwealth Trans-Antarctic Expedition that I proposed to write about.

The participants themselves contributed to the pool of knowledge that I was able to tap into, as did the works of some who had access to the contemporary records of the time such as diaries and notebooks kept by the expedition members. It transpired, as my investigations began, that several august institutions also held relevant material in their archives. Most of this had been donated by the explorers or their descendants for safekeeping and generally speaking was available to the public. I will come back to these organisations a little later in this section.

Initially I turned to the internet as a search tool and it led me to a number of the people with the closest links to expedition members. Foremost among them was Mary Lowe, closely followed by Peter and Sarah Hillary. Others were to emerge as I sought out the copyright holders of a number of photographs not held by Mary Lowe or Sir Edmund Hillary's son and daughter.

Acknowledgements

Mary Lowe's husband was the celebrated official photographer of the expedition. His collection of superb photographs now resides at the Royal Geographical Society in London. It is a selection of these that forms the core of my illustrations and a very big thank you goes to Mary Lowe for her most generous gesture of allowing me to make use of the collection without a copyright fee. Her generosity did not stop there; she invited me and my wife to her home to see other memorabilia that her late husband had collected in his travels across the world, including to Mount Everest, and then she lent me a number of items that I have been allowed to include in this book. From my first contact with her, she has kept an eye on the book's progress and generously given of her time in reading a draft copy of it and suitably correcting a number of mistakes before they were committed to print.

Peter Hillary and his sister Sarah have, between them, granted me the free use of some of their late father's excellent photographs, which were taken during his time spent in the Antarctic leading the New Zealand party from the Ross Sea all the way to the South Pole; these photographs are kept in the safe custody of the War Memorial Museum in Auckland. They too provided me with unstinting help in reproducing the selection I made for inclusion in this book at no extra cost; both gestures were much appreciated. So many thanks to Zoe Richardson and Shaun Higgins.

I was able to contact Dr David Pratt. He was in charge of the mechanised side of the crossing party, and conversations with him were most interesting, but sadly came too late for inclusion in the book.

Others who gave their kind assent to me using photographs were Dr Rainer Goldsmith, the expedition doctor, and Mrs Helen Lenton, whose late husband participated in the three years the expedition lasted as radio operator. The family of Hannes la Grange were contacted by Ria Olivia of the Antarctic Legacy of South Africa. Hannes also took part in the three-year exploit as the senior meteorologist. Then from Australia came permission by Sara Bucher to use two photos taken by her father Jon Stephenson, the youngest member of the expedition as a newly qualified geologist.

For failing to trace the whereabouts of anybody related to the late Dr Allen Rogers I should apologise here.

I mentioned the RGS as the repository for George Lowe's photographs, and, following a series of emails to that organisation, I spent three days in London and scanned through the 8,000 slides of which the collection comprises. My thanks are now due to Joy Wheeler for her diligence and patience in providing me with the reading room facilities to enable me to make my selection. Her services were again in demand as I selected the photos that would eventually find their way into my book when she kindly scanned and sent me proof copies of the original batch. These in due course were sent to my publisher in a suitable format for insertion into the book. In the days that I attended the RGS all the staff I had dealings with were most polite and helpful, answering my endless questions.

I have to admit that the task of tracing documentation relevant to the writing of this book could have been further protracted if I had followed up all the leads that I discovered. Travelling to the various sites in Cambridge, London and elsewhere was never an option for me so I resorted to email or telephone enquiries, and to the following organisations may I say a collective thank you for the help given: the Scott Polar Research Institute and the British Antarctic Survey, both in Cambridge, and the Royal Naval College at Greenwich all hold material about the expedition and contributed in various ways to the book's compilation. Thank you for that assistance.

Moving on, an old friend of mine, Derek Mathews, has always encouraged me to keep going when there was a tendency to falter. He has written a number of books on such diverse subjects as Tommy Steel and the hangman of Great Britain in late Victorian times, William Marwood. Derek motivated me to keep at it.

I have, of necessity, used a few quotations from other books where my own words were inadequate. These have included a book published by Erskin Press called *Eight Men in a Crate* written by Anthea Arnold; a small extract from John Behrendt's book *Innocents on the Ice*; and a similar small extract from Reinhold Messner's *Antarctica*; these provided background information that was relevant to the sections where they were used. I am very grateful for their use.

One of the greatest hurdles to overcome for a new author is that of securing a publisher. So many of them require an intermediary such as an agent and so few agents respond to an enquiry. Amberley Publishing have proved the exception. Their response was immediate and positive. They wasted very little time between my submission and agreeing to the publication of my book. They have extended their help to me on numerous occasions when, as a new author, I have floundered through the process of bringing a book to its conclusion. All the members of the publishing team I have dealt with have been extremely helpful and here I need to mention a few of them: Alex Bennett, Jonathan Jackson, Shaun Barrington, Cathy Stagg and Nikki Embery, in particular, have been very considerate of my needs. I just hope all their efforts have not been in vain.

Copyright is a subject that can lead to invisible pitfalls and I would beg of any person who feels that I have stepped beyond the limits to accept my very sincere apologies. No offence was intended and I have tried to give credit where it was due for any inclusions I have made.

My gratitude must also extend to others who have made this book possible and who I have accidentally missed out.

Most importantly, my wife Cas has been very tolerant of the hours I have spent putting this book together.

By the time you have read this section of the book you should be aware of the effort others have made into getting this volume off the press and I trust you will enjoy the read. I hope it will inspire you to look at the bibliography and search out further books about the expedition, ones that will exceed my effort in bringing before you the magnificent accomplishment that was achieved in 1958 when the Commonwealth Trans-Antarctic Expedition was brought to a successful conclusion.

Early International Co-operation

The Commonwealth Trans-Antarctic Expedition (TAE) of 1955 to 1958 took place against the backdrop of the worldwide International Geophysical Years (IGY), scheduled to take place in 1957/8. The TAE was a huge success for Great Britain and her Commonwealth partners and the IGY exceeded all expectations for the participating countries, producing a huge amount of data that took many years to collate and disseminate. The IGY proved that even potentially mutually inimical countries could co-operate in the interests of science. The IGY had been planned for some time to bring together scientists from around the globe to collaborate in discovering more about the complex relationship between the Earth and its weather systems and magnetic field, and how the sun influenced our environment. Bases were set up in various locations across the continents to simultaneously monitor any magnetic, solar, seismic or other effects that could be detected by the scientific instruments and by observations taken by the scientists at the bases involved.

In the Antarctic alone there was a proposed list of 44 sites where 12 countries would set up experimental stations to carry out the research envisaged. Across the world as many as 4,000 other sites were to be manned by many thousands of scientists and other technologists trained in various fields of science and research. The participating states that set up bases in Antarctica were Argentina, Australia, Belgium, Chile, France, Great Britain,

Japan, New Zealand, Russia and the USA. Russia and the USA had several bases. The Americans were stationed at the South Pole itself while Russia chose the Magnetic Pole and the Pole of Inaccessibility, the point furthest from the ocean in any direction, for two of their stations. Both countries had several other bases distributed across the continent. The United Kingdom had chosen the Weddell Sea as the site for its IGY base at a point on the Filchner Ice Shelf that was called Halley Bay. The British Antarctic Survey (BAS) later established one of their bases there, in 1983. The BAS was the organisation that succeeded the Falkland Island Dependency Survey (FIDS) in running all British bases in Antarctica. The Royal Society (RS) set up and ran the British research station at Halley Bay that was part of this country's contribution to IGY.

The Commonwealth Trans-Antarctic Expedition was the brainchild of Dr Vivian Fuchs, taking shape from as far back as a Falkland Island Dependency expedition he undertook to the Graham Land Peninsula in 1949/50. Dr Fuchs hoped to base the activities of the TAE in the Weddell Sea close to the Filchner Ice Shelf. The two expeditions were to run concurrently but as separate entities and from their own bases. Their organisations were completely independent of one another and apart from some sharing of personnel and logistical support they would remain that way throughout the entire period of their existence.

The years of 1957 and 1958 were chosen mainly because it was predicted that solar activity would be at a peak. The co-ordinated study of subjects such as solar eclipses, sun spot activity, aurora displays and magnetic storms would help in identifying why these phenomena affected radio communications, which had become such an important issue. Specific days were earmarked throughout this 18-month period so that a concentrated effort could be used to synchronise the observations and measurements from all over the world. But this international effort was not new.

As long ago as 1875 an Austrian naval lieutenant called Carl Weyprecht had garnered support for the first such international effort following his own Arctic Expedition in 1872. He had sailed north in the *Tegetthof* on an Austro-Hungarian expedition led by himself and Julius Payer. They were searching for a route across northern Russia, which came to be known as the North East Passage, to reach the Bering Strait from the Barents Sea. The ice closed in on their ship and they drifted, held in its clutches for nearly 11 months. In the course of the drift they did discover new land, which they named, after the Austro-Hungarian Emperor, Franz Josef Land. The expedition ship remained trapped in the ice and the men had to resort to the ship's boats to save themselves. Weyprecht left a record of the expedition that was found 100 years later by an exploring party from the USSR, which now administers Franz Joseph Land. On their return Weyprecht found that any results they had obtained were soon discarded by other explorers as each separate expedition sought to seek out its own path to glory and possible riches.

Although Weyprecht did not live to see the fruits of his labours, he campaigned for several years to bring organisations and societies together so that a unified effort could be put into action to harness all the exploration that was going on and to draw together results for all to benefit. His early efforts did finally result in the first International Polar Year, 1882–83. Weyprecht had contracted tuberculosis and he died in 1881 and his companion Julius Payer had resigned from the Navy to take up painting. The baton for organising the final details fell to a close associate of Weyprecht called Georg von Neumayer.

The first Polar Year took at least three conferences to finally formulate but by 1882 Austria combined with Hungary, the Scandinavian countries and Holland and Russia were amongst the first to sign up and they were followed by Great Britain co-operating with Canada, the USA and Germany.

Fort Rae on the shores of the Great Slave Lake in Canada was the chosen site for the Anglo-Canadian effort. Although no Canadians actually participated in the scientific studies that took place they helped with the organisation of the survey, Hudson's Bay Company employees assisting with the transportation of the four British soldiers and their equipment that formed the scientific party. The

HBC post at Fort Rae was chosen as the nearest Company depot to the Magnetic North Pole, and as the Earth's magnetic field was a major part of the research taking place it made sense to establish a site in its vicinity.

The four soldiers that made up the scientific unit were led by an officer called Henry Dawson. He and his three subordinates were all drawn from the Royal Artillery and were chosen by a leading scientist of the day, Sir Edward Sabine. He had been a senior officer in the Royal Artillery and was closely associated with experiments to do with magnetism and the behaviour of a pendulum at various experimental stations along the way. The soldiers made their way to Toronto where they visited the Observatory and then moved on to the route along the extensive network of rivers and lakes that had been used by fur traders. Having left Liverpool in May of 1882 they finally arrived on the shores of the Great Slave Lake in September of the same year. They were looked after by the staff at Fort Rae and given all the help they needed to set up their instruments and convert an existing cabin into a suitable building in which to conduct their magnetic observations. Their records were subsequently sent to the Observatory at Kew in London to be analysed. Twelve countries took part with a total of 14 stations manned over 12 months from September 1882.

There were two stations set up on the islands north of Canada for this first year of scientific observations. (Canada at this juncture in history had not laid claim to any of the islands that lay to the north of her mainland.) Baffin Island was chosen by the Germans for their contribution. For all the wrong reasons, probably the most notable of these efforts was the American station at Lady Franklin Bay located at the northern end of Ellesmere Island. The leader of this expedition was Lieutenant Adolphus Greely. Towards the end of the second summer, the first and second relief ships had still not arrived so Greely decided they could not wait any longer for a relief ship to take them home and the 25 men set off south down the Ellesmere Island coast in a small steam launch, for which they only had a limited amount of coal, and two ships' whaling boats, to try and reach depots that were supposed to have been laid in the event of the relief ships failing to get through. Apart from a few supplies left along the way, they failed to locate any substantial depots and when they reached Cape Sabine they realised that they would have to overwinter. It was only a matter of time before the weakest began to succumb, and when rescuers finally found them the following year, there were only seven men left alive – and one of these died on the rescue ship. Later reports stated that evidence of cannibalism was found. Such was the dire situation in which they found themselves, one of the last to die was on Greely's orders because he had constantly stolen from the meagre supplies they had and was becoming a danger to the few who were still alive. He was taken out and shot and the men who carried this out had a pact that none of them would ever say which of them actually killed the offender.

Although the scheme was counted a significant breakthrough in international co-operation between rival countries, it was to be another 50 years before they could muster up the willpower to do so again. It was 1932 before such an endeavour would again see that level of co-operation between countries.

With the advent of telegraphic and radio transmissions in the aftermath of the First World War it soon became evident that there were natural forces at work in the world that could seriously disrupt transmissions at times. Further international research would be required to study the effects of the earth's magnetic field as scientists demonstrated more and more that this was the reason for the problems experienced. As 1932 was the 50th anniversary of the first Polar Year it became the date for the Second International Polar Year. The number of participating countries more than trebled. This time the emphasis would be on worldwide coverage to record, in particular, magnetic influences, sun activity and aurora displays.

With the stations spread all over the globe the undertaking was going to be on a scale as yet unseen. Tides, currents and sea temperatures would be monitored, as would air pressures, rainfall and air temperatures. Seismic and other earth movements were to be measured. In addition to magnetic and meteorological studies, the higher layers of the Earth's atmosphere were also going to be studied for magnetic fields or any electrical disturbances that could be detected across the world on specified dates and times to create a global picture. Many of these measurements could not have been carried out in the 1882 Polar Year because the scientific instruments were either too basic or did not exist at all.

Sad to say, a lot of the information would be lost in archives with the advent of the Second World War, as countries that had genuinely sought to unite in a common cause suddenly found themselves on opposite sides of the conflict.

Operation Tabarin and
Its Aftermath

Under the code name of Operation Tabarin, bases were established in during the Second World War as part of a strategy by Great Britain to thwart any enemy force from creating supply depots in the far south for servicing warships or submarines that could interfere with Allied shipping that was taking much-needed war material to armed forces in the Far East via Cape Horn.

The numerous islands lying midway between the mainland of Antarctica and South Africa and Australia, such as Crozet, Kerguelen and the South Orkneys, were all potential hiding places for enemy raiders and consequently a search was carried out in 1939 by the Royal Navy to see if any covert activity had been instigated. No evidence was found.

When hostilities began in 1939 the German High Command was aware of the potential for establishing a base somewhere in the Antarctic, and early in 1940 the German Navy began operating a warship called the *Pinguin* in the vicinity of Kerguelen Island. They did this very successfully for nearly a year. Between July 1940 and May 1941 the *Pinguin* sank a dozen merchant ships belonging to Great Britain and captured the Norwegian whaling fleet, until she was finally sunk in an action with HMS *Cornwall*, a British cruiser. No further enemy activity was reported in the area following this engagement.

Although the Royal Navy was eventually successful in eliminating the immediate threat, the possibility always existed that the

Germans or even the Japanese might again try to sabotage supply lines, even to the extent of gaining a base by invading the Falkland Islands.

In 1942 Britain was being gradually strangled by the U-boat threat to the Atlantic convoy route, and this brought the Antarctic once more into the spotlight. Should this also become threatened by enemy action, Britain would be hard pushed to recapture the likes of the Falklands or even have a base of her own from which to fight.

With the elimination of the Norwegian whaling fleet the by-products of the whale were at a premium as part of the British food supply and for various industrial applications. It was therefore paramount that Britain kept a military presence in the Antarctic waters to safeguard this industry.

Another variant in the equation was the possibility of neutral Argentina persisting in her claim to the same portion of Antarctica as Britain. The last thing Britain wanted was to have to come into conflict with another country over an issue that would drain her resources unnecessarily.

It took until the middle of 1943 to begin gathering a group of men from the various services to be brought together ready to be despatched to the far south. Like all exploring parties run by a government agency, a committee had to be formed to oversee the setting up and eventual running of the enterprise. Luckily, three prominent members of this committee were chosen for their intimate knowledge of all things polar. James Wordie, Brian Roberts and Neil Mackintosh became involved. James Wordie was of course a Shackleton man, Brian Roberts had been with John Rymill back in 1934 as an ornithologist and Neil Mackintosh had cut his Antarctic teeth as a prominent member of the *Discovery II* investigations connected with the whaling industry in Antarctic waters.

The main brief of the party that was to go south was of course to report any signs of enemy activity, but under no circumstances were they to engage the foe. Indeed, they were not armed for any sort of conflict but were merely there as observers. However, if there was to be a presence in the area, and if the men who had been sent down were suitably qualified in fields related to exploration, then why not use their knowledge to carry out some scientific work at the same time?

The team leader chosen was known to all the three polar men on the committee. He had accompanied Sir Ernest Shackleton on the Quest Expedition as a Boy Scout and went on to qualify as a zoologist before also becoming employed on the marine and whaling studies of the *Discovery* investigations. At this juncture he was a lieutenant in the RNVR. His name was James Marr. His initial role was to recruit suitable men to serve on the expedition and finally lead them into 'action'. A total of fourteen men were selected and plans were put in operation to sail down to Deception Island in the South Shetland group via the Falklands to establish what became known as Base B.

Once the group was assembled and the stores gathered together, loading could commence and they could get ready to embark. Renamed the *Bransfield* after an earlier explorer in the Antarctic, their ship started life as a Norwegian sealer named *Veslekari*. Built at the end of the First World War, she had seen extensive service in Arctic waters and with her hull strengthened for ice work she was thought to be suitable for the task ahead. As the loading progressed it became apparent that her holds would not be large enough to take all the material assembled on the quayside. Marr had to find another vessel going in the same direction that could take the surplus equipment. Finally the problem resolved itself with spare capacity being found on a merchant vessel voyaging as far as Montevideo in South America.

Setting sail in the middle of November 1943, it was not long before the *Bransfield*'s pumps were in action, and problems continued so that by the time she made Falmouth the decision was made that she was not safe enough to continue on her way. Meanwhile, another ship was being readied for sailing to the Falkland Islands, with troops being sent down to bolster the island's defence force, and she had spare capacity that could accommodate the expedition. The only snag was that this alternative transport was moored on the other side of the Cornish Peninsula at Avonmouth. The mammoth job of getting all the stores back out of the *Bransfield* and transported over to the *Highland Monarch*, waiting in the

Severn Estuary, took several weeks and it was not until the middle of December that they finally sailed south.

At Port Stanley in the Falklands another transfer of the expedition stores and equipment had to take place. This time two much smaller ships were involved. The *Scoresby* and the *Fitzroy* were readied to take the expedition further down into Antarctic waters. They reached Deception Island in the South Shetland Group and once inside the natural harbour, formed by the flooded caldera of an almost extinct volcano, a sight of absolute desolation revealed itself. The rusting remains of a lost working environment – the old jetties, corrugated iron sheds and redundant, miscellaneous pieces of machinery – were littered all along the shoreline together with the grotesque skeletal remains of countless dead whales. It was obvious that there were no alien forces present, and apart from evidence of the Argentines' attendance at some stage in the past, all was quiet. Five men would remain here while the remainder were transported further down towards the Antarctic Peninsula itself. Their ultimate destination was to be Hope Bay, situated at the extreme northern end of the peninsula.

The approach to Hope Bay was littered with brash ice so, leaving the weaker *Fitzroy* behind, the *Scoresby* forced her way through the ice and nosed into Hope Bay. James Marr could see the possibilities of this site and realised that most of the advice he had been given before the expedition's departure from Great Britain now made sense. The beach area would enable the ships to discharge their cargo safely, and at a distance Marr could see that access to the hinterland would not present too many problems to enable them to man-haul their sledges further afield for exploratory work.

On regaining the *Scoresby*, the ship made ready to rejoin the *Fitzroy* to plan the landing. This turned out to be a false hope as both the *Fitzroy*'s captain, Keith Pitt, and the Falkland Islands' representative Captain David Roberts stressed the peril of the *Fitzroy* entering any area where the ice might impinge on her hull and cause irreparable damage.

To Marr's despair, they sailed away from Hope Bay to seek another site further south. Eventually they sighted a suitable bay. Port Lockroy on Wiencke Island in the De Gerlache Strait gave them a chance of establishing a base for the coming winter, and soon all was hustle and bustle to unload the two ships and get the hut built, plus the myriad of other jobs requiring attention before winter drew her frozen hand across their activities.

This site was to be called Base A. Being on an island, it would preclude any exploring to be done on the mainland due to the fact that the strait between them and the Graham Land Peninsula was known to be ice-free most of the winter. This was a bitter pill for James Marr to swallow, and ultimately the strain caused by this change of plan would get the better of him and result in his eventual early retirement from the expedition. Ironically, the next season's plans were put in place to add to the number of stations to be manned, and Hope Bay was included. To facilitate this, the organising committee in the UK managed to secure the services of an ice-strengthened sealer from Newfoundland called the *Eagle* and it was hoped she would be able to cope with the adverse conditions in Hope Bay that had rebuffed the *Fitzroy* the previous year. Hope Bay was given the designation of the letter 'D'. Deception Island and Port Lockroy would continue to be maintained.

Tragedy nearly caused the loss of the *Eagle* whilst anchored in Hope Bay. A gale-force wind blew with such intensity that both anchor chains were snapped and she was driven by the force of the gale into the path of a huge iceberg that had floated into the bay. The wind carried with it not only the ship but also such a dense cloud of snow that the skipper and his crew were unable to see where they were being driven. Following a horrendous impact with the berg that shook the ship from stem to stern, the bow section was wrenched away, leaving a gaping hole through which the sea could enter as the ship bucked about in the turmoil.

Fearing the ship might sink, and with the pumps struggling to reduce the water that threatened to inundate her, the only option appeared to be an attempt to beach the craft in the hope that she could be repaired and later re-floated. Then a small miracle occurred; the pumps started to get ahead of the incoming sea water, and after a hasty consultation with the crew the skipper steered the ship out of the bay and signalled to the shore party that he was headed for Port Stanley in the Falklands for critical repairs to be carried out. Fortunately, those left ashore were well stocked with provisions as the ship had discharged most of the essential cargo – but the feelings and thoughts of those left behind were as unsettled as the storm that had deprived them of the ship.

Several days later, Hope Bay base received a radio signal telling them that the *Eagle* had safely made passage to Port Stanley. Maybe Captain Pitt of the *Fitzroy* was right after all to refuse to take his ship into the bay the previous year.

In 1946, after two years of solitude and with the war now over, the men who had been the spearhead of Britain's secret war in the Antarctic were relieved and plans were instigated to carry on and actually expand the programme of exploration that they had started. For the time being more bases were to be established, but the two existing ones would have mixed fortunes. Stonington Island and Marguerite Bay would feature in the next phase of Operation Tabarin. That name would fade from the headlines as the new enterprise was to become known as the Falkland Islands Dependency Survey (FIDS), and that in its turn would become the mother of the British Antarctic Survey (BAS) that we know today.

This brief account of Operation Tabarin sets the scene for the future events that would lead to the expedition known as the Commonwealth Trans-Antarctic Expedition. Sir Ernest Shackleton had dreamed of this as being the 'Last Great Journey in the World'.

The arm of the Colonial Office responsible for administering the sector of Antarctica that the UK had laid claim to was the Falkland Island Dependency Survey. This organisation was given the task of setting up the forthcoming expedition to the Graham Land Peninsula. People were soon applying for the vacancies in the scientific team to be sent down to the Antarctic. Dr Vivian Fuchs was encouraged by the Revd Launcelot Flemming to apply for one of the geological vacancies and, as he had just returned from his latest African expedition and was looking for something else to tackle, he allowed his name to be put forward. Launcelot Flemming at that juncture held the very influential post of Director of the Scott Polar Research Institute in Cambridge. He had been a member of John Rymill's British Graham Land Expedition that had explored all along the Graham Land Peninsula's coast between 1934 and 1937.

Dr Fuchs's forte was geology, and over a number of years he had gained an excellent background in this field. His interview must have gone exceptionally well, because at the end of it he was offered overall command of the expedition. He was to be based on Stonington Island in charge of the team of 27 men, mostly scientists, who would form the various parties exploring the area.

Towards the end of 1947, the FIDS explorers assembled at Tilbury Docks in London to find that their ship was in a chaotic condition, with cargo strewn all over the decks. As they got organised they were delayed for several more days by a Board of Trade notice served on them stating that they were undermanned and that extra men had to be recruited to the crew before the ship could be released. Their ship, the *John Biscoe*, left Tilbury docks in December 1947 and reached Port Stanley in the Falklands towards the end of January 1948. The *John Biscoe* had started life as a net layer built in America in 1943 for laying anti-submarine nets in waters where enemy subs were likely to patrol. Her hull was of wooden construction so that she would not attract mines. After the war she was bought by FIDS for about £40,000 and refitted for use in the Antarctic. The accommodation on board for the men was so cramped that they had to sleep in bunks placed in the holds and stacked three high.

The journey gave the scientists a chance to get to know one another, as it appears they were nearly all strangers at the outset. The voyage south served as a shaking down period and it gave Dr Fuchs time to assess his men and allocate them to the various bases to be manned.

On their arrival, Dr Fuchs split the expedition members into various groups and the ship set them down at the selected sites that had been established under the Operation Tabarin deployment. Dr Fuchs and his party of 11 scientists based themselves on Stonington Island just off the mainland coast where they carried out a series of journeys to establish the geological composition of George VI Sound. This is where Alexander Island runs southwards from about 68° South and parallel to the Graham Land Peninsula for nearly 300 miles. This sound had been explored for the first time by three of John Rymill's men. One of these three was Launcelot Flemming.

The *John Biscoe* failed to relieve the expedition during the following summer due to bad ice conditions setting in earlier than usual and so the various groups settled down to another winter of isolation. The party of 11 men at Stonington were well stocked with food for themselves, but fuel and dog food was another problem. They planned nevertheless to continue carrying out their exploratory work. Before this they set out to some nearby islands to cull enough seals for dog food during the oncoming winter months when the seals would be scarce. Having accomplished this, the survey work continued with extensive sledging trips further south using the dog teams they had brought down with them. Caught in a blizzard during one of these exploratory trips, Vivian Fuchs and his travelling companion Rae Adie lay up in their tent to wait for better conditions and it was during this enforced delay that talk between the two of them came round to what they should do after returning home. They were not really in a position to formulate a comprehensive plan whilst sat in the tent, but the germ of an idea for a trans-Antarctic crossing was sown in this desolate environment.

Having spent year longer in the Antarctic than was originally planned, Dr Fuchs returned to an England that had significantly changed since he left it two and a half years earlier. The country was still experiencing wartime rationing of certain commodities such as sugar. The Labour Government of Clement Attlee had also introduced nationalisation for the steel, coal, gas and electricity industries amongst others, and there was now a fledgling National Health Service in operation.

To further his idea for the audacious plan he and Rae Adie had mooted in the tent during the recent expedition he arranged to meet a man with very influential connections whom he thought might be able to help him. That man was Professor James Wordie, Fuchs' former tutor from Cambridge University, who had helped him in many other ways during his time as an undergraduate.

Early in Vivian Fuchs' career, and while still at Cambridge, he had met the professor, who had an impeccable pedigree in polar exploration. He had been with Sir Ernest Shackleton as his chief scientific adviser on the ill-fated *Endurance* voyage to the

Weddell Sea in 1914, which attempted an audacious crossing of the Antarctic continent just as the world had plunged into the First World War. Sir Ernest Shackleton and his men were headed towards a high latitude deep in the Weddell Sea to establish a base from where it was hoped they could strike out across the Filchner Ice Shelf onto the Antarctic mainland. They intended to force a way through unknown territory to reach the South Pole and then cross the Polar Plateau to pick up depots which had hopefully been laid down by a party of men who had worked their way across the Ross Ice Shelf to the foot of the Beardmore Glacier. From this point onwards Shackleton would be wholly dependent on these vital supplies if he and his men were to make it through successfully to the Ross Sea side of the continent.

As everyone knows, the *Endurance* never made it to the proposed anchorage. She was caught in the pack ice and drifted helplessly to the north in the ice for many months before being crushed and sunk, leaving the men stranded on the frozen ocean. Using three open boats salvaged from the ship the 28 men struggled across the sea ice to reach open water and then sailed to Elephant Island. From here Shackleton and five companions managed to reach South Georgia in one of the *Endurance*'s boats that had been modified by McNeish, the carpenter for the sea crossing. Once they reached the west coast of South Georgia, three of them led by Shackleton set out across the unmapped mountains that formed the backbone of the island to get to the Norwegian whaling station at Stromness on the eastern side of the island. This trek took them 36 hours to complete. They had only stopped to heat up a little food and some water for a drink. They slept briefly at one stop but were off again soon after. Finally the journey came to an abrupt end with them sliding down the rope they had brought with them through a freezing cold meltwater stream to reach the shore behind the whaling station. Shackleton sought the whalers' help and subsequently rescued all the remaining men from Elephant Island and the three that had been left behind on the west coast of South Georgia, where they had made their original landfall.

After the war James Wordie became the senior geological tutor at St John's College, Cambridge, and he would be knighted for his services to Polar exploration in 1957 after the success of the trans-Antarctic expedition, which he helped to promote and guide through its early formulation.

When the meeting between James Wordie and Dr Fuchs took place, Wordie explained to Fuchs that he felt the time was not quite right for such an ambitious project; the reverberations of the Second World War were still very evident around the globe, and raising the huge sum of money the project needed would be a step too far at this stage.

So Dr Fuchs resumed his career with FIDS, where he was now in charge of the co-ordination of the whole of the FIDS programme of work to bring it into a cohesive unit with a structured plan for future exploration.

Vivian Fuchs and Early Plans for the Trans-Antarctic Expedition

The happiness of Dr Vivian Fuchs' childhood was cut short by the First World War. His English mother, Violet, had married a German against the wishes of both families. Eventually, the couple set up home in the Kent countryside where Vivian's father, Ernst, built a modest home for his wife and only son and farmed a few acres as a market gardener. In October 1914, two months after hostilities began, all German nationals living in Great Britain were rounded up and transported to tented camps. Ernst Fuchs was allowed out on parole after a period of detention, during which time the family moved to the Isle of Man, but before he could start earning a living he was taken away again. Mother and son had no means of support, and seem to have lived on a small allowance that the government paid after they had sequestered the family's savings. This was a consequence of the mixed marriage, and the authorities were oblivious to any destitution the policy caused.

As the war rumbled on and on, the authorities became aware that manpower was at a premium and so any fit men being held in internment camps who could be vouched for by a sponsor were released into the sponsor's custody. In Vivian's father's case, he would be allowed to work as a gardener. Ernst's sponsor was actually his wife's cousin.

After the war the Fuchs family found their way back to Kent. Vivian moved school several times, and each new school brought new challenges, but he never gave up and by 1926 had survived all that could be thrown at him in the way of prejudice relating to his German heritage, and he was accepted for a place at St John's College, Cambridge.

Towards the end of his studies Vivian Fuchs was approached by James Wordie and asked if he would like to go to Greenland on one of Wordie's summer expeditions. These were organised to give young geology students field experience. Vivian Fuchs went, and this was the start of a lifetime of exploration that would eventually lead to his greatest exploit.

In Greenland, the expedition that launched Vivian Fuchs' career as an explorer was confined to a few short summer weeks in 1929. James Wordie planned to tackle what was then the highest known mountain in Greenland, Petermann Peak, situated in the coastal mountain range along the east coast.

Setting off from Aberdeen in a small Norwegian sealer called the *Heimland*, they crossed over the North Atlantic until they reached the Denmark Strait, which borders the east coast of Greenland. This coast is always difficult to approach by ship due to the pack ice from the Arctic Ocean moving southwards during the summer breakup. The ship entered the ice but very soon became beset, and for a week the captain, Lars Jakobsen, fought to get her free. When escape was achieved, they sailed further north for about 200 miles to try again. The ship was again caught, but eventually they managed to push through more than 100 miles of ice and gained the ice-free water near the coast. The expedition had lost most of the summer by now, so the race was on to get ashore and try to find the mountain that they had come so far to climb. Franz Josef Fjord, well over 100 miles long, running from east to west into the heart of the East Greenland mountains, gave them a watery highway to get closer to Petermann Peak, and after landing and organising their campsite no time was lost in setting off in pursuit of their lofty target.

The party consisted of six men led by the professor. One notable member of the team was August Courtauld, son of the industrialist Samuel Courtauld. The climb took nearly a week before they were successful, and then it was a hurried descent so that they could reach their ship before the sea started to refreeze.

Neither Fuchs nor Courtauld gained the summit, remaining about 100 feet below to look after the party's equipment in case of any unseen eventuality. Petermann Peak is 2,940 metres high, and this was the first time it had been climbed. In 1935 August Courtauld climbed the highest mountain in Greenland, Gunnbjorn Fjeld, during an expedition he personally financed. August had another claim to fame when in 1931 he manned a weather station alone in the centre of the Greenland Ice Cap for five months. He was part of Gino Watkins' expedition to research the possibility of a route across Greenland for aircraft travelling from the USA to Europe. This enterprise was known as the British Arctic Air-Route Expedition and part of the programme was to monitor the weather systems that prevailed on the Greenland Ice Cap for a whole year. Various team members manned the station for a couple of months at a time, but when it came to the third changeover, owing to extreme weather conditions the relief party could not leave sufficient supplies for two men, so Courtauld volunteered to stay alone and continue the records. His own relief was delayed by foul weather and it was only at the second attempt that his rescue was accomplished. It came just in time as he was out of fuel and candles and down to his last few biscuits. From 22 March to 5 May the snow had built up round his entrance to such an extent that he could no longer get outside. (Gunnbjorn Fjeld is 3,694 meters high and other mountains subsequently discovered since that first climb have pushed Petermann Peak down to eighth place in the league table.)

After the expedition's return to England, Vivian Fuchs completed his university studies in geology and it was at this juncture that he met and made friends with Louis Leakey. This friendship was to lead Vivian Fuchs onto the next phase of his career as an explorer, but not in the frigid regions of the world that were eventually to bring him international fame.

Louis Leakey had been brought up in Africa where his parents were missionaries. He completed his doctorate and became a Research Fellow at St John's College in Cambridge. He devoted most of his career to archaeological and palaeontological studies in East Africa, where he discovered some of the earliest human bones ever found, establishing the fact that the human race as we know it today had its roots on the African continent.

It was in 1930, again on the recommendation of James Wordie, that Vivian Fuchs was offered the position of geologist as part of a four-man party going to East Africa to study the lakes in the Great Rift Valley. The team travelled down to Mombasa and then headed for Nairobi. They planned to drive into the interior along the rutted and potholed tracks to reach their first exploration area near to Lake Naivasha. Louis Leakey was there to meet them and lent one of his lorries to help them on their way. The old Ford and Dodge trucks they used to ferry all their supplies and camping equipment struggled along the dusty and at times flooded roads. Frequent punctures and breakdowns held them up but eventually they reached the lake, where they set up their first camp. The group spent the next 12 months exploring the area, even crossing into the Belgian Congo from Uganda. It was during this expedition that Vivian Fuchs was laid low with an attack of malaria, which was initially diagnosed as typhus. Recovery was slow but sure, and after eight or nine weeks he was back with the other team members.

There followed a series of three other expeditions to Africa, and just before the one in 1934, Vivian Fuchs married a distant cousin called Joyce Connell. They shared the same interest in travelling to faraway places, and so she accompanied him as he set out for Africa for the third time. He continued the association with Africa, on and off, for nine years.

The Second World War intervened in Vivian Fuchs' career as an explorer and he served for the duration, including getting involved in helping to plan the D-Day operations. After the capitulation of the enemy forces, there followed a period with the organisation that was tasked with the job of rebuilding the infrastructure of everyday life in war-torn Europe. Such issues as sorting out refugees, establishing law and order in the vacuum that existed in most of the Central European States and the repatriation of prisoners of war were among the priorities to be dealt with.

Early in 1953, at the instigation of James Wordie, a meeting was arranged for Dr Fuchs to put his ideas for the TAE to Sir Miles

Clifford. Sir Miles was then Governor of the Falklands and the two men had had a working relationship for several years through Dr Fuchs' involvement with the Graham Land expeditions carried out by the Falkland Islands Dependency Survey, so the rapport between them was very good. At least two other schemes were being proposed for similar ventures, but once the details became known and Sir Giles had seen them, he eventually decided to back Dr Fuchs' proposal as being the most practical.

An outline plan was produced which wasn't too far removed from Sir Ernest Shackleton's original plan, only this time mechanised transport would be the key to crossing the continent. The vehicles used would be supported by small aircraft capable of landing and taking off from selected sites on snow or ice to bring in vital stores, spares and personnel when required. Shackleton, of course, did not have the luxury of air support bringing in fresh stores. He knew from his previous expedition in 1907 when he had attempted to get to the South Pole that his team would have to carry much of their supplies with them. He also realised that there was only one way he could cross the continent and that it entailed a series of depots being laid down across the Ross Ice Shelf as far as the foot of the Beardmore Glacier. This could only be accomplished by a back-up team working their way south from a position close to Scott's old Discovery Hut. This was situated on the edge of McMurdo Sound on the opposite side of the continent. In this way he would have a continuity of food depots for him and his five companions plus fuel for cooking and, crucially, seal meat for any of the dogs that had survived the crossing up to that point.

Dr Fuchs' had formulated a similar scheme whereby he and his team could pick up depots laid from the Ross Sea to a point about 500 miles north of the South Pole. This would enable him and his convoy to restock their depleted reserves once past the South Pole. He also wanted an easier route down off the plateau than the Beardmore Glacier that Scott and Shackleton had used. The back-up team would be given the task of reconnoitring a new and safer glacial route for him to follow. His plan also saw the need to establish a base on the Weddell Sea coast in the year before the actual crossing was to take place. From here they could move inland 200–300 miles to establish a satellite base where a plane could land safely so that it would be able to ferry vital fuel and other supplies to the far side of any coastal mountains that might impede their initial push into the interior.

Dr Fuchs was asked to prepare some costs and he worked out an initial figure of £500,000 as a target to aim for, the equivalent of something like £12 million today. (Though such equivalencies are notoriously approximate – £12 million sounds like a bargain for such an undertaking; and sure enough, it was not sufficient.) Another part of his overall strategy was to include other Commonwealth countries, in particular New Zealand, into whose sector of the Antarctic continent the expedition hoped to reach as it completed the crossing. At this time the continent was divided up into segments by the various countries who felt that they were entitled to have a claim on the sector nearest to their own land mass or through the early claims of their explorers. The New Zealand sector ran from 150° West to 160° East, a total of 50° of longitude, and took in the whole of the Ross Ice Shelf together with the Victoria Coast along the edge of the Ross Sea. Scott and Shackleton had also established their huts in this sector because it presented one of the best and shortest known routes to tackle the journey to the Pole. Great Britain had been one of the first countries to carry out exploration in this sector through the exploits of Scott and Shackleton. Together with the relative proximity of New Zealand to this same sector, this provided the basis of a territorial claim, which Britain had passed on to its colonial partner.

The area was originally discovered by Captain James Clark Ross in 1841. He named it Victoria Land after the queen. The discovery was subsequently ratified with an Order in Council in 1923 as being a possession of the Crown by an Act of Parliament called the British Settlements Act of 1887. This order defined the area involved and was recognised by other claimant countries. The Governor General of New Zealand was appointed as governor of the territory and given administrative rights over the claimed area. It was known as the Ross Dependency.

Although the TAE project was not part of the IGY, it conveniently dovetailed itself into the overall plan. The starting and finishing points would be on territory claimed either by New Zealand or the United Kingdom, as would the path to be taken during the crossing. This would make it into an exclusive Commonwealth enterprise. The route would cross a completely unknown area of the continent and Dr Fuchs hoped it would lead to the establishment of whether the landmass of Antarctica was all one, or possibly two or more parts separated by huge chasms filled with a permanent ice cap. To test this, he proposed to carry out a series of seismic measurements every 30 miles during the crossing to determine the ice thickness so that when compared to the altitude readings it would be possible to measure how high the underlying ground was. Mapping and geology would form integral parts of the journey, as would meteorological data taken along the way.

Now that Dr Fuchs had laid out his plans and they had been accepted in principle, the next step was to start on the organisational side. To this end a committee under the chairmanship of Sir John Slessor of the RAF was set up in 1955 in London to attract key people and to work out how to include other Commonwealth countries. Subcommittees were also necessary to tackle the scientific programme's financial funding and the selection of personnel.

A large boost came in the form of a grant for £100,000 from the British Government, and once the expedition was made public, money was donated by New Zealand, Australia and South Africa. Other donations were secured as the news spread, including the pledge by British Petroleum (BP) of supplying all the oil and fuel requirements for the land, sea and air transport used by the expedition. Private financial help, which used to be the mainstay of earlier expeditions, could not be relied upon any more but a continual round of lectures and sponsorships from schools and other like-minded bodies did help towards the overall cost.

Any expedition that received the blessing of the Royal Geographical Society could be assured of support from other august bodies; but even so there was considerable resistance from some influential organisations and prominent people to start with once the overall plan was published. The detractors felt this was not going to achieve anything meaningful and might even end ignominiously. Canada had already voiced her concerns and thought the project would be a waste of public funds and as a consequence stood back and let the opportunity pass her by.

One of the first tasks carried out by the organising committee was the forming of a Limited Liability Company. This enabled the expedition to become a charity so that all the rights associated with the enterprise could be exploited by the Trust to raise money for the project without the fear of the organisation having any claims laid against it, or the money raised being subject to fraudulent use, or tax. These rights included newspaper, film and magazine articles and ultimately the book describing the whole project. All the money they raised for the trust went towards the funding of the expedition and paying off its debts afterwards. Despite the doubts that had been voiced, a positive plan had by this time been formulated and with the guidance of the various committees a timetable was drawn up.

An initial completion date of no later than the end of January 1958 was set. This was to be the latest date when the crossing party should safely arrive on the Ross Sea side of the continent and still leave time for the expedition's ship to pick them up and return to New Zealand before the winter could begin to freeze over their escape route across the Ross Sea.

During Scott's first expedition in 1901 to 1904 his ship *Discovery* had been frozen in during the winters of 1902 and 1903 and it was only with the help of two other ships, the *Morning* and the *Terra Nova*, using explosives that an escape was accomplished at the end of their third year. As they set sail for home on 22 February 1904, the Ross Sea was already starting to freeze over. With the prospect of spending another year in the south, a directive had been issued in London that the *Discovery* should be abandoned and all the men brought home if she could not be extricated in time. When Scott went south for a second time in 1910, the expedition of course ended in tragedy when he and his two surviving companions succumbed to the terrible weather they experienced out on the ice shelf just 11 miles from a depot and probable safety. The date of his last diary entry as the three men lay huddled in their sleeping bags was 29 March 1912.

Whilst waiting for the Pole party to arrive the expedition ship the *Terra Nova* had departed northwards from the base hut to pick up another party of six men led by Victor Campbell; they were known as the Northern Party. These six explorers had been originally landed at Cape Adare, the first land base for overwintering under the leadership of Carstens Borchgrevink in 1899. Victor Campbell and his five companions spent the winter at Cape Adare using Borchgrevink's hut and the second year the *Terra Nova* collected them and transferred them to another site called Terra Nova Bay. They should have spent six weeks here on geological studies, but when the time came for them to be picked up the ship was thwarted in its attempts to get close enough to the shore to rendezvous with them. They were condemned to spend a miserable second winter in an ice cave, mainly eating frozen penguin and seal meat cooked over a primitive stove fuelled by the blubber from the carcases of the animals they had killed. The sooty smoke from the blubber stove coated the inside of the cave so that every time they touched the sides with their worn and tattered clothing they also became blacker and oilier. Naval tradition was maintained throughout their incarceration in the form of a dividing line across the floor of the cave delineating the men's quarters from those of the officer and the two scientists.

After failing to collect the six men of the Northern party, the *Terra Nova* returned to Ross Island and the members of the main expedition party who had completed their tours of duty were taken aboard. She sailed for New Zealand on 7 March 1912, still with no news of Captain Scott and his companions. The remaining men under the command of Dr E L Atkinson RN saw out the winter and early in November set out across the barrier to search for any evidence of the lost polar party. At this juncture the base party still had no idea where either group of missing men were. They buried Scott, Wilson and Birdie Bowers where they were found and erected a cross fashioned from a set of skis surmounting the top of the burial cairn that had been created using blocks of snow.

The Northern party finally rescued themselves with no further loss of life whilst all this was going on.

Of course the TAE organisers did not want a repeat of either of these situations. Either scenario would have severely stretched their budget and would have caused wide spread condemnation from the 'I told you so' group who had disparaged the expedition from the beginning.

New Zealand's Dilemma

While Dr Fuchs had been fostering his ideas of a trans-continental journey, the Antarctic Society of New Zealand had also been mulling over a similar plan that might be carried out using their resources and those of Australia. This society had its origins in the 1930s and the idea had run hot and cold for a number of years. With the advent of the Second World War it had been in abeyance until it was resurrected in 1953 by a memorandum sent to the New Zealand Prime Minister, Sidney Holland.

New Zealand had already laid claim to the Ross Sea sector of the continent, and the society felt it was incumbent upon their country to utilise this claim and establish a permanent presence for research and administration purposes. The society also felt the issue needed to be addressed before another country could forestall them and set up a permanent base and deny New Zealand her claim. A similar scenario had occurred in Greenland where Denmark had established a counter claim to Norway. An international court had awarded them administrative control and sovereignty over Greenland despite Norway's claim, which had been based purely on its historical record of hunting and trading connections over hundreds of years going back to the days of the Vikings. Denmark had won their case because they could prove that they had maintained a permanent presence there for a number of years, with district governors in the larger settlements. The Danes also supplied a limited amount of healthcare and education and where possible sustained some basic industrial activity to help supplement the income of local Inuit communities.

Great Britain had, to her cost, ignored the Graham Land Peninsula and the Falkland Islands Dependencies for a number of years prior to the Second World War, and almost too late had found out that both Argentina and Chile were setting up permanent bases on the peninsula with the express purpose of declaring their claims to the area. Argentina had also maintained a weather station for many years in the South Orkney group of islands. This had been the base hut established by the Scotia Expedition of 1902 to 1904 led by William Speirs Bruce. Initially it was offered to the British Government, but it was turned down and the Argentines took over.

Another reason for some meaningful activity, especially in the field of geology, was the ever-present desire to find another Klondike. Any commodity such as oil, coal or procurable metal ores – or better still, uranium, gold or diamonds – that could be commercially extracted would be an inducement to raise capital to finance the cost of the exploration envisaged. The Antarctic Treaty of 1961 was still several years away and this would eventually exclude any mineral extraction, plus a number of other undesirable activities.

The New Zealand Society were also casting a nervous glance at the possibility of a foreign government putting armed forces in strategic places on the continent to further their own claims. The relative geographical nearness of Australia and New Zealand to Antarctica compared to other countries might mean that they would have to tolerate a foreign country with possibly aggressive tendencies being too close to their southern shores.

Before a move could be made to mount any sort of expedition the question of costs would be bound to prove a hurdle and estimates would have to be submitted. A figure of £25,000 to £30,000 was bandied around, based on the costs Australia had incurred for setting up its station on Macquarie Island. The scientific societies around the world were being made aware of the forthcoming International Geophysical Year in 1957 and this was acting as a spur. New Zealand's Antarctic Society was no exception, and the memorandum to Prime Minister Holland was the spearhead of their thrust to get things moving.

The New Zealand committee's chairman, Arthur Helm, had contacted Dr Fuchs following a press announcement relating to Dr Fuchs' proposed exploit but many months seem to have elapsed before a response was received. Finally, in reply to the New Zealand enquiry, Dr Fuchs stressed that he always hoped that the two countries and other interested Commonwealth countries would join forces to undertake the project.

Dr Fuchs proposed an initial timetable for the venture as he envisaged it unfolding. December 1955 would be the starting date when an advance party would leave Great Britain to sail south and establish their base as deep into the Weddell Sea and as near to the Filchner Ice Shelf as possible subject to a satisfactory landing site being found. The advance party would be able to construct a hut and man it for the winter of 1956 while the ship returned to Great Britain for a second load of supplies and all the personnel that a crossing party would need. The main party hoped to arrive back at the Weddell Sea base by February 1957 and, with the aid of two aircraft brought down as deck cargo, fly inland several hundred miles to build up a depot of supplies at a satellite base for the forthcoming transit later in 1957 and into 1958. During the second winter a small team based in this satellite station could probe further inland to reconnoitre as far as possible for a route that the others could follow the next summer and also get some valuable data on the weather in the area.

By early in November 1957 the trans-continental party would set out for the South Pole and beyond to rendezvous with the support party from the Ross Sea and then both teams were to try to complete the journey by the end of January 1958 and be evacuated to New Zealand by the expedition ship early in February 1958. In his reply to the New Zealand committee Dr Fuchs stressed how he would welcome New Zealand input and asked them to manage the backup expedition coming from the Ross Sea side of the continent to meet the main party.

Once a commitment had been made to raise funds for the two-pronged attack on the crossing, the whole operation moved up a gear. With New Zealand having selected Sir Edmund Hillary of Everest fame to lead their side of the expedition, the selection of team members in both countries could begin in earnest. At the same time, the hunt for the money continued. Various estimates were bandied about but as with all these projects most of them proved inadequate. On top of the £100,000 subscribed by the British Government, New Zealand made it known that they would contribute £50,000, Australia came in with £20,000 and South Africa parted with £18,000. Canada was conspicuous by her absence and felt that the money would be better spent elsewhere. With the ever-expanding ambitions of the Ross Sea endeavour it soon became apparent that even the New Zealand Government's contribution would not suffice and time after time they generously dipped into the treasury giving a final total of not far short of a quarter of a million pounds.

Sponsorship provided the next tranche of income, both in Great Britain and in New Zealand. Massey Ferguson, the tractor manufacturer, chipped in by instructing their New Zealand agents to supply seven of their tractors and carry out modifications to change them to full- or half-track drives. These tractors became the workhorses of the Ross Sea party and Hillary was extremely impressed with them – perhaps too impressed, as this would lead to later controversy.

Fuel for these tractors had to be modified to ensure that all the expedition vehicles could run on the same mixture. Dr Fuchs was planning to use Sno-Cats, Weasels and a Muskeg tractor. British Petroleum, who had agreed to supply the expedition, came up with a solution. They created a complete, standardised range of lubricants for all the vehicles. This enabled all the petroleum-based materials to be sent in suitably marked containers to simplify the logistics of storing and transporting the fuel, oil and grease, etc.

Aviation fuel presented an equally difficult but separate problem as the two Austers, the Beaver and the Otter aircraft used different fuel mixtures. BP developed a standard fuel for all. Bearing in mind that temperatures out on the ice cap could reach as low as -70°F and most lubricants will start to congeal well above this temperature, then the task seemed impossible; but BP rose to the challenge and provided what the expedition needed and in the huge quantities that they were likely to consume. A Sno-Cat, for instance, could use a gallon of fuel for as little as one and a half miles in difficult terrain, and Dr Fuchs had four of these giant tracked machines. The total distance travelled will never be known because on many occasions they had to backtrack to avoid obstacles across their path. Added to the overall total was the reconnoitring journey from Shackleton to South Ice before the crossing even got underway.

The Polar Plateau presented an additional problem as once the two teams had climbed up to it they would be travelling across endless snow fields all the way to the South Pole at an altitude of anything from 8,000 feet to a maximum of nearly 10,000 feet; and of course some of the route was completely unknown. This higher altitude would result in a reduction in the horsepower being developed by the engines and this needed to be sorted out before the traverse could begin. Tests were carried out under laboratory conditions in Great Britain, and the Norse Polarinstitutt kindly agreed to run a series of outdoor trials for the vehicles up on the inland ice cap in central Norway. This helped to prove that the engines would still be able to haul the large sledge loads they proposed to take with them. Most of the weight was the huge quantity of fuel that they were going to need.

The continuing need to raise money went on unabated in Great Britain as well as in New Zealand. The New Zealand approach was based on a regional fundraising effort. By designating a town, city or rural area, the committee set targets for that area to achieve and left it to local organisations to plan their own ideas for achieving their goals. Most of the rural areas exceeded expectations and the urban ones still managed to raise respectable amounts. In Great Britain the fund raising was done in a more traditional manner, where ticket sales for a talk or lecture by a member of the expedition's organising committee contributed a steady flow of income, and schoolchildren would be asked to sponsor a dog or sledge for the expedition to use.

Food manufacturers were enticed to contribute supplies with the proviso that their name would be associated with the expedition and hopefully its success would repay the firm with enhanced sales. Similarly, manufacturers were lured into donating equipment: footwear, gloves, socks, coats, tents, sleeping bags and countless other commodities. Engineering firms gave freely of their time and resources, as did scientific organisations which donated or lent expensive instruments and navigation equipment such as compasses and radio receivers.

No one could have asked for more from the two countries and their people.

Transport – There Are No Roads

The question of fuel and lubricants has been mentioned, and a crucial part of this or any expedition venturing into the most inhospitable area of the world is the transportation of its men and equipment in the most efficient manner possible.

From Sir Ernest Shackleton's first expedition in 1907 right up to this trans-polar expedition the leaders have taken with them an assortment of motorised transport to supplement the ever-faithful husky and of course manpower. Although Sir Ernest had chosen Manchurian ponies as his main form of transport, he was ever mindful of the advance of technology and included on board the *Nimrod* was a 12–15hp Arrol-Johnston open-topped car with a four-cylinder air-cooled engine. He knew from his time spent with Scott and Wilson on their southern journey in 1903 that the Ross Ice Shelf could provide a suitable surface over which a car might travel. In Shackleton's own account of his expedition, *The Heart of the Antarctic*, he mentions that the car was one of the first items to be unloaded, but he used the ponies for transporting the stores up off the ice shelf, and all other journeys were by dog- or horse-drawn sledges. The car gets very little mention. The rubber tyres on the wheels proved an ineffective form of traction and the car, apart from its novelty value, contributed nothing. In 1960, restoration work was being carried out at Shackleton's old hut and some remnants of the Arrol-Johnston car were discovered amongst other debris littering the site.

The famous Australian explorer Sir Douglas Mawson sailed to Antarctica in 1911 equipped with what started life as an aeroplane but for him became a wingless one. He and his men had a slightly more successful experience with their motorised transport and it managed to pull a reasonable load of up to four sledges. After a few trial runs a party of four men set out to explore the coastal area near Adélie Land but had not even completed the first day's travel when the engine of the 'Air Tractor', as the device became known, developed a strange knocking noise and then stopped completely, breaking the propeller with the suddenness of the stall. It had to be abandoned but was later dragged back to base at Cape Denison, where upon examination several cylinders were found to be seized. Just as happened with Shackleton's car, the remains of the air tractor were located by a group from an organisation called the Mawson's Hut Foundation doing archaeological and restoration work at the hut site over half a century later.

Captain Scott led his second foray to Antarctica in 1910 and with him he took three specially designed tracked vehicles for use on his attempt at the South Pole. The original tracks had been especially developed from the original idea, which had been for a farm tractor; but muddy fields were not the same as ice and snow. Slats of wood were attached to the metal links and to all intents and purposes seemed to work quite well in the trials that were carried out when they took the prototype to Norway. Reginald Skelton had been instrumental in the modifications to the Wolseley tractors. He had been chief engineer with Scott on the Discovery Expedition. Later, when Scott was selecting his Terra Nova Expedition men, he did not include Skelton, passing him over in favour of Teddy Evans, much to Skelton's chagrin. Mechanical failure of the gearboxes resulted in only very limited use being made of the two tractors that survived the unloading onto the ice shelf; the best one fell through the ice to the sea bed before it could even begin service.

Tracked transport developed at a rapid pace over the intervening 40 years up to 1955, and as the old saying goes, necessity is the mother of invention. Following the two world wars and the development of tanks and other tracked vehicles for the war effort it was not a great leap of the imagination to see similar means of transport being utilised for travel in the lands bordering the Arctic Ocean and on the Antarctic continent itself.

The largest of Dr Fuchs' snow vehicles was the Tucker Sno-Cat, which was called the 743 because it was a 700 series model with four tracks and three doors. It was powered by an eight-cylinder, petrol-driven Chrysler engine that developed 200hp. Each Sno-Cat weighed just over three tons and could carry 90 gallons of petrol, so together with all the ancillary equipment the vehicles weighed a total of nearly four tons each. Then there were two sledges being towed behind each of the Sno-Cats, which could carry between them a load of up to three tons each, most of which consisted of fuel for the vehicles. The vehicle's cab provided a reasonable level of comfort for the driver and navigator but travelling in the rear, as was the case when the expedition started to abandon broken-down vehicles and their drivers required transport, was none too comfortable.

The Sno-Cats had four pontoon caterpillars, each with its own drive shaft, and to manipulate a turn to the right or left the driver had to brake one of the front caterpillars, allowing the opposite one to keep moving. In this way the vehicle would, in effect, start to spin slowly about the track that was being held back by the brake. There was always a small time lapse before any directional change became obvious but with patience and practice just the correct amount of braking could be made to change the direction in which the driver wished the Sno-Cat to go. The four pontoons were capable of independently moving up and down in a seesaw action and this allowed the Sno-Cats to cope with the irregularities of the surface caused by the wind. These irregularities took the form of frozen waves called sastrugi. They are very similar to the sand dunes formed in desert areas. The four pontoons and their flexibility whilst driving became even more indispensable when the Sno-Cats were to cross the crevassed areas they were to encounter during the traverse.

Starting off from Shackleton Base near Vahsel Bay in the Weddell Sea with four of this type of vehicle, it is a testimony to their design that they all completed the journey of 2,150 miles in 99 days to reach Scott Base on the Ross Sea. They all required a great deal of maintenance on the way, and in the conditions under which David Pratt and Roy Homard had to work, the two men were deserving of every accolade that came their way.

Incidentally, the Americans under the command of Finn Ronne had also established a base on the Filchner Ice Shelf which they called Ellsworth Station, named after a famous American flyer who was one of the earliest men to take to the air in the Antarctic. They carried out a traverse of the ice shelf using Sno-Cats and Weasels, to determine the thickness of the ice in the same way that the TAE proposed to do. Using explosive charges and taking readings with the aid of sensitive monitoring equipment, they could calculate the density and thickness of the underlying ice down to the bedrock underneath and even the depth of ocean below the ice.

A typical seismic test would involve a lot of ground work before the actual test took place, and some notes taken from John Behrendt's book *Innocents on the Ice* give some idea of the complexity of the procedure:

> We spread out two 1,200 feet long cables and attached geophones, or jugs, to each of 12 pairs of wire connectors at 100 feet intervals. We shot off the explosive charges in a hand drilled hole about 4 inches in diameter and anywhere from 6 to 45 feet deep. Charge size varied greatly from a pound or two for a reflection (echo) from the sea bed or ice-rock interface to 1,000lbs for long distances from the shot to the recording system. When the geophones on the snow surface vibrate in response to the reflected sound (seismic) wave, a small voltage was generated and received at the recording instruments. Half the measured time from the shot to the recorded reflection, multiplied by the velocity of sound in the ice and snow, which we measured independently, gave the thickness or the combined ice and water thickness on the floating ice shelf.

He goes on to explain that the equipment they were using on the Filchner Ice Shelf required a lot of manual work to put it in place. For instance; there were 24 amplifiers and six of these in a specially designed aluminium case weighed 50lbs. The control unit also weighed in at 50lbs, as did the 24-volt converter box. Then there was the oscilloscope camera, giving an additional 70lbs to lug about. 1,200 feet of heavy cable scaled in at about 300lbs. There would also have been boxes containing the explosive charges and detonators. All this equipment was carried in one of their Sno-Cats, and once the test had been carried out the film from the camera had to be developed as quickly as possible due to the low temperatures. This was done aboard the Sno-Cat, where hopefully they could maintain a high enough ambient temperature so that the water used to wash the prints did not freeze and spoil the results. During the Americans' stay on the ice shelf all their vehicles experienced a range of mechanical problems similar to the British expedition. Their Ellsworth base was part of the American contribution to the IGY programme.

The measuring procedure was very similar to that carried out by Vivian Fuchs and his seismologists, the only major difference being that the Americans were for the most part operating across a floating ice shelf and the TAE were crossing the continent and consequently were measuring ice depth down to bedrock. Fuchs had one of his Sno-Cats adapted to ferry all the apparatus needed to carry out the seismic testing.

The TAE also took another American-made tracked vehicle called the Weasel. Made for transporting troops and equipment during the Second World War, it could also be used as a Bren gun carrier. Weasels were considerably lighter than the Sno-Cats and differed in that they only had two sets of tracks. They were made by Studebaker. Two versions were made for wartime use, one of which had flotation bags for amphibious use. Dr Fuchs took two of each. They weighed a little over two tons, and could carry three passengers in a rear seat and a driver in the front seat. Powered by a six-cylinder petrol engine that developed 70hp, they were capable of travelling at nearly 20mph but more normally over the terrain they encountered during the traverse they seldom exceeded 10mph. Most of the time the Weasels were used to pull just one sledge carrying anything up to two tons of stores but they were capable of pulling more if required. The vehicle itself could also carry an additional load of half a ton but at the expense of having no passengers. The batteries were only 6 volt initially but were later altered to a higher rating because during very cold temperatures the 6-volt system could not cope especially with starting in the lower temperatures on the Polar Plateau. Other expeditions had used Weasels and so they were a proven if slightly vulnerable type of vehicle for the work ahead.

The Australian National Antarctic Research Expedition (ANARE) set of expeditions from 1947 onwards used Weasels extensively once they had established a permanent base in Antarctica which they called Mawson after their most celebrated explorer. They landed at Horse Shoe Point on the coast of Mac Robertson Land where they unloaded three Weasels and set up their base. They finally reached their farthest point south at the Prince Charles Mountains. Here they abandoned one unit and managed to retreat to their base in the other two.

The Australians persevered with Weasels over a period of years and another trip to the Prince Charles Mountains in 1957 during the IGY led to an unusual experience. The members of the party travelling to the mountains tried steering the Weasel using ropes connected to the steering arms of the vehicle but with the driver standing on the trailer being towed, so that in the event of the Weasel falling into a crevasse the driver could escape before plunging down with the unit. During a spell of this style of driving the inevitable happened and the Weasel lurched into an unseen crevasse, the 'steerer' jumped off the sledge as it too was about to disappear into the gaping channel. To his horror, he saw the Weasel manage to grip the far side of the crevasse and haul itself out with the trailer still in tow. This left the driver on one side whilst the Weasel started to gently rumble off on the other side. Desperately the driver sought a way across and finally set off in pursuit of the wayward caravan. Luck was on his side and he brought the runaway to a halt before any lasting damage was done.

The British Greenland Expedition of 1952–54 led by Commander James Simpson set out to negotiate a way onto the Greenland Ice Cap to carry out a very similar programme of tests as the TAE would attempt to do under Dr Fuchs. They were going to do seismic testing of the ice to determine its thickness but needed to have vehicles capable of covering long distances and carrying all the necessary heavy equipment. Having chosen Weasels, the next problem, again similar to TAE, was to get the Weasels onto the ice cap. Eight were landed on the east coast of Greenland but, due to the extent of the sea-ice conditions, not as close to their chosen route as they would have liked. This meant that a tortuous route through the coastal mountains had to be negotiated. Although the RAF could help with supply drops, it was the mechanics in the party who had to repair the Weasels and, when necessary, improvise to get them up onto the plateau.

Having succeeded in their primary task of getting onto the ice cap, the rest of the summer was given over to the seismic testing. The rough terrain gradually took its toll and depleted the vehicles in number. The leader of the expedition, Jim Simpson, had planned that after the last seismic test had been completed they would carry out a traverse of the ice cap and finish up at the huge American air base of Thule on the western coast of Greenland. The last surviving Weasel faded away almost in sight of their destination, leaving its seven sisters scattered across the vast expanse of the Greenland Ice Cap and the rugged mountainous approach up which they had battled the previous year.

The best outcome of this expedition from the point of view of TAE was that three of its members found their way onto Dr Fuchs' expedition. They were Sergeant Major Desmond 'Roy' Homard, who provided the backbone of the engineering personnel that kept the TAE mechanised transport going; Hal Lister, a glaciologist responsible for the seismic testing; and Lt Commander 'Dicky' Brooke, who joined the New Zealand contingent at Scott Base as a surveyor.

Interestingly the Sno-Cats had a lower weight footprint than the Weasel by a two to one ratio; in other words the Weasels exerted twice as much pressure on the ground per square foot and consequently were more likely to break through a snow bridge over a crevasse than the heavier Sno-Cats were. Dr Fuchs, who drove the lead vehicle all the way from Shackleton to Scott Base, nearly always used a Sno-Cat. The Weasel had been out of production for quite a few years when the expedition was looking for tracked vehicles and so the ones taken south for TAE in 1956 were second-hand and most of the spares had to be cannibalised from other old units in Government Surplus depots around the country, or junkyards. The engines and transmission units were overhauled and some modifications were carried out to the cabs and tracks but a lot of the bodywork was original and little of the total was tested before shipment to Antarctica.

The other tracked vehicle used by the Weddell Sea party was the Bombardier tractor, known more commonly as a Muskeg tractor. The TAE had one of these on its traverse from Shackleton Base. It was powered by a Chrysler petrol-fuelled engine which had six cylinders giving over 100hp. It weighed two tons unladen and could haul its own weight of two tons on a trailer/sledge. An endless rubber belt reinforced with fabric was used for the caterpillars. Steering was similar to most tracked vehicles in that the brake is applied to one track and this causes the machine to drive forward on the other side. The expedition found this machine very useful in the unloading from the ship as it was easily manoeuvrable and relatively quick to operate from ice edge to base site. The Muskeg that the expedition took for the traverse was the first vehicle to actually be abandoned at a camp, 100 miles out from South Ice, the satellite base they had established 270 miles inland from Shackleton. This was part of a plan to dispose of vehicles as and when they became surplus to requirements. The next day one of the two remaining Weasels broke a track and, as they did not have any more spares, a crew were sent back to retrieve the Muskeg and leave the cannibalised Weasel to the solitude of the ice cap.

The Muskeg was designed and built by a company owned by Canadian industrialist Joseph-Armand Bombardier, founder of aerospace and transport company Bombardier Inc. Production had begun in 1953 so this vehicle was relatively new when purchased for the TAE expedition. The Cree Indian word *muskeg* means boggy ground. Of the four types of vehicles used, this last was the most improbable choice but it worked far better than anybody anticipated. It started life as the workhorse of many farms across the world and would be instantly recognised by many people today. It was an ordinary farm tractor, though not quite the one we see in fields – the wheels had been modified to take tracks, or, more correctly, some were half-tracks and the rest were fully tracked. The traditional wheeled version could not cope with snow or ice while the half-tracks were satisfactory until they were driven into soft snow, and that is why the full-track version became the type chosen by Edmund Hillary to lay the depots on the way to the Pole.

Massey Ferguson, the British manufacturer, modified and supplied seven units free of charge through their New Zealand agents C B Norwood Ltd. Five finished up going to Scott Base on the Ross Sea and the other two were taken on the expedition ship *Theron* and used around the other expedition base on the Weddell Sea. Their relatively diminutive engine size of less than 30hp, which was developed from a four-cylinder petrol engine, could haul loaded sledges weighing up to two tons, which was an impressive performance. Having a relatively short track length made them more vulnerable to disappearing into crevasses, but on the whole they coped extremely well. One of the two tractors that were delivered to the Shackleton Base was accidentally lost when the ice shelf broke away in a storm and deposited it, together with most of the fuel drums and other strategic stores, somewhere in the unforgiving ocean to the north.

Sir Edmund Hillary played a large part in the development of the Fergies, as they were affectionately called, and he placed so much faith in them that, as will be told in greater detail later, they played a more significant role in the expedition that anyone had envisaged.

The distribution of the vehicles between the two bases was as follows. At Shackleton, Dr Fuchs started out with four Sno-Cats, three Weasels, one Muskeg and two Ferguson tractors. In addition he had several teams of dogs and two aircraft, one an Auster and the other a De Havilland Otter, both with single engines. The Ross Sea Base started out with five Ferguson tractor units, two Weasels lent to them by the Americans, a large number of dog teams and two aircraft, one of which was also an Auster, the second a Beaver. The Otter and the Beaver were made by De Havilland but of Canadian manufacture.

The two Austers had a relatively limited range and could at most accommodate just two people, but due to their short take-off and landing feature they were the perfect choice for aerial reconnaissance from sites out on the ice cap and close to a sledging party doing field work who might need help with scouting the terrain, bringing in some basic supplies, or any other servicing needs.

The Otter flying out of Shackleton Base had a far superior range, especially when fitted with the extra fuel tanks. It could carry a good payload and had seating for at least four personnel in a heated cabin. This plane was used to carry forward mainly fuel for the traversing convoy. But when South Ice was being built it brought up the base hut in sections, extra men to help with the construction and much-needed stores and provisions. Dog teams alone would not have coped with the timber frame and sheeting required for the hut's construction, and probably several weeks would have been needed to cross the mountainous terrain with dogs between Shackleton and South Ice when time was at a premium.

The Ross Sea party at Scott Base used their Beaver in a similar way to the Otter. All the planes were fitted with skis once the two base camps were established, as from now on the take-off and landings would be from snow or ice surfaces. Both of the Austers had pontoons to start with because they could be lowered over the side of the ships onto water to enable them to take off from the sea and do the scouting that was so essential when the pack ice was presenting the ships with problems crossing the Weddell or Ross Seas. The New Zealand party had seen the wing of their Auster severely damaged as the *Endeavour* left Lyttelton harbour and subsequently had to wait for a replacement to be ferried down to them by the ever-obliging Americans flying from New Zealand to their own station on McMurdo Sound.

All four expedition aircraft were piloted by RAF or RNZAF qualified pilots and the two air forces had also seconded air crew for servicing the planes. It is testament to the flying skills of all the pilots that none of the planes were lost or even damaged during the expedition.

Both halves of the expedition were equipped with the traditional Antarctic form of transport, huskies, and they were to form a vital part of the crossing. Their strategic role was to push ahead of the mechanised transport and survey the unknown territory that had to be negotiated and then their handlers could radio back any problems that might be encountered, such as crevasses or unsuitable terrain that it would be advisable for the motorised units to avoid. When the supply depots were being set up on the Ross Sea side of the continent it would be the dog handlers who would make radio contact with the air crews and advise them of where to bring in the supplies for the various depots and also locate good landing sites for the planes close to the depots.

After the backup depots had all been set down, the New Zealanders prepared to carry out a series of mapping and geological surveys radiating out from Scott Base. Many thousands of miles were covered by the dog teams during the two seasons they were in Antarctica, and unlike previous expeditions there were no occasions when they needed to be sacrificed to save the personnel in the exploring parties. Apart from a couple of fatal accidents involving crevasses, all of them returned to base after completing their trips.

Dr Fuchs had obtained his dogs from Greenland but had also been given four puppies that had been born at Whipsnade Zoo. Disappointingly, only one of these turned out to be suitable for the work and weather they were likely to experience in the months to come. Sadly the other three were dispatched with as little distress as possible to the animals concerned rather than let them suffer in the hostile environment they were about to endure. The Greenland huskies performed very well and the men formed close bonds with their hairy companions.

The New Zealand group had taken about 60 dogs with them and these had come from an assortment of places. In 1956 the Australians had taken Harry Ayres, one of the New Zealanders, down with them to their Mawson Station to gain firsthand experience with their dogs, and on his return he brought back with him about twenty adult huskies and five pups. Fifteen additional huskies were already in training in the Southern Alps in New Zealand and these had come from a breeding programme started in Auckland Zoo. Most of the huskies were of Greenland origin. An ongoing breeding programme resulted in the number of animals multiplying. This idea had been used by many other expeditions, and as a young dog of over six months onwards could be put to work with more experienced dogs, new team members could soon be inaugurated into the existing packs.

Under the Antarctic treaty signed in 1961 all dogs had to be withdrawn from the continent as they were not an indigenous species, but this was not implemented until 1994 following the departure of the last two teams participating in one final trip from the BAS station of Rothera on the Graham Land Peninsula. The surviving two teams of dogs were then repatriated to Canada and given to an Inuit community living at a settlement called Inukjuak. They were mushed from Hudson's Bay for the last 300 miles to their new home where they received an emotional reception.

Sledges of various sizes and forms of construction were taken down to both main bases. The dog sledges were mostly of a traditional construction and consisted of wooden runners and cross braces lashed together with leather thongs. They were based on a sledge that Fridjof Nansen had designed when he crossed the Greenland Ice Cap in 1892. The front and rear of each sledge had an upturned prow to enable it to ride up and over ice and snow obstacles such as sastrugi. The back end was raised up to create a pedestal that acted as a handlebar for the driver. A small step at the base of the pedestal was used as a platform on which the driver could stand when the team was coping with the task in hand but from which he could easily step off to control the sledge across an uneven surface or help them in the event of their struggling to pull the sledge. A crude but effective brake was also fitted to the rear end, enabling the driver to put his foot on it and so plunge a spike into the ice in the event of the sledge over-running the dogs on a slope or merely to hold the team when a halt had been called. Cross ties strapped some 10–12 inches above the runners acted as a platform on which to secure the articles being conveyed. By using this construction, repairs in the field could usually be effected by the simple remedy of tightening or replacing damaged thongs and changing any broken struts that might occur.

The sledges varied in length, and of course that and the number of dogs employed dictated the payload that could be accommodated. A common size would be in the order of 12 feet long with the distance across the bottom runners being 20–24 inches. The surface of the runners was treated with resin originally but by the 1950s the explorers had adopted various types of plastic to reduce the frictional drag on the ice. A loaded sledge could carry nearly half a ton but the rule of thumb used to work out the practical weight was a simple calculation of 80–90lbs per dog.

The friction between the runners and the surface over which the sledge was to travel varied enormously. Strangely enough, it was the downward pressure of the sledge and its load being able to slightly melt the snow or ice as it passed over it that allowed a very thin film of water from the melted ice to form, and the more efficiently this action took place the easier the sledge moved. In the Arctic the Inuit had made this significant discovery hundreds of years earlier and their solution to the problem was simply to form a layer of mud about an inch thick to coat onto the underside of the runners and allow it to freeze. By scraping it flat they achieved a very passable running surface. Even when travelling over rocky or gravelly surfaces they found that their sledges could travel much more easily. Repairs could be carried out whilst on the trail by relining the runners with more mud. Their runners were not very often made of wood but of the material they had to hand and that was usually whale bone or even Caribou antlers.

The sledges pulled by the Sno-Cats, Weasels, Muskeg and Ferguson tractors had to be far more robust in construction. For a start they were expected to carry at least two tons each. The payload could be fuel in large 45 gallon drums or food boxes weighing about 40lbs each. Other items were as diverse as explosives for the seismic test shots, dog food in the form of pemmican, surveying equipment or even rock samples collected by the geologists for later analysis.

The TAE sledges were based on the Maudheim design first used by the joint Norwegian/Swedish/British expedition that was operational in the Antarctic in the late 1940s. The original Maudheim sledges were constructed from hickory and were made in Norway. These sledges had to withstand the more strenuous work they were subjected to when being pulled by mechanical means. The wooden version measured 14 feet long by 5 feet wide with 6-inch broad runners but when metal was used in the construction it was found that a longer chassis could be made and would be more appropriate for the work that it was likely to be called upon to do during the TAE expedition; the salient features of the hickory version were nevertheless retained.

The sledges were still constructed of wood but not of the weight-saving dimensions used on the earlier Nansen type. Now built for robustness using seasoned timber, they were still lashed together but, in addition, there were steel brackets bolted at strategic places to strengthen them for the extra loads they would have to carry. (Their construction can be seen in some of the photographs in the plate section.) Tow hitches of steel were also bolted on to enable the sledges to be coupled to the towing unit and other sledges. These hitches would have to endure the exceptional strains imposed on them as the convoy tackled the hardened sastrugi surfaces and the crevassed areas.

The bottom runners were lined on their underside with a relatively new composite material called Tufnol. This was made from a linen base material impregnated with resin as a bonding agent.

To provide a small crumb of comfort on the journey, two of the sledges were converted into a form of mobile home where, during severe weather or rest periods, the members of the expedition could seek shelter from the elements. Cooking, sleeping, radio communications and medical treatment could be carried out in the Caboose provided.

These sledges were considerably longer than the ones drawn by dog teams being about 20 feet. The longest items carried were aluminium ladders or lengths of timber that could be used to help extricate the vehicles from crevasses. By placing these supports under the stricken vehicle and jamming them into the crevasse walls, they provided a platform on which the tracks of the Sno-Cats and other vehicles could gain a purchase and with other tractor units hitched to the towing points, a concerted effort from up on the surface would haul out the downed unit.

In 1989 Reinhold Messner and his companion Arved Fuchs (no relation to Vivian Fuchs) set out to replicate the Trans-Antarctic Expedition but to carry it out in the way of the old-time explorers – by man-hauling their sledges. Messner was a famous mountaineer who had climbed Mount Everest twice, once without the aid of oxygen, and many other 8,000-metre peaks in the Himalayas. He was critical of the mechanised transport that the TAE employed:

> Man-hauling versus engine power, was for him about the human dimension and not about unlimited possibilities of technology. Whosoever moves in the Antarctic with motor vehicles, helicopters and aircraft, is like a car tourist who squats in his capsule and feels nothing of his surroundings. He who wants to experience the Antarctic intensively must get far away from aircraft and sno-mobile; even though we need aircraft to get to the ice.

The two men used sails to assist them in their task and Messner justifies his use of sail power, which was in the form of a highly developed kite-like sail, to help him and his companion on their way by pointing out that both Scott and Shackleton had also employed wind power when they could. The Golden Age explorers usually fixed up a tent groundsheet mounted on a ski or tent pole in the shape of an old Viking sail secured to the sledge. Messner and Arved Fuchs would have harnesses attached round their waist and shoulders with the sail billowing out ahead of them. He freely admits that on their first good sailing day they made a total of 57 kilometres, far in excess of anything Scott or his contemporaries could have achieved.

In the past Arved Fuchs had crossed Greenland by dog sledge, and in the same year as he tackled the Antarctic crossing he had also walked to the North Pole. Additionally, he had carried out numerous sailing expeditions, including completing the famous North West Passage.

Recruiting Personnel – Who to Take

Applications to join soon followed the press announcement and the task of sorting the grain from the chaff could begin in earnest. Experience in the fields of science relevant to the expedition's aims took top priority, as did anyone with polar experience. In London the first group selected included David Stratton, David Pratt, John Lewis, Gordon Haslop, Peter Weston and 'Taffy' Williams. Each man was given charge of his particular speciality so as to split the overall workload and enable each to concentrate on obtaining the best equipment or supplies for his requirements.

David Pratt had been in a tank regiment during the war and was very conversant with tracked vehicles. He became responsible for all the mechanised operations, including selecting which type of vehicle would be best suited for working across the snow and ice.

John Lewis had piloted small aircraft during his stint at Deception Island and other Antarctic bases back in 1950. He worked closely with the RAF and the Air Ministry, who were to supply the two small aircraft, the radio sets and various spares for the planes. The planes had to be adapted for landing on snow, ice or water and therefore had to have skis or floats fitted. Another adaptation for work in the Antarctic was that each aircraft was supplied with specially designed thermal jackets to keep the deep cold out of the engines, and others to protect the movable parts such as the ailerons. These had to be removable for the planes to fly but sufficiently compact to be carried aboard when flying between destinations.

The Auster could be used for reconnaissance and the De Havilland Otter became the workhorse of the Weddell Sea-based part of the expedition because it had a greater range than the Auster and could carry a payload of about a ton. Gordon Haslop was offered the post of second pilot and coming from New Zealand helped to bring that country into the fold. His flying experience with the RAF had given him the chance to operate aircraft all over the world and fly into all sorts of strange landing sites.

Peter Weston was the third member that the RAF seconded to the expedition. He had extensive knowledge of servicing planes and had even been to the Antarctic during a combined expedition carried out by Great Britain and the Scandinavian countries of Sweden and Norway in the early fifties. This expedition was given the unsurprising title of the Norwegian-British-Swedish Antarctic Expedition under the leadership of Captain John Giaever, a Norwegian with many years of polar experience behind him. They had various means of transport available to them including the use of two Auster aircraft and Weasel-tracked vehicles.

The Air Ministry allowed Taffy Williams who had been trained in the RAF to participate and, as chief radio operator, he would have overall responsibility for communications. In his mid-30s he was the eldest member until then to be taken on. Most of the others were only a few years younger so quite a camaraderie developed as they all got to know one another.

The final member of the first selection was an experienced surveyor. He had gained a considerable amount of experience and knowledge of the Antarctic while serving on several FIDS expeditions in Graham Land and the Falklands. His name was David Stratton and Dr Fuchs made him his second in command, with the immensely responsible task of gathering together much of the stores and equipment the expedition would require and liaising with various companies and organisations so that any modifications or special needs could be attended to well before the departure date. David Stratton had worked at Hope Bay on the Graham Land Peninsula with Ken Blaiklock and George Marsh. He had his pilot's licence so was a useful backup to the two chosen pilots, this and his experience as a manager for British Petroleum made him the best choice for Dr Fuchs' second in command, especially in the light of the immense financial support that that company gave to the expedition. After TAE he resumed his career with BP but in 1972 tragically died after contracting poliomyelitis in North Africa where he had been working.

The New Zealand committee was also in the process of choosing suitable personnel. They, too, needed an advance group to be able to assess the problems their team was likely to come up against. Remember that New Zealand had neglected its Antarctic territory and was now trying to assert its claim as well as help with the project of crossing the continent. With this scenario in mind they picked their leader carefully. It was at this point that George Lowe, Hillary's climbing partner from Everest days and Vivian Fuchs' choice as the expedition's photographer, lobbied successfully to persuade the New Zealand committee to choose the charismatic conqueror of Mount Everest, Sir Edmund Hillary. He had already been serving on the committee that was looking into what part New Zealand would play in the forthcoming adventure.

Hillary was born in 1919, and after school (where he was classed as average) he joined his father working in the family beekeeping business. This tended to be a summertime occupation and to fill in his spare time he got interested in climbing in the Southern Alps of New Zealand's South Island. He was conscripted into the Royal New Zealand Air Force in 1943 and served in the Pacific theatre of war as a navigator on Catalina flying boats, until repatriated to New Zealand following an accident in which he was badly burnt. Recovering from this indisposition, he resumed working for the family business but in due course met Harry Ayres, one of New Zealand's foremost guides and climbers.

They climbed together and under Harry Ayres' tuition Ed Hillary scaled a number of impressive peaks in the Southern Alps. This fortuitous meeting, and the experience Hillary had gained, led to him accompanying Eric Shipton to the Himalayas in 1951. At the time Shipton was the most highly respected mountaineer in Great Britain and he had been sent out to reconnoitre a route for a possible attempt on Mount Everest in 1953. The rest of that story should not need retelling here.

Seven men including Hillary were to form the spearhead of the New Zealand group. Three were to accompany Vivian Fuchs down to the Weddell Sea to help set up the UK base being established there; three more were to travel to the Ross Sea and work with the Americans who were already established in McMurdo Sound close to where the New Zealand committee wished to build their own station; and the final member of the seven would spend a year with an Australian expedition that had based itself on the Mac Robertson coast in the segment of Antarctica claimed by Australia but as yet not really explored. It was Harry Ayers who was seconded to the Australian Mawson base. The Australians needed a competent mountaineer and in Harry they had one of the finest in the southern hemisphere.

Ayres' association with Edmund Hillary was recommendation enough, but his expertise in climbing didn't stop him being called upon to perform another task. On his return to New Zealand he was to bring back several teams of battle-hardened huskies to form the nucleus of the dogs that would be required once the TAE started in earnest. This meant that while he helped the Australians with tackling any mountains they wished to climb, in return they instructed him on dog handling. On one climb with two Australians he was leading up an icefall when he heard a shout from the second man on the rope; without looking down, he instantly dug in his ice axe, whipped the rope that held the three men together tight around the shaft of the axe and checked the fall, saving all their lives.

The first of those venturing down to the American base at McMurdo Sound was Bernie Gunn, probably the most versatile member from either side of the TAE. Like Harry Ayres, he was an alpine guide and a very seasoned climber. He was a skilled photographer and skier. His aptitude for things mechanical led to his sorting out problems with the tractors and mending equipment that had broken. He was also a radio operator. On top of these numerous skills he was also a qualified geologist.

During the field work that ran in conjunction with the TAE support party, Bernie Gunn and Lt Commander Dick Brooke made the first ascent of Mount Huggins, which stood over 12,000 feet high, up above the Skelton Glacier. The Scott expedition of 1901 to 1904 discovered it and named the mountain after Sir William Huggins, the president of the Royal Society at the time.

Teaming up with Bernie Gunn on the first leg of TAE was Lt Commander W J L Smith of the Royal New Zealand Navy. His brief was to search for a suitable berth for the expedition's ship *Endeavour*. His occupation in the navy was as a hydrographer. He had had a remarkable war; just one of his exploits was to navigate a miniature submarine into the approaches to Singapore Harbour and set mines on a Japanese war ship that was acting as a floating gunnery platform defending the harbour. The two-man sub succeeded in its task and caused considerable damage to the ship before escaping back under the mined and netted approach. For his part in this extremely dangerous mission he was awarded the Distinguished Service Order medal. The submarine's commander received the Victoria Cross. Bill Smith was to become Second Officer on the *Endeavour* during her trips with the TAE expedition so the experience he gained on this first sortie would prove invaluable the next year when the expedition set out in earnest to assemble on the Antarctic continent.

When the FIDS programme developed into a larger organisation, and because of the *John Biscoe*'s limited cargo-carrying capacity, she was eventually replaced by the RRS *Shackleton*. The New Zealand Navy purchased the *John Biscoe* for £20,000 and renamed her HMNZS *Endeavour*. Her usefulness as a supply ship for the New Zealand base in Antarctica came to an end in 1962 and she was sold on. Her new owners used her for nearly 20 more years as a sealer in Arctic waters off the Newfoundland coast. In 1982 she was wrecked off that coast.

The organising committee in New Zealand decided to include a wider spectrum of exploration into the programme and to integrate various field parties that could carry out surveying, mapping and geological work. This was strongly supported by Edmund Hillary, as he saw it as an opportunity to establish his country's claim to the Ross Sea sector. With this in mind the third man chosen to accompany Bernie Gunn and Bill Smith needed to be from a scientific background and also a potential leader of the IGY group that would eventually accompany the TAE party. Dr Trevor Hatherton had all the right credentials, with a degree and subsequent doctorate in geophysics awarded in England before his move to New Zealand. Here he took up a post with the Scientific and Industrial Research department. He was a competent climber, having gained experience in the Alps.

Edmund Hillary and J H 'Bob' Miller were to fly to Montevideo and join up with Dr Fuchs and his advance party. They would then travel down to the Weddell Sea in the expedition ship and gain some much-needed experience of working and living in the Antarctic in preparation for their own expedition to the Ross Sea the following year, 1956. Dr Fuchs was on his way from London to South Georgia and then on to the Weddell Sea in the Expedition's ship, the *Theron*, calling at Montevideo to pick up the two New Zealanders.

Bob Miller was selected as second in command of the New Zealanders because of his wide experience in surveying and mapping, which were to be the primary objectives during the expedition's stay in Antarctica. He had graduated from Victoria College in Wellington and became a surveyor. War interrupted his career and in 1940 he joined a Field Artillery regiment, which served in North Africa. In 1943 he was wounded and sent home to New Zealand. He resumed his work and this led to him carrying out some expeditionary work, surveying a little-known area of New Zealand.

He was knighted in 1979 for the services he had rendered to Antarctic exploration. Known nearly all his adult life as Bob, he became Sir J H 'Bob' Miller. His mediation skills whilst on the expedition led to him being likened to Edward Wilson on Scott's two expeditions.

Squadron Leader John Claydon was the Committee's first choice for the post of senior pilot. He had been a serving officer in the RNZAF during the war with a fighter squadron operating in the Pacific theatre. Achieving a special distinguished pass when graduating from flying school, he was always destined to be an exceptional pilot. He became commanding officer at the Wigram Flying School. Having been picked for the expedition he was also nominated to be one of the three New Zealand participants to accompany the vanguard party to Vahsel Bay under Dr Fuchs in 1955.

Continuing with the Ross Sea Committee's choice, Flying Officer Bill Cranfield was to be their second pilot. Bill was only 22 when selected but he had amassed an impressive number of flying hours and was a flying instructor at the Wigram Flying School, where John Claydon had been commanding officer. Bill had had a lot of experience with various aircraft and in particular the Auster, which was to be one of the two reconnaissance planes.

Filling the third slot of the RNZAF contingent was Sergeant Wally Tarr. Trained as an aero-engine fitter, he was exceptionally talented in his field and his expertise with the two aircraft kept them fully operational throughout the whole period. He also worked at Wigram and, like Bill Cranfield, probably knew John Claydon. Wigram Air Base seems to have been the source of all the RNZAF personnel to accompany the expedition because Corporal Peter Tate was based there (he was to join the expedition for the second season). He had experience with aircraft maintenance and in addition could operate radio equipment.

Back in London the expedition organisers needed to select a suitable ship for taking the 1955 contingent down to the Antarctic because the old FIDS ship *John Biscoe* had been disposed of and a replacement had not yet been bought. The committee managed to secure the services of MV *Theron*. She had been used as a sealer working in Canadian waters. Her hull had been strengthened to withstand moderate ice conditions and under her skipper Captain Harold Maro was to be put to the test time and again as the expedition fought its way through the Weddell Sea.

The *Theron* sailed from Millwall Docks on 14 November 1955 with a crew of mostly Norwegian sailors and a complement of nineteen expeditioners. On board was of course leader Dr Vivian Fuchs, who even as a child had always been known as 'Bunny'. There was David Stratton, Bunny's second in command. John Lewis the chief pilot, Gordon Haslop, second pilot, Peter Weston, aircraft mechanic, Taffy Williams, radio operator and David Pratt the tracked vehicle expert, were there. Then there were the four

New Zealanders: Sir Edmund Hillary, always referred to as Ed, his second in command Bob Miller, George Lowe, Hillary's long-time mate and expedition photographer from Everest days, and John Claydon, chief pilot.

Details of the other men aboard will give an idea about how diverse a group they were. Dr Rainer Goldsmith was appointed medical officer for the advance party. After the first year when his term of engagement was completed he returned to the UK on board the *Magga Dan* to resume his career in the field of physiology. His background was as a newly qualified physiological researcher and this meant that he was always interested in how the human body reacted to extreme environments. The advance party suffered only a few minor injuries, mostly snow blindness and frost bite, so he was not too stretched in the medical department. Sergeant Major Desmond Homard, known as Roy, was chief mechanic for the advance party looking after the vehicles. He had gained the necessary experience for this during his two years on the Greenland Ice Cap with the North Greenland Expedition between 1952 and 1954. The training he received as a serving soldier in a Royal Electrical and Mechanical Engineers (REME) detachment with the Army during the North African campaign during the Second World War additionally stood him in good stead. He stayed on for the duration of the expedition's three years and worked in conjunction with David Pratt, the other engineer, during the final year of the crossing.

There were to be three meteorologists chosen to be among the eight men who would form the advance party. Peter Jeffries, aged 24, had gained field experience on weather ships stationed in the Atlantic. Primarily interested in upper air studies, he found himself thwarted when all the gas for his balloons and their inflation apparatus were lost when the ice shelf calved after the *Theron* had left. He did not take part in the crossing but moved to the IGY site at Halley Bay for the second year, where he was able to partake in their meteorological studies.

Tony Stewart was working as an instructor at the Pangbourne Nautical College when chosen and he became the senior meteorologist for the advance party, but returned to England before the crossing took place.

A young South African by the name of Hannes la Grange made up the trio of weathermen. South Africa had donated generously to the original plea for money and Hannes became their representative on the project. He would complete the crossing and subsequently led a South African expedition back to Antarctica a couple of years later.

The penultimate member of the advance party was Ralph Lenton. He travelled down on the *Theron* ostensibly as a radio operator but his skills at carpentry made him indispensable, especially when it came to building the Shackleton Base hut that first traumatic winter. He was also with the party that moved out to South Ice to help construct the hut there, but returned to Shackleton for the second winter. He gained his radio communication skills whilst serving in the Fleet Air Arm during the Second World War. Afterwards he had spent several seasons with FIDS so he was well qualified to participate in TAE and he went on to complete the crossing.

The final member of the octet and one of the more senior members of the expedition in terms of polar experience was Ken Blaiklock, whose connections to Bunny went back to the early FIDS exploits when they were together at Stonington base in 1949/50. Ken completed the team that were to overwinter at Shackleton Base that first winter. He was appointed as one of the surveyors and was in charge of the advance party for that first life-threatening winter. When South Ice was established he helped to man and build this outpost, carrying out some survey work in the mountains to the south of their hut and, in partnership with Jon Stephenson, drove two dog teams all the way to the South Pole during the crossing. This made the pair of dog mushers the second and last team to make it to the South Pole after Amundsen in 1911. He was only 20 when he first went down to the Antarctic prior to TAE and after it he carried out several other Antarctic expeditions. He was awarded the Polar medal with three bars and finally an OBE for services to scientific polar research.

As part of Bunny's strategy for including the Commonwealth countries in the TAE, George Lowe joined the Weddell Sea party. He was from New Zealand and a personal friend of Ed Hillary. They had been on Everest together. George Lowe was in the main support party on the final assault to conquer the highest mountain in the world. He was not only a very competent climber but a very talented photographer. George did not overwinter in the Antarctic with the advance party but came down again in the following year and completed the crossing to the Ross Sea.

Although not included as one of the team to partake in the actual crossing or the advance base operations, Derek Williams made his way down with the *Theron* party as the representative of British Petroleum. As previously noted, BP had agreed to supply all the fuel requirements for the expedition and Bunny had asked Derek Williams along for the first season so that he could make a start on the official film to document the beginning of their historic attempt. The remainder of the expedition's photography would rest with George Lowe, and their combined work would result in the official film of the expedition. George Lowe played a major part in its final production, with his name on the film's credits. Derek Williams had made many documentary films in his career, several of which received Oscar nominations in the short film category. The film he and George made about the crossing of Antarctica had a private showing at Buckingham Palace.

Heading South aboard
the *Theron*

Built in 1950 on the River Clyde by Messrs James Lamont for the Canadian company of Christensen, the *Theron* was designed for the sealing trade and her cargo space had room for 30,000 seals in temperature-controlled holds. 180 feet long by 33 feet beam and drawing 17 feet, she was of a compact design and her marine diesel engines developed 1,300hp. She had a multi-station steering facility which enabled the captain to control her from the wheelhouse, the compass platform or even the crow's nest: essential features for navigating in ice-strewn waters.

Theron's voyage down the Atlantic to Montevideo in Uruguay was fairly uneventful. She set sail on Monday 14 November 1955 from Millwall Docks. The expedition had not been allowed to take on board the explosives they would require for the seismic tests and these had to be picked up as she passed out of the Thames estuary at Greenwich. Her deck cargo differed from other Antarctic expeditions. None before could boast a crated Sno-Cat and two Auster aircraft, one crated with the wings in a separate container and the second lashed to the deck ready for immediate use. This second plane can be seen in the plate section, as *Theron* left Millwall docks, but both Vivian Fuchs' book and Stephen Haddelsey's describe how in South Georgia the wings were assembled onto the fuselage prior to a test flight. This story is confirmed in George Lowe's version of events. However, in Haddelsey's book *Shackleton's Dream*, he has a photo of the plane leaving the Port of London with her wings in place so this is difficult to explain. The fully crated Auster does not appear to have been used once the expedition reached the Antarctic, probably because there was just not enough time to get it airworthy. It was returned to England and eventually shipped down to New Zealand for use in the Ross Sea sector.

There were so many fuel drums that no one could move about on deck without having to detour round them. The only obvious common ground with other ships going south was the twenty or so Greenland huskies. Their accommodation of wooden boxes was piled on top of the Sno-Cat crate. Down in the three holds, normally reserved for the thousands of seals that would have been caught, were stowed the bulk of the stores, which included two Weasel tracked vehicles and two Ferguson tractors. The inventory read like a warehouse closing-down sale.

The Cape Verde Islands provided a short interlude while the *Theron* was watered and then it was on to Montevideo where Bunny had already arranged to meet up with Ed Hillary and Bob Miller, who had flown in from New Zealand via most of the other countries in South America. This rendezvous brought together the four New Zealanders: Ed Hillary, Bob Miller, George Lowe and John Claydon.

Before reaching Montevideo, a shadow was cast over the ship after one of the engine staff coming on deck for a breath of fresh air decided to have some sport with an albatross that had been shadowing the ship in its own silent, circumspect way. He shot it with the gun he was cleaning. *The Rime of the Ancient Mariner* came to the minds of all who heard of the incident.

After a couple of days' respite from the rolling action of the top-heavy vessel they set out from Montevideo and were now sailing in a direct line to Grytviken in South Georgia. The British Government had installed a magistrate here as part of the establishment of the UK's claim to that sector of Antarctica.

The whaling station was still in operation at the time of the visit, and for those men who had never seen the process of dismantling a 70-ton monster it must have been a sobering experience. From the huge torso first making its appearance on the slipway to its despatch into the various pieces of apparatus that disposed of its body to making way for the next unfortunate carcass took little more than an hour. After skinning the body and flensing the blubber off it for the oil, it was stripped of the meat which was then cut up and cooked and the bones were crushed for fertilizer. Whatever slid into the sea from the slipway where the whale once lay was devoured by the myriad sea birds constantly hovering around for their share.

Bunny already knew Robert Spivey, the magistrate, from their two years together at Stonington between 1948 and 1950. There were other familiar faces at the station to meet them, and, as can be imagined, a reunion was the order of the day.

George Lowe, in his book *Because It Is There*, remembers visiting Kenneth Butler, the English manager of the Norwegian whaling station, and marvelling at the style in which he lived. Members of the expedition were entertained at his personal residence with drinks from a cocktail bar, they were waited on by two white-jacketed servants and after an elegantly served meal, which he doesn't elaborate on, the group relaxed in comfortable chairs and the conversation inevitably came round to whales and whaling. George found it all fascinating. Walking back to the ship, he excitedly anticipated the prospect of sailing on down towards the Antarctic and crossing the convergence where the sea changes colour from the dark blue of the South Atlantic to the greener hue of the colder waters of the Antarctic Ocean.

Grytviken Harbour provided the ideal place to give the Auster a trial flight, and the aircrew set to and put the plane into flying trim. Using floats, the test flight was carried out by John Lewis. His first run was abandoned due to rough water but a second attempt saw the plane lift off, circle round a couple of times and come back to a near perfect landing. The plane was quickly re-stowed, allowing the *Theron* to navigate round to Leith Harbour for taking on fuel. This was followed by a further stop for filling all the water tanks, and, with a final farewell, she steamed out of the harbour bound for the great white south.

The ship's rails were lined by most of the expedition members at the first mention of icebergs. These were sighted only a few days out from South Georgia and were to become a permanent feature of the seascape from now on. Captain Harold Maro, the *Theron*'s long-serving skipper, soon became a favourite of the expedition not only for the competent way he sailed her but his ability to entertain the team by telling them stories of his experiences during his time sealing in the icy waters off Labrador and Greenland.

The approach to the frozen Weddell Sea was presaged by the brash ice that they encountered on 22 December. The ship ploughed through these small ice islands with no apparent slowing of progress but this was to change dramatically within a few days. They crossed the imaginary circle drawn so precisely on all maps denoting the line around the world where at summer solstice, 22 December, in the southern hemisphere, the sun is above the horizon for a full 24 hours.

The ice started to get more dense and this had a calming effect on the ship's motion, much to everybody's relief, but soon a course had to be selected on which the ship would head down into the Weddell Sea. Bunny had studied all previous efforts by exploration ships trying to penetrate as far south to as high a latitude as they could get in this relentless accumulation of ice. He had formed the opinion that the Weddell Sea had two contra-rotating currents moving the ice in two circular paths leaving a channel that could be exploited approximately down the middle of them. Captain James Weddell had navigated this route on his spectacular penetration as early as 1827, when his sailing ship the *Jane* had achieved the incredible latitude of 74° South. Against this theory lay the fact that William Speirs Bruce during his Scottish National Expedition in 1904 had found a relatively ice-free lead along the eastern boundary of the Weddell Sea and had reached a southerly latitude similar to James Weddell before retreating to the South Orkneys to beat the onset of winter.

The Weddell Sea lies approximately between the longitudes of 20° West and 60° West. The east coast of the Graham Land Peninsula forms the western boundary of the Weddell Sea and more loosely the Caird Coast of Coats Land forms the eastern boundary. William Speirs Bruce named this part of Antarctica Coats Land after his sponsors, the wealthy Scottish brothers James and Andrew Coats, who had been the main financial backers of his expedition. They had made their fortunes in the cotton industry. The Caird Coast was subsequently named by Sir Ernest Shackleton after the sponsor of his proposed trans-Antarctic expedition, Sir James Caird.

Wilhelm Filchner, the German explorer, had penetrated even further south on a slightly more western approach to the one Speirs had taken and almost reached a bay in 1912 that he called Vahsel Bay. This bay was named after his ship's captain. He planned to spend the winter in the region and successfully set up his base camp but had not allowed for the vagaries of the ice and before the party could move into their hut they had to speedily dismantle it and re-embark with as much of their stores and equipment as they could salvage. The ice on which they had chosen to place their camp broke away from the rest of the ice shelf and threatened their destruction. Shortly after setting off to the north they became trapped and had to spend the next eleven months embedded in the ice. They were so fortunate not to suffer the same fate as Shackleton did just four years later. Shackleton had also taken the western approach based on Filchner's and Speirs' experiences and although coming within 70 miles of Vahsel Bay his expedition was to experience a far worse threat to survival, but they did all make it, thanks to his superhuman efforts and determination.

The Swedish explorer Otto Nordenskjold's expedition also came to grief, but this time along the Graham Land Peninsula's east coast. He was attempting to find a route along the western edge of the Weddell Sea in 1902–4. How he extricated his expedition is almost as remarkable as Shackleton's story. Under his command a wintering party of six men set up a base camp on Snow Hill Island while their ship the *Antarctic* returned to South Georgia and then onto South America to winter and stock up with fresh supplies for the expedition. The following summer under the captaincy of Carl Larsen, a professional seal hunter, the ship was caught in the pack ice as she ventured south to pick up the men that had been left for the winter and she was eventually crushed. The wintering party on Snow Hill Island were unaware of this catastrophe. Prior to the *Antarctic* being destroyed Larsen had landed three men at Hope Bay after his ship had become trapped; the same Hope Bay that Operation Tabarin had wanted to use. They were instructed to try to work their way south to make contact with the wintering party and explain the ship's situation. These three men could not get through due to open water and they waited many months in a stone igloo they built for a rescue to come. Meanwhile, the wintering party, realising that something must have happened to the expedition's ship, set out on foot to probe northwards from their base for any sign of their comrades and against all odds they came across the three refugees living in their stone igloo. They all returned to Snow Hill Island to live out yet another winter. Rescue missions were mounted from a number of sources because the *Antarctic* had not returned to the Falklands as planned. Argentina sent a naval ship called the *Uruguay*. A search party from the Argentinian ship managed to locate Nordenskjold and his eight men and rescue them and by another coincidence they also picked up a group of four men from the stricken *Antarctic* who had set out from Paulet Island where they had been marooned and were attempting to make contact with the original wintering group. They had managed to sail down towards Snow Hill Island in one of the ship's open boats intending to rendezvous with the southern party. From these men Nordenskjold now knew the location of the survivors of the *Antarctic* and the *Uruguay* with those already rescued made its way to Paulett Island to pick them up. Coincidences do happen and the saving of the lives of all the expedition members would not have been possible without quite a number of them.

These expeditions were really all that Bunny had to base his decisions on; he reasoned that if the central approach was possible, then the *Theron* would only have to sail down one side of a triangle instead of sailing first eastwards to Cape Norvegia on the Caird Coast and then south-west along that coast, which would add considerably to the mileage they had to travel before arriving at Vahsel Bay. Bunny must have discussed this with his ship's captain, whose knowledge of ice navigation was one of the best in the world. Ed Hillary in his book *No Latitude for Error* states that in conversation the ship's captain, Harold Maro, had told Ed that he would have preferred the western, coastal route but Bunny wasn't prepared to budge. So both men deferred to the leader.

The *Theron* had been strengthened for working in ice conditions so all appeared to be possible. The Auster was not used for any reconnaissance prior to the *Theron* entering thicker ice probably because the open ocean was too rough to allow this to take place and once in the ice it would be difficult to find room for taking off. Whatever the reason for not doing this, it was soon to be regretted. At the end of the third day they were virtually prisoners of the ice.

Progress for the first 24 hours was good and about 160 miles were ticked off, and on the next day, 24 December, they were still making some headway but by the evening the ship's progress slowed. Eventually they were brought to a standstill by the presence of a lot of icebergs and the closeness of the pack and with visibility deteriorating rapidly, Captain Maro, who had been spending long hours in the crow's nest to navigate his ship, gave the order to close down the engines – and at least celebrate Christmas, wait for an improvement in the visibility and see if they could try again in a couple of days' time.

Christmas Day was celebrated in the usual manner and the tension in the atmosphere aboard the ship eased for a precious few hours. The whole ship's company enjoyed chicken noodle soup, roast turkey with all the trimmings followed by strawberries and ice cream washed down with Uruguayan wine. The New Zealand contingent of Ed Hillary, John Clayton, George Lowe and Bob Miller rounded off the convivial affair with a rendition of Maori songs.

Boxing Day brought better visibility and the engines were restarted. Slow progress was made until they entered a space where it might just be possible to launch the Auster. John Lewis successfully took off and flew south for about 30 miles, coming back to disclose that there were open leads and a water sky ahead once the next mile or so of ice could be broken through. A water sky is the reflection of open water thrown up onto the underside of clouds at some distance from the viewer, indicating a break in the pack ice. Despite repeated efforts, the ship became trapped for several hours before eventually breaking out; but by now the open leads ahead were a thing of the past, the ice having closed up to stop the ship again. George Lowe can recall lying in his bunk listening to the ice as it pressed hard against the ship. The ship's superstructure became strained under the enormous pressure. Everybody was starting to realise the predicament that was creeping up on them and the tension could be felt throughout the ship's company.

This failure to capitalise on the aircraft's ability to survey the route ahead meant that the *Theron* was at the mercy of the ice. All they could do was wait and see what the next few days would bring. Ed Hillary's comment on the continued delays was: 'All you need here is a timepiece that tells the time in days.'

Bunny calculated that the ship was being dragged to the west and north, away from his hoped-for shortest route to Vahsel Bay by the ice cage that they were trapped in. On 8 January they were given a small chance to determine their own destiny and the ship resumed her direct assault on the ice by driving at the nearest flow. The prow would rise onto the ice and slowly the ice would crack and with luck split to allow another charge to be mounted. The progress was minimal, however, and the strain on the propeller and hull could not be maintained indefinitely.

Bunny had been in contact by radio with the leader of another British Antarctic expedition. They were currently making excellent progress down the ice-free channel that Bunny had forsaken. This expedition was the United Kingdom's entry into the IGY, organised by the Royal Society. They had left South Georgia a few days after the *Theron* and by 6 January had started unloading their ship, the *Tottan*, at what would become known as Halley Bay, a future British Antarctic Survey (BAS) base situated some miles further to the east of Bunny's planned base site. It must have been galling for him to realise that the *Theron* was still stuck and the summer was passing them by. Soon after Bunny had discovered how well *Tottan* had progressed he had the first good news of the trip so far. HMS *Protector*, the Royal Navy's ice patrol vessel, contacted them offering assistance. She had on board two small Westland helicopters and a sophisticated radar system that would enable her to locate *Theron* and guide her to safety.

Fate had not dealt kindly with the TAE but was about to produce a couple more body blows. For a number of days some of the men had been over the side onto the ice trying to saw, hack and finally blast a way through, and had succeeded in displacing several chunks of ice, which were being disposed of to the stern area using the ship's winch and a steel hawser, when suddenly the hawser came loose from the block and whipped back alongside the ship. It fell into the water and sank down, to be picked up by the propeller and become tangled round the prop shaft. It was impossible to untangle the hawser and every time the blade turned so the loose end spun round and thrashed against the steel hull with a reverberating, clanging sound. As the end gradually decreased in length so the noise was reduced but all aboard the ship had to put up with the uncertainty as to whether the hawser would give up before the hull was punctured.

The second mishap occurred whilst trying to manoeuvre through some narrow leads in the ice. The ship's rudder came into heavy contact with a substantial ice floe and was bent off centre. The *Theron* could not now be directed to port. Captain Maro knew that the only chance of rectifying this was to put into practice a stunt that his father had employed when confronted with a similar situation; he backed the ship until her rudder lay against a large piece of ice and reversed into it. At first nothing happened and after several goes he gave another but more forceful push. Remarkably, he had virtually re-aligned the rudder and the ship could proceed.

During this period of virtual imprisonment two things arose that George Lowe linked to the albatross incident during the *Theron*'s voyage down to Montevideo. Bunny carried out a request he had received from the family of Joseph Miller, who had been bosun aboard the research vessel *Discovery II*. They had asked if his ashes could be committed to the Antarctic Seas. This service was carried out with suitable dignity and the casket was committed to the deep.

The second incident concerned a white windsock that was being flown from the mast. The almost total white background of the surrounding pack ice made it very difficult to pick out the white wind sock from the aeroplane and so the sock was soaked in seal's blood to make it more obvious. The Norwegian crew were not too happy with this and one of their officers asked for the sock to be replaced. Although the Norwegians made no direct mention of the albatross incident, the inference was clear that blood being flown from the masthead was something that the seamen were suspicious of. The committal was also seen as an ill omen. The sock was removed forthwith.

On 19 January 1956, after fighting for every yard of progress in a northerly direction, the ship forced its way into a small area free from ice and following a consultation with the two pilots it was decided to try a flight. The pool was barely 350 yards long and even this was not all in a straight line. This flight was to be taken by the New Zealand pilot John Claydon. He was expected to do a dummy run to check the feasibility of the task ahead but instead as he ran down the open water he made the decision that he could successfully achieve his objective and pulled clear of the ice at the far end with just a few yards to spare.

Claydon was airborne for nearly three hours, and on his return he could report on more favourable conditions. They were still not free of the encompassing ice, but if progress could be made in a westerly direction for about 2 miles through the fairly heavy pack, by then turning north-west for some 18 miles of looser pack they should be able to finally turn north, where there was a navigable way out of their problem. At this point they should be able to meet up with HMS *Protector* and then her helicopters would be capable of finding a path through the ice so that the *Theron* could use the same channel that *Tottan* had found.

The ice still threatened the ship even as they were receiving the good news that there might be a way out. Following the incident with the bent rudder the ice started piling up against the sides of the ship and because she was so low in the water, with all the extra cargo she had on board, the ice even threatened to spill over onto the deck. Later the ship was reprieved as the ice relented and she was again free to float on an even keel.

The first serious encounter with the ice had taken place on 26 December 1955 and it took until 25 January 1956 before a southerly course could once again be followed. So this episode in the expedition's journey had cost more than four weeks of the short Antarctic summer, with repercussions that could only be fully realised when they were setting up their base. Not only had they lost so much time but the ship had taken a severe beating; her hull had been pierced above the water line and the internal damage caused the ship's water tanks to leak. Much of the drinking water had been lost or spoiled by sea water resulting in restrictions until a source could be found.

Bunny had once before been trapped in the ice many years earlier when sailing to Greenland with Sir James Wordie and he had also experienced being isolated at an Antarctic base for an extra 12 months because a relief ship could not get through due to an early freezing of the sea. Shackleton had lost his battle with the Weddell Sea, as had Nordenskjold. Filchner needed his share of luck to finally escape the jaws of the ice. It was surprising, then, that Bunny chose to seek an unproven route through the ice based purely on his own theory, instead of a route that offered at least a better than even chance of success. His argument about the shorter distance now meant nothing. Speed was now of the essence.

Cap Norvegia at the extreme top end of the Weddell Sea was reached on 26 January 1956 and from here Captain Maro could turn his ship southwards to follow what in hindsight should have been their course from the beginning. Now under nearly ideal sailing conditions the spirit of the party lifted perceptibly. Within 24 hours they reached Halley Bay, where the *Tottan* had disgorged the men and supplies that were to be the Royal Society's expedition base camp for the next two seasons. *Tottan* had tried to sail further down the coast line but had been turned back by ice conditions causing some consternation amongst the *Theron* party.

The *Tottan* was an old hand at servicing Antarctic bases; in 1951 she had gone to the aid of a French expedition working on Terre Adélie. This island is part of the Sub-Antarctic group called the Kerguelen Archipelago. Her mission was to evacuate them to Australia. The Australians also used her to ferry the members of their Heard Island relief expedition in 1952 and bring back the party that had been in residence for the previous 12 months. She returned to Heard Island in 1953 to effect a change-over of personnel. On her way back to Melbourne she encountered 60-foot waves and winds of well over 100 miles an hour for more than 48 hours. The captain never left the bridge for the duration of the hurricane.

The IGY did not possess an aircraft and now for the second time Bunny was able to make suitable use of the Auster. The features that were needed for the TAE base would be easier to spot from a plane rather than from on board a ship and should comprise a level and not too high ice flow attached to the main ice shelf to enable unloading from the ship to take place; a practical way of getting the stores from the ice shelf up to a position that would be safe to build the expedition's hut; and a way through to the hinterland for the proposed crossing that would be attempted the following year.

The Halley Bay site was nearly 200 miles from Bunny's preferred landing place at Vahsel Bay. After an air reconnaissance, the *Theron* set off to the west on the final leg of the tortuous journey from South Georgia that had begun on 22 December 1955, nearly six weeks earlier.

Eight Men Perched
on an Ice Shelf

The Auster took off from the sea at Halley Bay near the IGY base camp and flew inland to see if it might be possible to use Halley Bay as a starting-off site for the crossing. If the expedition could not find anything better further to the west where Vahsel Bay was located, then this might have to be the choice. Unfortunately, at Halley Bay the way further inland was severely blocked by a heavily crevassed and disturbed area that it would be extremely difficult to get the vehicles over, which might even prejudice the whole operation and then the crossing would be still-born. The Royal Society expedition that had chosen this site did not need to penetrate further inland, so the obstruction of crevasses and mountains was not a problem for the members stationed here. (Halley Bay is located at Latitude 75° 36′ South by 26° 40′ West. Vahsel Bay is about 200 miles south-west of Halley Bay at Latitude 77° South by 35° 49′ West.)

A low cloud formation for the next two days meant that no useful flying could be accomplished. It was now a case of all aboard and try to make a determined attempt to reach Vahsel Bay. They kept the ship as close to the ice edge as possible while Bunny and his men scanned the shore line with their binoculars looking for any suitable landing place. Gradually the scene changed and they were forced to move further out because they were passing the snout of the Dawson-Lambton Glacier that rose high above them. This glacier received its name from Ernest Shackleton as a tribute to one of his sponsors, Elizabeth Dawson-Lambton. There were a number of icebergs that had calved from the glacier and were drifting away from it giving Captain Maro a good reason to steer away from the hazard. There was the constant presence of brash ice but the ship pushed her way through and from the crow's nest Captain Maro was still able to see his way ahead.

Nearing Vahsel Bay they again launched the Auster and this gave Captain Maro, who went up with John Claydon, an excellent opportunity to see for himself the state of the ice and assess the extent of the risk.

Satisfied that there was a very good chance the ship could press on, they sailed towards Vahsel Bay. Meanwhile the Auster was again employed to search ahead and radioed back that the ice shelf some distance beyond Vahsel Bay sloped down towards the sea with a fairly level surface behind it. Vahsel Bay proved to be unsuitable due to the ice lying in it but an ice-free passage still existed to the west.

The ship rendezvoused with the plane at Vahsel Bay and following the observations taken on the next flight by David Stratton and John Lewis, the plane was swung aboard and they pushed on for the next 20 miles or so to the spot indicated by the aerial survey. Here, as predicted, they found an almost perfect landing spot with the requisite level ice shelf backed by a higher and safer level that could be gained up a fairly steep but not unmanageable slope. Docking took place and, after securing the *Theron* to the ice edge, the order was given to start the process of getting the expedition really underway. Several senior members of the expedition, including the advance party leader Ken Blaiklock, were taken up in the plane to gain their impressions of what lay inland of the ice shelf. There was never going to be a perfect place and time dictated that now they must capitalise on this, the best area yet seen.

Bunny and his deputy, David Stratton, walked over the lower level of the ice shelf and inspected the slope up onto the next level about 150 feet higher, looking for an area on which to build the hut for the advance party. They were seeking a place from where the sea could be seen and the ice shelf observed in case it calved. At the same time they had to have a safe surface where the snow was compacted and not liable to subsidence on which to build the expedition's hut.

The final choice put the base hut about 2 miles from the unloading site. Bunny estimated that the ice shelf here was well over 1,000 feet thick and although Wilhelm Filchner when he reached his chosen camp site on the ice shelf had thought it was safe enough to set up his hut he soon found out that the ice was about to calve, causing his party to make a speedy evacuation. Bunny felt that this place would be safe for the foreseeable future and being less than 2 miles from the unloading point, should make the transporting of material not too onerous a job.

The clock had been ticking all this time and the date was now 30 January 1956, nearly four weeks after the *Tottan* had landed the Halley Bay Expedition and discharged all of their stores. The dogs were the first item to be unloaded from the *Theron* and how they revelled in their new-found freedom, rolling in the snow and barking for joy. The deck cargo of the Sno-Cat and a myriad fuel drums had to be shifted before the holds could be reached.

It was essential to bring out the hut timbers and sections as quickly as possible but to move these to the hut site required the use of the Weasels and tractors. Unfortunately to get at the transport many other items had to be removed first. The loading plan in London Docks appears to have been loosely organised and this was about to become apparent with repercussions that nobody had foreseen. At least a day was lost before the sledges could be loaded and hitched up to the tractors and even then the half-track Fergusons were not capable of hauling loaded sledges up the ramp to the top. This meant that only the Weasels could be employed for the ramp and a shuttle of sledges between ship and ramp was devised, the Weasels taking over from the Fergusons. Then just as the system started to work smoothly a Weasel shed its tracks and it turned out that the spares were in another hold and nobody could get at them. Ed Hillary was taking note of these problems and later, when he in his turn set up Scott Base ready for New Zealand's operations to begin, he made sure that the loading of his ship was more logical.

On 1 February, just two days after the unloading had started, there was a dramatic rise in temperature and a change of wind direction, ominous signs for the unloading process. The amount of discharged cargo was accumulating on the ice shelf faster than it was being removed and now that a number of men were engaged moving supplies up the ramp and indeed at the hut site where preparations were being made for the base of the hut to be put down, any threat to the ship from worsening weather could prove most inconvenient to say the least.

The wind was picking up and *Theron* started to pull at her moorings. Captain Maro became increasingly worried about the situation and now had only one option. He gave the order to cast off and sailed out to the open sea where he could ride out the storm that had broken. Sea water was being swept over the ice shelf and it was not long before every available man was straining to move the cargo away from the area that was being inundated. If this was not accomplished and the temperature dropped again, all the stores could be encased in a cladding of frozen ocean spray, from which it would be a mammoth task to salvage anything.

Some of the lighter crates were afloat and the men found themselves wading around in water at or near freezing point up to 2 feet deep. George Lowe recalls struggling with a crate that had a message stencilled on its side 'Handle with care, property of the BBC'. He could not help but chuckle over the pathetic situation both he and the crate were in.

From the ice edge it was not possible through the murky conditions to know how far away the *Theron* might be and with a huge sigh of relief Bunny saw her re-emerge about half-an-hour after withdrawing.

She edged in as gently as possible so as not to collide with the ice and damage her bows and at the closest point the captain shouted through a megaphone for anybody who could to scramble up the hastily placed rope ladders and netting that had been thrown down the ship's side to get aboard because he might not be able to get back if the storm persisted. How they all achieved getting back on board without any accidents beggars belief; but all those who had witnessed the *Theron* disappearing were now safe and could get into dry clothes and enjoy some warm food and shelter. It was a very different story for the five men who were up at the base site because everything had happened so quickly that the message to retreat back to the ice shelf had not reached them in time.

The five refugees – David Stratton, David Pratt, Roy Lenton, Bob Miller and Peter Jeffries – had been held hostage by the storm near the base site and had spent the night huddled in the cab of one of the Weasels with nothing to eat. They had attempted to drive the Weasel down the slope but lost the marked route in the swirling snow driven by the storm and sensibly decided to stay where they were. As the visibility improved and they could make sure they were on a safe course to continue, they ventured down onto the ice shelf and the realisation dawned on them that they were alone, the *Theron* had gone; but for how long?

Was this a temporary situation or worse? Had the *Theron* left them as *Aurora* had been forced to do to the Ross Sea party of Shackleton's Trans-Antarctic Expedition in 1914? Were they in fact in a much worse predicament than that? Were the stores that lay around them of any use for survival? What could they contain? How likely was there to be food and fuel and spare clothes in any of them? And as for shelter, the hut had not even risen above ground level. They were wet, cold and hungry but they must not lose hope.

Rather than waste valuable time they found an emergency food ration and a primus stove probably from the Auster and with this they managed to concoct a mixture of sardines, tinned tomatoes, margarine and sugar. After a quick assessment of the situation confronting them they decided to resume where the others had left off and rescue as many of the cases still marooned in the slush down near the ice edge as they could and as the day passed their immediate danger receded because in the afternoon the storm had abated as quickly as it had risen. The sea was unusually calm and Captain Maro brought *Theron* back in to the ice shelf edge. All five climbed gratefully on board to a press of handshakes and back slaps. As soon as they had changed into warm dry clothes they were regaled with a hot meal, all the while telling their story.

The consequences of the storm were not lost on Bunny and his men, this had been a close call and the expedition could have ended there and then. Captain Maro was now distinctly edgy about the prospects of staying on much longer and Bunny, sensing this, set his men to the task of getting everything out of the holds and onto the ice. Owing to the erratic stowage in the Port of London items were coming ashore and being put down on the ice wherever room could be found. The unloading sequence went out of the window, and the area around the ship was a complete shambles. All the men were involved with the activity of unloading. Gradually, some semblance of order started to return as the stores were sorted and moved into heaps ready for transhipment to the base site. This had taken them five days to achieve. On 5 and 6 February the ice could be seen advancing on the landing place. Captain Maro was taken up by John Lewis to scan the sea and see for himself what the ice was doing. Bunny even found time to go aloft and search inland for any problems that might hinder the first step the expedition would take on its 2,000-mile journey.

As John Lewis swung the Auster in a wide arc inland they were able to discern far away on the horizon the evidence of a mountain range that until now had never been seen before. Fuel for a long flight was insufficient so they turned for home and on 7 February Bunny sent his chief surveyor, Ken Blaiklock, up with Gordon Haslop to make an aerial reconnaissance of the mountains seen on the 6th. Flying directly towards them Ken soon established that there was indeed a substantial range of unknown mountains rising as best as he could estimate about 4,500 feet or so high. The range ran in a general north-east to south-west direction with substantial glaciers debouching from it. Beyond this first range it appeared that a second and higher range existed.

Unknown to the two flyers they arrived back at the ship in the middle of an emergency. The pack was making a move against the *Theron* and Captain Maro could not wait much longer. As soon as the plane returned it was quickly stowed aboard the ship. Final instructions were given to the eight men who were to form the advance party. Amidst all the hustle and bustle the eight men needed to retrieve any personal gear they had left on board, scribble a few final letters to be taken away with the ship and somehow grasp that this was the moment when their world would change dramatically for the foreseeable future. They would be alone apart from a radio that up to now had not been very reliable and the next 10 or 11 months would be the greatest test any of them would ever be called upon to endure. There was little that those who were leaving could say to their comrades as the ship pulled away from the ice edge. Final handshakes and hugs had smothered any words that were mumbled. Waving bravely but forlornly from the ice edge the eight-man team gradually receded from view until they were just black specks that could as easily have been penguins, and then they were gone. The *Theron* departed from Shackleton Base on 7 February 1956, earlier than when William Speirs Bruce turned back in the *Scotia*, which was 23 February 1905 from a point 70° South.

Ken Blaiklock was left in charge of this small group. He had a number of seasons of polar exploration under his belt, as had two of the others – Roy Homard, the mechanic who had been in Greenland for two years, and Ralph Lenton who had spent five seasons with FIDS on the Graham Peninsula. As for the other five, Peter Jeffries, Tony Stewart and Hannes la Grange at least had some experience in carrying out their meteorological work in remote and isolated places. This left Taffy Williams the radio operator who could boast of a good few years of military service behind him, and the last team member, Rainer Goldsmith their doctor, newly qualified in physiology but with very little field experience.

Once the silence had re-established itself after the three blasts from the ship's siren had faded away, the little group made their way back up the slope to establish the camp they were going to live in for as long as it took to build the hut. The Sno-Cat crate was not large enough to allow them to use it for sleeping quarters and had to be dedicated for use as an area for working, writing up diaries, keeping records, a dining room, a cookhouse and a radio shack; in fact any occupation that needed to be undercover except sleeping.

For sleeping they erected four two-man tents and these flimsy affairs would have to suffice nearly all the way through. During the six months from 7 February until 7 August 1956 they would have to sleep in them. Then Ken Blaiklock and his tent mate Rainer Goldsmith would spend their first night in the partially completed building that was still not weather-proofed and did not have any heating. Temperatures had reached as low as -40°F during May, with an average of -35°F.

Cooking was on a rota basis, as is usually the case when the party is not large enough to justify a full-time cook. Every member of the group took his turn and for his trouble he could at least sleep in the Sno-Cat crate. This gave them all a chance to feel warmer for the four days they were on duty. They could bring their sleeping bag into the crate with them, where it was possible to hang them up during the day and get them dry, although a couple of days back in the tent would soon mean that the condensation from their bodies had made them just as damp as before.

Eight men working about ten hours each every day sounds a lot but when the list of jobs that had to be accomplished was considered, then it can be appreciated how stretched the labour force was. Of primary importance were the two main tasks that were to take up most of their time: shifting the stores from the ice shelf and building the hut.

Out on the ice shelf was something in the region of 300 tons of stores. It was all precariously positioned. Mechanical failures to the Sno-Cat and one of the Weasels would slow down the movement of the crates up the slope to the base site. The Ferguson tractors did not cope at all well with the soft snow that lay on the slope and with only the one operational Weasel they were restricted to about 15 tons of cargo being moved in any one day; and this was with a full team helping out. Roy Homard spent all day and every day crouched over one machine or another wrestling with breakdowns. The spare parts he needed were often in crates still on the ice shelf. He frequently had to remove his mittens to carry out the fitting of small parts, which led to several nasty bouts of frostbite. Ralph Lenton concentrated on making a start on the hut's construction and due to the complicated design and the size of some of the components that went into making it, he would have to secure the services of several other men to fulfil the task. In between helping Ralph with the hut, Taffy Williams was trying to establish radio contact with any other station that might pick up his signals, be it *Theron* on her way home, the IGY base 200 miles away to the north or even one of the American bases being established as part of IGY.

On a good day, this left five men to shift the stores and of course one of those would be duty cook, or getting ice for water, or feeding and attending to the dogs, or searching the pile of stores for some particular requirement.

Under temperate weather conditions a considerable amount of progress could be made but these were not temperate, they were hostile and starting to get worse. Every time the wind got up the chill factor increased, adding several degrees of frost and making it at times too cold to be out on the ice shelf for very long. Loose snow also caused a big problem by blowing in their faces and as it drifted along the surface it could obscure obstacles left lying around. The ramp up which they had to haul all the stores had been marked out with bamboo stakes to prevent anyone straying into the crevassed areas in certain places along its length. The drifting snow sometimes covered over the track and the men had to be constantly vigilant as they moved up and down the inclined track for fear of falling into one of the hidden traps.

The advance party set about prioritising their work schedule. They spent the first few days shifting the most vulnerable and essential stores up to the base area, including a small portion of the fuel drums and any food crates that they could identify. All the crates and drums had to be manually shifted into a suitable place before they could be lifted – again by hand – up onto a sledge that they had towed down the slope. Hardly any of the men involved in moving the cargo had ever driven a tractor, let alone a Weasel or a Sno-Cat, so there was a very steep learning curve

It was backbreaking work. A routine started to evolve and after getting ready in the morning, by nine o'clock, if conditions allowed, they were out and about until about two in the afternoon when the duty cook would call them in for a lunch break. The Sno-Cat crate had been rebuilt up on the base site and all the team would repair to this for about an hour. Resuming again after their stop there would be a further four or five hours toil and then all of them would reconvene for an evening meal cooked on the two primus stoves. By 10.30 they would shuffle off to their tents and start the process of struggling into their frozen sleeping bags. Each tent had its own primus stove and as soon as they could safely make room for it to be lit they could at least enjoy half-an-hour or so of warmth before curling up for the night and trying to get some sleep. When the outside temperatures dropped and without the heat from the little primus stoves, they found it harder and harder to do so. Despite several layers of a new blanket material called Terylene that had been designed and donated by Imperial Chemical Industries, their double-layered sleeping bags and the thick sheep's skins on which they lay, the cold still penetrated into the bedding.

After four days of dragging stores and drums onto sledges and off again at the base site Ken Blaiklock turned some of their energies towards erecting the hut. Ralph Lenton was the obvious man for leading the team in its construction. He was the only carpenter amongst them. He was very meticulous in his work and this could sometimes lead to resentment but without his expertise the building work would have taken much longer and if it had not been completed when it was, no one knows what the consequences might have been.

The temperatures were gradually falling during the rest of February but progress on the hut was maintained. The biggest hold-up was the complicated design. Trying to align pre-drilled holes in several components at the same time would have been difficult enough back in England when all the wood was straight and new but down in Antarctica after the sea, snow, and frost had taken its toll there was many an oath spoken or whispered that accompanied the construction process.

The designers had built extra strength into the frame to withstand the weight of snow that had been predicted. The base site was not in the heavy snow-belt as it turned out, but it did suffer from drift, with the ever-present wind driving what snow did fall into frustratingly large heaps that had constantly to be shovelled out of the way.

If the sea passage down to the Antarctic had been kept to its original schedule this would have allowed at least four and possibly five weeks to establish the base but of course this didn't happen. Time was lost in the ice of the Weddell Sea when the *Theron* was trapped there; and there were additional days lost with the stopover at the IGY base of Halley Bay and because Bunny wanted to secure the best possible unloading area and future base site, so of course a couple of days went by during this period as well. The expedition had at its disposal about 40 men, which included the ship's crew, to help unload the *Theron* in an organised way, transport a vast amount of the stores up to the area where the base hut was to be built, safeguard the advance party for the coming winter by constructing the hut and even carry out some reconnaissance into the region they were to traverse the next season. Very little of this was accomplished and the burden of blame must fall on the leader because he was ultimately responsible for the organisation of the whole expedition.

All through February the dogs had been tethered down the bottom of the slope on the ice shelf and to save some time from now on they were brought up to be nearer the base hut. The men realised that as the days shortened, venturing down a snow-strewn ramp in darkness could put them in unnecessary danger. The men employed the one serviceable Weasel to facilitate the move and by leaving the dogs still attached to the spans they were tethered to, the Weasel simply led all the dogs in one go up to the base area. They could then be staked out until a tunnel system could be dug which would give the dogs a substantial shelter when the worst of the weather came along.

From Rainer's diary it appears that the wind had turned to the north on 6 March and although the temperature had risen by nearly 10°F there was so much drifting snow about that work was called off for the day. This was the first full day spent in the shelter of the crate that they now called the Sno-house. There were to be many more in the forthcoming weeks.

A couple of days later worked had progressed to the point on the hut where some of the trusses were fitted into place but without any lifting gear they struggled to manhandle the parts onto the tops of the side frames. Having experienced their first day of idleness due to the weather they pressed on as quickly as possible when the outside conditions permitted. With the framework of the hut complete they were looking forward to adding the roof panels and the sides, which they had manoeuvred into position alongside the framework. On the morning of 21 March they woke up to the wind blowing the snow around into drifts at a very low temperature and this persisted until 27 March. All they could do was survive. Apart from the essential duties of feeding the dogs and the Met men taking their readings, there was never an opportunity to carry out any outside work. By the time they had spent so many hours together in the Sno-house there had developed a certain amount of tension among some members of the little community and the atmosphere, already thick with fumes from the primus stoves and the lack of ventilation, needed the calming influence of the senior members to maintain equanimity.

They finally ventured out on 28 March to a scene of huge drifts and much of the hut filled with many tons of snow and the crates containing the hut panels completely buried under the drifts. Taking one of the Weasels, two of the men, Ken Blaiklock and Tony Stewart, ventured down to the ice shelf to bring back some of the seal carcasses for the dogs and any other items that might be useful. The scene that they encountered was devastating. The storm had done its worst and the heavy swell that it had brought to bear on the ice shelf must have battered away at the zone where the ice had been held together, sought out the weakest point and taken a large portion of the ice shelf away to the north, to be broken into a thousand pieces. The fractured ice had taken with it most of the stores that the eight men had trustingly left for a later date while they toiled with the hut's construction. This meant that the oil drums of fuel, one of the Ferguson tractors, fuel for the coal-fired range yet to be installed into the hut, much of the dog food, a small rowing boat, timber with which they hoped to build the scientific hut and many other sundry items had been taken from them.

On top of the feeling of desolation which they had to overcome, they were faced with a situation that could even now physically overwhelm them. The hut was far from finished and they had something in excess of 60 tons of snow to clear out before they could resume work on it.

The Sno-house presented them with another problem when the temperature rose unexpectedly a few days later. All the hoar frost that had collected on the ceiling started to melt and water dripped continuously down onto the table, the bench seats and the cooking area, so that the men had to put up the hoods on their weatherproof jackets until some insulating material could be secured to the ceiling as a stopgap.

To help counteract the eternal snow drifts they dug a labyrinth of tunnels around the camp site and as they extended the network they joined them into one system and were able to start storing food boxes, spare clothing, miscellaneous stores and dogs. Each dog had its own cell and they even created a nursery for the newly born pups. In the event of a fire or some other catastrophe damaging the hut or Sno-house they would at least have a safe place to seek refuge in, with a reasonable stock of supplies to keep them alive until the return of the other expedition members the following summer.

April faded from memory and May looked as though it would continue the depressing streak. The first bright spot came on 7 May when after endless hours of patient application Ralph Lenton disturbed the near silence in the Sno-house, where they were all gathered carrying out mundane jobs to while away the time, with a triumphant shout that he had made some contact on the radio with the outside world. A thousand miles away on the Falkland Islands a radio station located in the capital Port Stanley must have heard the call signal and although the connection finished almost before it began, their perseverance had won through in the end, three months after the *Theron* had left them. They had not even been able to contact the IGY base at Halley Bay, their nearest neighbour, only 200 miles away.

Morale was suddenly boosted; compare the situation with that of the *Endurance* expedition over 40 years before. Here they were on the edge of the Antarctic continent with a radio set that should have been capable of transmitting and receiving messages from all over the world but still not able to send or receive any messages, whether by voice or Morse code to let the world and their loved ones know they were well and relatively safe. Shackleton and his men on the *Endurance* had been locked in the ice for many months in 1915, a few hundred miles north of the TAE base; but the expedition had no means of making contact with the outside world. It must have been a case of frustration on the part of one expedition and a sense of forlorn hope on the part of the other.

During the first 10 days of May the eight men played Scrabble and chess, wrote up their diaries or read what had already been read. Some turned their hands to darning and mending worn-out clothing that had not really stood up to the treatment it had been designed for. The only consolation to this enforced idleness came by way of the radio link. Messages could now be passed through the Port Stanley station to London and then onto their loved ones at home. Incoming messages consisted mainly of telegrams that were several months old to start with, but at least it was news.

One of their first out-going cables told of the disaster they had been confronted with when the stores on the ice shelf had disappeared during the storm that had kept them housebound in March. They could not know yet the full extent of the loss until an inventory of all the crates still to be opened had been carried out, but the major items like the fuel drums and the tractor and the upper air apparatus and gas were listed in the message. Despite all that had gone wrong and how they were struggling to make progress, and the fact that several times it looked as though they would be woefully short of the target that had been set for them, never once does a message to London outlining their plight seem to have been sent. It became apparent later in the year when the relief party arrived that they were totally unaware of the extreme difficulties that these eight men had overcome.

After the latest hold-up the little wind generator that was now installed on the *Dexion* mast gave sufficient output to light up several lamps in the Sno-house or it could supply electricity to some flood lights outside, so that with the shortening hours of daylight some progress was possible on the hut's construction.

Several times the snow drift meant that the four tents that they were still using for their dormitories had to been taken down and put back up on the new snow surface because they were being overwhelmed by the snow pressing in on the sides. During the day they were still living in the Sno-house right through June and July. They intermittently carried on with the hut but only when the ferocious weather permitted. So many days had been lost that some members feared that they would never complete the project. Mid-winter's day provided a brief respite and the eight men congregated in their Sno-house to celebrate an Antarctic Christmas in the traditional way. An oven that had been designed by Roy Homard and made out of an assortment of sheet metal salvaged from some discarded drums was formed into three layers, a bit like a Russian doll and between each metal layer a further layer of fibreglass insulating material was inserted. This provided the means for baking the Christmas cake. Other delicacies included turtle soup, boiled ham and vegetables for the main course followed by a traditional Christmas pudding with rum butter, all washed down with wine and brandy.

The oven passed through several evolutionary stages before it performed almost perfectly but all the cooking that took place whether by using the cooker or the open primus stoves in the unventilated Sno-house had its undesirable side-effects. Carbon monoxide gas built up as a consequence of the primus stove fumes and the unfortunate man on cooking duty suffered from headaches and feeling nauseous. To open the ventilator only allowed the ingress of wind-driven snow that soon covered and then wet any surface it settled on, so it was kept shut as the lesser of two evils.

Following a message that the men had sent out during the Christmas break they received one from the Queen expressing her thanks for the greetings that had gone out to her and telling them that she would be following their progress with interest. Goldsmith simply says in his diary, 'very nice'.

By 6 August one end of the hut was nearly complete but as yet it had not been insulated. Despite the lack of the insulation Rainer Goldsmith and his tent companion of recent weeks, Ken Blaiklock decided to move in. It was generally colder than their tent because the small primus could not possibly hope to heat such a large space, nevertheless it was a move towards normality.

The sun put in its first appearance after nearly four months on 23 August. This inspired a more positive attitude and almost immediately thoughts turned to other outside activities than just building the damned hut. The tractor would be needed to back up the Weasel that they had managed to keep going most of the winter but it had become buried in frozen snow and would take some time to extricate. But at least a start was made.

Three Men Venture South

By early September the weather had moderated quite considerably, so a decision was made to bring the dogs back to the surface and start getting them into harness for some gentle training. The dogs had other ideas and every time they were put together a fight would ensue. Eventually, some progress was made and Ken Blaiklock persevered for the next few days with short runs along the ice shelf. The long months of inactivity meant the dogs were very unfit but the nature of the beast is never far below the surface and they were soon starting to pull as a team.

With the hut nearing completion, or as near as it was going to get, they decided to leave their beloved Sno-house and transfer all the essentials over into the hut. One of the victims of the ice shelf disaster was the loss of the anthracite they were to have burnt on the new stove and as a substitute they began sawing up any surplus crates they could lay their hands on. The heat output from the stove in the unfinished hut barely kept pace with the heat loss through the various gaps that still existed as a result of not being able to find all the parts that had been buried under the snow drifts. From now on they could dispense with the four tents and no more would they have to brace themselves to seek out the refuge of the Sno-House during a blizzard when getting up in the morning or going to bed at night.

Towards the end of September Ken notified the others that he would be attempting a relatively short journey to Vahsel Bay to look for seals with which to feed the dogs. He was the only person amongst them who had driven dogs before. He chose Rainer Goldsmith to go with him. All was set for a departure on 25 September but it got off to an inauspicious start with the dogs fighting one another, the sledge overturning several times and a general melee most of the time. As the dogs tired some progress was made but the overall effort did not really pay any dividends and certainly no seals were procured.

Communications were improving all the time, especially with the generator now installed in the hut together with a larger transmitter. Halley Bay had finally been contacted and there had been an exchange of news that revealed how well the IGY party had settled in. News from London revealed the names of the party coming down on the *Magga Dan* and a shuffle of personnel at Shackleton was also conveyed to the eight men there. Peter Jeffries was asked if he would like another season but this time at Halley Bay, where he would be able to resume his upper air experiments that had been curtailed after losing most of his equipment when disaster had struck in that first storm of their stay. Tony Stewart had completed his year's work and would be going back to England, as would Rainer Goldsmith, who by now had grown to quite like this strange life. He rather resented the way the information was relayed to him; through a 'general order of the day', rather than a signal sent personally to him, but that was the way the Committee in London seemed to deal with all the organisational matters.

Life went on and the next target that the eight-man team hoped to achieve was the laying of a small depot about 50 miles to the south, as a precursor to something a bit more ambitious before the others turned up. Again it was Ken Blaiklock who led the three-man party, the others being Rainer and Peter Jeffries (Jeff as he had become known). They had been warned by London of the presence of a huge fissure very near the hut that had been detected from aerial photos taken from the Auster when the expedition first arrived to set up Shackleton Base. Although the three men kept a sharp lookout for any sign of it they never did discover its whereabouts. They were away for nine days and left a small depot of fuel and food for future use.

Three days after the depot party had returned the news came through that the *Magga Dan* had set sail from the UK and was finally on her way south carrying the men who would comprise the remainder of the crossing party and all the supplies and vehicles they would need to accomplish it. Until they reached Depot 700 that Hillary and his team were going to put in on the other side of the South Pole, they would have to be self-sufficient from the time they left their advance base at South Ice.

With the depot trip out of the way they started readying the tractor, Weasel and Sno-Cat for operational duty. The Sno-Cat in particular needed many, many hours spent on it owing to the amount of time that it had lain idle. Apart from the enormous quantity of frozen snow that had accumulated around it which had to chipped off, there was the additional problem of having to remove so many of the cabin and engine covers to access the mechanical parts of the vehicle before any maintenance could be carried out. The wind chill factor was still relevant, despite there now being 24 hours of daylight to work by.

Ken was organising a second trip to the 50-mile dump and had already chosen the same two men to go with him. This did not endear him to the other five, who rightly or wrongly felt that all the party should have a chance of seeing a bit more of the continent. This was all the more appropriate as both Rainer and Jeff would be going home soon and an opportunity to gain some valuable field experience was being lost.

Having apparently already antagonised the men who had not had a chance of some exploring, Ken again chose Rainer to accompany him even further afield to explore the mountains that were first seen from the flight made by Bunny and John Lewis the day before the *Theron* was forced to sail for England. Bunny had christened them the Theron Mountains after the ship. One of the purposes of this planned trip was to do some geology work and route surveying, neither of which Rainer, the group's doctor, was qualified to do. This trip into unknown territory of just two men could be calamitous: any mishap, such as one of them falling into a crevasse, would almost certainly have resulted in the death of one man and possibly the other as well. When Captain Scott attempted to explore the Ross Ice Shelf to try and find a way onto the Polar Plateau in 1903 he was accompanied by Dr Edward Wilson and Ernest Shackleton. As Shackleton's strength deteriorated due to the onset of scurvy it became a race against the clock for the other two to drag him on the sledge for many miles on their return journey. Even with a team of dogs there wouldn't have been a great margin for safety, but with the dogs also failing, it was left to Scott and Wilson to complete the rescue. It is obvious then that any two-man party would be in jeopardy.

Apart from the discovery of coal seams, Ken and Rainer were really surprised to find a colony of snowy petrels nesting high up among the craggy ledges of the cliffs. These birds would have to fly over 200 miles out to the sea and the same distance back to bring in food to rear their chicks. Departing on 7 December they spent Christmas Day at the 50-mile depot and returned to Shackleton base on the 27th.

The *Magga Dan* reached Halley Bay on 4 January 1957 and the men listening in to what was happening on the air waves tapped into a radio conversation Bunny was having with an American expedition that was setting up its base a few miles to the west of Shackleton. The Americans had already paid a courtesy call by helicopter to the TAE base in the early hours of 30 December and the advance party was upset that their expedition leader could make time to talk to the newly arrived American team but did not attempt to speak with them at Shackleton. This sort of apparent arrogance had grated with the men on a number of occasions during their lonely vigil. Even as the *Theron* was on the point of leaving Bunny had apparently given the eight men some sort of lecture as to what they should achieve in his absence and on another occasion over the radio he had sent a couple of very impersonal telegrams. It was as if he knew he had to say something but it never came over as he wanted to say it. Another example of this is an entry in Bunny's book *The Crossing of Antarctica*. He covers the reunion of the two halves of the expedition in a few brief sentences that take up no more than eleven lines. Little interest seems to have been shown by the new members of the expedition as to the difficulties experienced by the advance party; George Lowe being the exception.

The Main Party Returns – Reunion at Shackleton Base

The arrival of the *Magga Dan* was preceded by the Otter flying into the base with John Lewis at the controls and Bunny, George Lowe and newcomer Donald Milner, the BBC correspondent, on board. The next day the *Magga Dan* berthed alongside the ice shelf bringing further new arrivals. Apart from the familiar faces from the *Theron* days, 10 men from the IGY base at Halley Bay who had completed their contract and were being returned to the United Kingdom on the *Magga Dan* came ashore to lend a helping hand. Bunny had arranged for them to help with any outstanding work, especially with the task of unloading all the new stores that had been brought down ready for the crossing the following summer. After 12 months of isolation, the members of the advance party resented this intrusion into their old way of life. Their privacy had been interrupted and a number of the things they had worked so hard to achieve were soon being either altered to suit the newcomers or criticised for the way they had been done. The hut immediately became the centre of attention as the kitchen, heating system, water supply, electrical wiring and many other components of the interior received first scrutiny then material attention to fit, change or modify what had taken the eight pioneers so long to achieve. The three members who were destined to leave found that they were being re-berthed on board the ship, so even this action was a severance from all they had known and the friendships they had made.

Whatever the misgivings the eight men from the advance party held, the expedition had reached a pivotal point and from now on the momentum would continue to build towards the final assault on the icy waste ahead of them. The *Magga Dan* sailed for England on 30 December, a little over a fortnight after arriving, and amongst those on board was Peter Jeffries who would be dropped off at Halley Bay for the next season, together with Tony Stewart and Rainer Goldsmith, who were due to sail back to England. Among the items Rainer took with him were his diary, a frozen emperor penguin and a frozen baby seal he had found dead on a beach. These last two items were due to be stuffed as specimens as memories of his stay in Antarctica. After some discussion he was allowed to place the two bodies in the *Magga Dan's* freezer for the trip home.

The *Magga Dan* brought down several new members, one being the expedition's new medical officer, Dr Allan Rogers. He had worked as a lecturer at Bristol University. When not involved with the members of his new practice at Shackleton his penchant for inventing useful gadgets was given full rein. This talent was an interesting bonus for the expedition. Another member was Geoffrey Pratt, 31, who was seconded from British Petroleum and as a trained geophysicist would be in charge of the seismic and gravity testing experiments to be carried out at regular intervals across the continent. Doctor Hal Lister came to the expedition as a qualified glaciologist. His two years with the British North Greenland Expedition had given him some vital and relevant experience of what was to come. He had participated on the Greenland trip with two other members of the present group, Roy Homard here at Shackleton and Richard Brooke, who was even now joining the Ross Sea side of the expedition. Finally, there was a young, recently qualified geologist called Jon Stephenson who was only 26 and the youngest member of the group. Born in Australia, he represented his country for the remainder of the expedition. Later he was to help man the satellite station still to be constructed 270 miles further south, with Ken Blaiklock and Hal Lister as his companions. Fifty years later he was to write a book about the crossing using his diaries and other sources to compile the narrative, called *Crevasse Roulette*.

The inclusion of a British Petroleum scientist for the crossing in this, the most important aspect of the project, and the huge resource that BP provided in the form of all the fuel required during the crossing, together with the documentary film made by Derek Williams, a professional film producer, indicates an immense investment by the company in the successful outcome of the enterprise and the results it might produce for them. Before the advent of the Antarctic Treaty and its banning of the exploitation of any mineral deposits for financial gain, it looked like an opportunity not to be missed by BP in the search for oil-bearing strata in this huge land mass, the publicity notwithstanding.

The *Magga Dan* had conveyed the expedition's second phase safely down through the Weddell Sea but not before she had also experienced a traumatic period of several days tangled up with the ice on a course close to the catastrophic one that the *Theron* had taken the previous year. This came about due to an error with the gyrocompass. The ship's captain had been maintaining a direction that was supposed to steer them clear of the one taken by the *Theron* when she became inextricably trapped in the ice for four weeks. An error of about 15 degrees now had to be rectified before the *Magga Dan* could resume sailing towards Cap Norvegia. Captain Pedersen calculated that this error had cost them about five days. His explanation was rather vague. He wondered if some Christmas reveller had switched off the electrical supply to the instrument giving rise to the error.

The *Magga Dan* was a much more powerful ship than the *Theron* and Captain Pedersen used this to batter away at the encroaching ice whilst trying to force a way through the pack ice that was now crowding round the ship. All the time the *Magga Dan* had been steaming south they were aware that the *Tottan* was also heading down through the Weddell Sea to relieve the IGY base at Halley Bay and a friendly rivalry had developed to see who could reach the base first. The *Tottan* had taken the proven route along the coast but the *Magga Dan* had fallen foul of the faulty gyrocompass and was now behind the *Tottan* in the race to Halley Bay. In the end both ships arrived on the same day, with just a few hours between them.

George Lowe, who had rejoined the expedition and was now the sole photographer, writes about the near calamity with the gyrocompass, as does Jon Stephenson, but Bunny does not attempt to explain the background, although he does record that the ship was trapped in the ice and the Auster was used several times to search ahead to find the best route out. Bunny had learned his lesson. He directed that the *Magga Dan* should sail straight across from South Georgia to Cap Norvegia and then follow the ice-free coastal lead. But he left the finer details out of his narrative. The *Magga Dan* finally tied up at Shackleton Base on 14 January 1957 after leaving South Georgia on 20 December 1956, a total of 25 days.

To compare the calendar of events of the *Theron's* visit to that of the *Magga Dan*: *Theron* arrived at the base site on 30 January 1956 having left South Georgia 41 days before, on 20 December 1955. The *Magga Dan* took just 25 days for the same voyage, setting off on the same date as the *Theron* the following year, and docked at Shackleton on 14 January. The *Theron* left Shackleton to return to England on 7 February just eight days after her arrival, compared to the *Magga Dan's* departure date of 30 January, having stayed 16 days.

South Ice – the Next Step

The plan had always been to establish a small manned station 250–300 miles inland during the coming season and keep it occupied right through until the following year when the mechanised convoy would begin its march. To transport all the materials inland, the De Havilland Otter would be the workhorse as it could carry a ton of material at a time. The first stage of the operation, which would take as many as 16 or more flights, entailed taking the three men and sufficient supplies to get them through the initial stages until the hut was habitable. Prior to this crucial flight, some reconnaissance was necessary and it took three successive flights and one that was aborted due to the weather, spread over 10 days, to get a good idea of what lay before them and where to site the base that was to be home for three men for the next nine or 10 months.

The first reconnaissance flight set out on 20 January 1957. It took five and a half hours during which the Otter flew nearly due south for 280 miles towards the second range of mountains that had been seen on the distant horizon during the flight taken a year earlier, when the base at Shackleton was being set up. Gordon Haslop, Ken Blaiklock and George Lowe accompanied Bunny, with John Lewis at the controls. They were looking for a suitable place to build the new inland base and at the extreme end of the outward flight there appeared to be just what they were looking for, a good flat expanse of snow for landing the plane and some local rock formations that could be used as location points for the plane as it brought in the various loads required. They also had a chance to see if they could find a way through the mountains for tracked vehicles and while this could only be established with any certainty using a ground party, from the air at least a rough idea of where to start the search would help. Two huge glaciers were discovered bringing the ice down from the Polar Plateau to the Filchner Ice Shelf. The first of these was named after the chairman of the London Committee, Sir John Slessor. The second glacier was later named 'Recovery' when on the second run to South Ice they recovered the Weasel that had broken its cam shaft and had to be left behind during the pilot run to South Ice in October.

Continuing the tradition of naming new geographic features after prominent people, the range of new mountains that they saw on this first flight was named after one of the most flamboyant and well-known explorers, Sir Ernest Shackleton. This range forms part of the Trans-Antarctic Mountains that stretch right across the continent.

After settling on a suitable site for Depot 300, as the new advance station was referred to, the first men and supplies were taken out on 5 February. This was only two days ahead of the schedule of the advance party when the *Theron* left them to their own devices on 7 February the previous year.

With the preliminaries of the reunion at Shackleton over and the unloading complete, the *Magga Dan* sailed away on 30 January 1957 for England and left the 16 men to start gearing up for the first step into the interior. Not quite the first step because Ken Blaiklock and Rainer Goldsmith had already done that just before Christmas, but this was to be the first real step to the South Pole and beyond.

The second flight, on 22 January, searched across the Theron Mountains looking for a way through this range. From the air it was possible to see the crevassed areas they would need to avoid. John Lewis even managed to land the plane for a closer inspection of a portion of the route they might be able to use. The third and final reconnaissance flight took place on 30 January. The plane had now been equipped with an extra fuel tank to increase its range and was airborne for over seven hours, enabling it to reach beyond the site chosen for Depot 300. They double-checked on the Theron range and flew further south to 82° 15′ before setting a course back across the mountains and returning to base camp.

February 5 was a good day for flying and for the previous week there had been a rush to gather together all the requirements for the four men who would erect the new base hut. John Lewis flew the Otter with as many stores as they could safely squeeze into the loading area and with Hal Lister, Ken Blaiklock, Jon Stephenson and George Lowe all crammed into the cockpit, the plane gathered speed across the ice and lifted clear of the take-off strip, a cleared area of ice with petrol drums delineating the runway. Rising into a clear blue sky, the pilot wheeled back across the base camp and with a gentle waggle of the wings swung inland on a course set for the new advance camp site. By 12.30 they were circling the area that had been selected for the new building. Coming lower on each run John Lewis searched the surface for any obstacles and as is always the case when passing over an unknown touchdown point, he had the final decision of where to bring the plane in to land – or not to land at all. Flying at such a low altitude and keeping an eye open for the exact spot required a very steady hand on the controls. The other four need not have worried because the landing, when it came, was an anti-climax. In fact, the surface was so good that Lewis taxied the plane towards what looked like higher ground seeking out a better site for the base; but on reflection the decision was made to return to the original landing place, unload and start getting ready for the first sections of the hut to be brought in. The four pioneers stood watching as the plane spun round and with a waggle went back to Shackleton for the next load.

Temporary living quarters was the first priority. They were going to have to live under canvas for the next few weeks and it all depended now on the weather as to how the hut would progress. The plane was due back by about 10.30 that evening but failed to arrive. The small hand-cranked radio they had with them seemed to be suffering from frozen condensation inside it and was discarded. The spades were soon in use because the plan for this hut was to dig a pit about five feet down, large enough to take the foundation timbers. The hut measured about 18 feet square so they had plenty to do, digging out more of the snow while they waited for the plane to return.

Worn out with the shovelling, fed up with waiting for the plane's second visit and with no way of contacting Shackleton to find out why there was a delay, they ate their supper and retired to their sleeping bags.

The radio was still stubbornly silent the next morning so it was back to shovelling snow. That evening they retired to the tents for something to eat and settle down for the night when the plane flew in low over them. The weather had clamped down at Shackleton and stopped the plane taking off safely the previous day. Now everybody turned to the task of getting the ton of supplies out of the hold and the plane on its way back to base. Ralph Lenton had also come up to the site, partly to help with the construction, (he had led the team that struggled to build the base hut) and also to check over the radio, as he was a very able radio operator.

Various flights came and went bringing in the hut sections, and each load came with its own challenges. The 7 February delivery brought the aluminium 'H' sectioned beams for the floor, all 21 of them had been cut into two pieces and each pair required 20 bolts to secure them together with fixing plates. They completed this task at 9.30 that night and crept off to bed with a supper of pemmican. The next day was even worse, as they were expected to secure a felt cover to all the floor panels; the tacks were so small that they could only accomplish this job with bare hands and so the difficulties continued. From a nation of inventive and highly skilled engineers, how was it that the design of this hut had been allocated to such an unthinking designer?

As each load was brought up from Shackleton, so various other expedition members visited the site to offer advice or contribute. Bunny came on 8 February bringing a replacement radio set. Nobody had bothered to check it out and, guess what, it was also unserviceable.

The weather had stayed remarkably stable at Depot 300 but there was a certain amount of frustration building up amongst the construction crew because the plane was not bringing in the hut components quickly enough, mainly owing to the weather often closing in at Shackleton.

With a lull in the building programme Ken the surveyor and the young Australian geologist Jon Stephenson made their way to the nearest rocks that could be reached from the base site about 6 miles away to see what the Nunataks consisted of. Ken was going to use these outcrops of rock to start a survey that would continue to the Pole and take in any mountain peaks that might be discovered on the way. Jon would try and establish what type of rock it consisted of and possibly its characteristics. After completing his calculations Ken reckoned that they were about 500 miles from the Pole at 81° 56′ South and some 270 miles inland from Shackleton. Later it was calculated that the altitude was 4,430 feet above sea level. Jon did not reach any conclusions about the rocks as they were severely broken up by frost damage.

There were no more flights until 13 February when the Otter arrived with Taffy Williams on board. He had brought and got working another transmitter, which he tested by contacting Ralph Lenton at Shackleton, this at last gave them the radio link that had been missing since their arrival nearly two weeks earlier. The next day's flight failed to materialise and now drifting snow was causing a daily problem as it kept infiltrating the hut despite the team tying tarpaulins around it to try and keep the snow out.

Despite atrocious conditions on the ground the plane made a further delivery on 18 February. Gordon Haslop astounded everybody by bringing in the plane even though his view of the landing area was lost in the swirling snow. This was the sixth of a planned sixteen loads and the weather was not improving as February was coming to an end. Bunny came in on 20 February to see for himself the progress that had been made and decided that now the hut was basically complete, George Lowe should return to Shackleton. This left Hal Lister, who was to be in charge of the base, together with Ken Blaiklock and Jon Stephenson. When Hal had been in Greenland he had spent time on the ice cap there helping to man the weather station they had built and lived in for a year as part of their scientific programme. They had called their station in Greenland 'North Ice' so he now appropriately christened their new abode 'South Ice' and it stayed that way for the duration of the expedition.

A safety precaution against bad weather closing in on South Ice was a navigation aid called SARAH, which stood for 'Search and Rescue and Homing'. This was a homing beacon that a receiver in the aircraft could pick up from 40 miles away and would enable the pilot to locate the new base and, once in the vicinity of it, give him a chance to assess the weather conditions around the landing zone before deciding on whether or not to try to land. This device was to come in very handy later on, when the Auster was forced down while taking the doctor to try and help an injured man at the IGY station at Halley Bay. The more powerful radio transmitter that had been installed at South Ice continued to work well and a permanent radio connection with Shackleton could now be maintained.

Each of the three men stationed at South Ice was ferried back to the main base in turn before the worst of the winter set in so that they could not only have a break from all the work they had done but to give them a chance to fraternise with other members of the expedition and relax away from the remoteness of their future home.

Whichaway to Go?
A Nearly Fatal Excursion

Before the period of darkness set in, a small trip by Ken and Jon to the 'Whichaway Nunataks' was organised. This outcrop of rocks was about 30 miles away from South Ice and was located near the Recovery Glacier. The rocks were hopefully going to give some vital clues as to what lay under the ice cap. David Stratton acted as a relief man at South Ice along with Hal Lister, who was already there for the duration of Ken and Jon's trip. Hal had pointed out to Bunny that he thought a fourth person should be stationed at South Ice for the forthcoming winter because the three men already stationed there had a mountain of scientific work to carry out and stoppages for cooking and other domestic duties would mean that their time would be severely compromised. Bunny on the other hand realised that he only had 13 men including himself to prepare everything for the crossing and with vehicles to overhaul, workshops to build plus all the other functions that needed to be carried out, he would also be struggling to cope with the manpower at his disposal. The request was declined. A total of 16 men formed the crossing brigade and of these only 10 would actually take part in the mechanised team. Ken and Jon were to use the dogs to pioneer a route ahead of the vehicle convoy. There were also the three aircrew members John Lewis, Gordon Haslop and Peter Weston. Finally Ralph Lenton the radio operator who would be left at Shackleton as the person responsible for all the communications.

The New Zealand contingent had at least five extra men, admittedly these five were the core of the IGY team but they were still available for the general duties normally carried out around the base. The other main difference in manning levels was that Scott Base did not require a three-man advance base, which Bunny's group maintained at South Ice. Ed Hillary did have a series of smaller expeditions planned, which took men away from Scott Base for varying periods once the better weather arrived, but throughout the dark period of winter he had a full workforce who could prepare for the depot-laying they would have to carry out in the coming summer season.

So on 3 March Ken and Jon were flown out to the Nunataks by John Lewis in the Otter with 10 days' provisions and camping gear to enable them to collect rock samples, do some surveying and try and fix the position of the Whichaways. When they had finished, the small radio transmitter they took with them could be used to signal that they were ready to be collected by the plane. In the event of the pick-up failing to be accomplished the two men were also equipped with a small sledge that would enable them to walk back the 30 miles to South Ice before their supplies ran out.

They were well provisioned for at least 10 days but anticipated staying for only about two and once they had landed they wasted no time in getting the tent erected and their various provisions stowed safely inside. Both men then set off to explore, Ken to climb the Nunatak and establish its position and Jon to collect rock samples for future analysis. They half expected the plane to return for them some time the next day so kept reasonably close to their tent. By the afternoon the plane had still not put in an appearance so they visited a more distant Nunatak and as the weather stayed bright and calm they were able to maximise their opportunity.

Circumstances out of the two men's control now started to dictate the course of events. The first two flights, one on 6 March and the second on the 9 March, to pick up Ken and Jon had to be aborted due to bad weather in the vicinity of South Ice and by this time the men's rations were getting to the point where they would have to make the decision to walk out.

117

Jon Stephenson in *Crevasse Roulette* tells the story. Hannes la Grange the meteorologist forewarned them on the radio of the deteriorating weather conditions at Shackleton and the difficulty of getting the plane airborne. By the eighth day they decided to prepare to evacuate themselves as planned. They still had four full day's rations and should be able to cover the 30 miles back to South Ice fairly easily. The first difficulty they experienced as they set off was the hard ice surface that the wind had created, which gave their footwear very little to grip on. They had come with a moccasin-type shoe that proved to be warm and comfortable but its smooth sole constantly slipped on the ice. The one pair of crampons they possessed was shared between them and they had not brought skis or snow shoes.

Ken took on the responsibility of navigator and impressed Jon with the accuracy that he achieved with the compass as they continued their journey. The constant wind direction helped to keep them on course but poor visibility prevented them seeing either behind them to the Nunataks or forward whilst trying to keep on a straight course.

Six hours of travelling began to tell so they camped and before retiring to double sleeping bags inside the small pyramid tent, they prepared a meal of standard pemmican and biscuits heated over their small primus stove. During their rest period the temperature dropped to -30°F and the chill soon permeated through from the snow and ice below the ground sheet.

Porridge and hot cocoa in the morning brought some relief and again they moved out into the cold, cloudy surroundings. Erecting the tent at the end of another day of difficult travelling they broke one of the four bamboo supports, which made the shape of the tent very difficult to cope with once they were inside.

Not being too sure how far they had come in two marches they reduced their meals to half rations and pushed on for the third day. Constantly having to remove gloves and mittens to carry out routine tasks, they were beginning to get frostbite to the hands. Their faces were always vulnerable as well.

On the fourth day the cloud lifted allowing them to see forward but the scene was virtually featureless. Looking behind they could just discern the mountains on the skyline so they hoped they were getting closer to their camp at South Ice.

The sun now set at about 7 pm so travelling later than this and having to allow time to make camp meant that the day was soon over. Food was now running out despite their going on half rations. Jon mentions in his book that at this juncture all the pemmican had gone and they only had enough food for one more meal, sleep was being interrupted by the cold they were having to endure and even the fuel supply had dwindled to a point where they were rationing their drinks, always a dangerous thing to have to do because dehydration soon sets in, with all its dire side-effects.

Sat in the tent eating the last of their supplies they were suddenly aware of a noise outside. Leaving the tent in a rush the relief was enormous as they watched the Otter circle the camp looking for a safe place to land. Jon admits to feeling quite emotional as the plane landed and their rescuers jumped down and advanced towards the two very cold and very relieved young men beside their rickety tent. It turned out they were still about 15 miles away from South Ice, but at least they had been heading in the correct direction.

The plane had finally managed to get airborne on 11 March but on reaching the original camp site Bunny and his pilot found no sign of Ken or Jon and realised they must have set out on foot for South Ice. So the plan was to search along the route the two men would most likely have taken and at least drop some extra food and fuel for them until a pick-up could be organised. The plane reached South Ice but its two occupants had seen no sign of Ken or Jon on the ground. Landing briefly to discuss the situation with Hal Lister and David Stratton, the plane took off and returned to Shackleton.

It would be 15 March before they could again resume the search and by now the food carried by Ken and Jon would be exhausted or at best on extremely reduced rations. The situation was getting desperate and fears were creeping in that the rescuers would have a major problem on their hands.

On this second mission they had flown back to the Whichaways and landed next to the vacated camp site where they were lucky enough to find a message left by Ken and Jon. From this information they gleaned the date the two had set out and the course they hoped to take. No sign was found of the men as the plane flew back towards South Ice, but on an instinct they doubled back on their flight path and by scanning both sides of the route a small black speck could be seen. This turned out to be the tent and as luck would have it a suitable place to land nearby allowed the plane to come down very close by.

No more flights were made to South Ice after 25 March and now the teams at both camps could concentrate on getting everything ready for the big effort as early in the next summer period as the weather would allow. Bunny's original plan was to set out on the crossing in early November 1957. The actual departure date for the final assault was 24 November, although the route had already been tried out in early October by Bunny attempting to take a Sno-cat and three Weasels all the way to South Ice. This proved to be a very sensible precaution because very little was known about the route they would need to take to clear all the early obstacles they guessed might lay in their path. Air reconnaissance had shown where some of the major crevassed areas were and Ken and Jon had started to break the trail with the trip they had made the previous Christmas using the two dog teams. Bunny and his companions would soon find out how fickle crevasses were within a few miles of leaving Shackleton and more importantly, how susceptible to breakdowns the vehicles were.

Before any move could be made by the small fleet of assorted tracked vehicles, the workshop had to be built to check them out prior to starting on their epic voyage. The building was smaller than the main hut but the construction was just as arduous because the design was very similar. Only now did the new members begin to appreciate the struggles Ken and his seven men had faced during the previous year. Fortunately, Ralph Lenton was on hand to guide them through the intricacies of the process but even he couldn't help them when it came to handling small components with freezing fingers and with their faces constantly bitten by the cold winds.

Once this facility was complete David Pratt and Roy Homard could set to and overhaul the vehicles. The workshop was fitted out with some machine tools such as a lathe, a drill and a welder, all run using the generator brought down in the *Magga Dan*. The workshop was large enough to accommodate even the biggest vehicle, the Sno-Cat. The two engineers responsible for the vehicles' well-being were kept busy every day, long after most of the other men had done their day's work. Some of the machines, especially the Weasels, were much used and their weakest points were literally their weakest links, the tracks that they ran on. During the expedition maintaining these tracks proved to be the most time-consuming of the breakdowns they experienced.

There were to be no exceptions made for cook duty, which lasted four days, and initially this period for those unfamiliar with culinary duties was approached with varying degrees of trepidation. This rota only came round every seven weeks or so and the degree of anticipation felt by the men before any meal was tempered by who was the chef.

Routine in the hut once the sun had disappeared for the winter soon settled down and apart from Hannes la Grange having to go out to take the weather readings and the engineers trekking to and from the workshop, the only other reason to venture out was to feed the dogs or get ice for the fresh water supply.

The hut layout can be more easily explained by looking at the sketch of it as supplied from George Lowe's book. It is not until the overall sizes are inspected that a realisation dawns as to the magnitude of the task that the advance party took on during the previous winter. At 73 feet long and 28 feet wide it must have been one of the largest huts ever built by the early explorers in polar history. The *Terra Nova* hut of Scott's second expedition was about 50 feet by 25 feet. Shackleton's hut at Cape Royds for his attempt at conquering the South Pole measured 33 feet by 19 feet. Scott's hut was built to accommodate 33 souls divided into two groups, the officers and scientists in one part separated by a screen of packing cases from the naval ratings. In the *Nimrod* expedition of Ernest Shackleton there were 15 men, but not segregated as in Scott's *Terra Nova* expedition.

If you put the areas of the Terra Nova hut and the Nimrod hut together they amount to about 1,900 square feet. The TAE hut at

Shackleton on the Weddell Sea works out at over 2,000 square feet in area for just 16 men, three of whom spent most of their time stationed at South Ice.

Early in July Bunny made known his plans for some spring journeys that he hoped to carry out. Three men, David and Geoff Pratt and Roy Homard, would accompany him in trying to drive a Sno-Cat and a Weasel to the depot set up 50 miles away by Ken and Rainer the previous year using dog teams. He hoped this would give some crucial driving experience across the terrain they were likely to encounter. (Bunny refers to six men and four vehicles making this journey in his own book.) If the weather was good then the next trip Bunny had planned involved the relief of South Ice. By readying the Otter, Bunny could be flown with Geoff Pratt and George Lowe down to the station and this would allow Jon and Ken to come back for a well-earned break. Geoff Pratt would remain at the base to work with Hal Lister and then Bunny, together with George Lowe, would be ferried farther south with sufficient supplies and a dog team, for about three weeks, to explore the mountains of the Theron range in more detail. Hal would be relieved on the return of the exploring party. Another planned trip would entail four vehicles attempting to break through the mountains and crevasses between Shackleton and South Ice as a precursor to the actual crossing of Antarctica. All these trips needed to be completed by early November and then Bunny hoped to be away from Shackleton by 14 November for the commencement of the crossing itself.

July and August returned some stubbornly low temperatures and gradually the proposed plan started to slip from its original schedule – but at least the sun had made its regular pilgrimage back to the Antarctic. It was first sighted on 20 August.

To bring the vehicles out of their cocoons of ice and snow ready for servicing was relatively easy, the difficult part was locating more than 40 wooden crates that held all the spares for them. These crates were submerged under several feet of frozen snow that had drifted over them during the storms and blizzards of the last five months.

The weather was causing a serious obstacle to the plans Bunny had laid out at the beginning of July and it soon became apparent that they would have to be altered. The first casualty was the 50-mile depot trip with two vehicles. Nobody was surprised by this decision but it did bring about a more sombre mood in the camp. This was the prelude to a period of criticism of the style of leadership that Bunny exhibited. The men felt that he and David Stratton were the only ones considered to have worthwhile ideas about how to overcome the obstacles that they experienced and any suggestions coming from themselves were not appreciated, in some cases even roundly denounced. Bunny had put an embargo on playing the gramophone for most of the time and would only allow it to be played during Saturday and Sunday evenings, giving as his reason that he felt it was an unnecessary distraction. Talking at mealtimes sometimes dwindled and most of the team would turn their attention to reading a book, of which there was an excellent choice, especially on the subject at hand, Antarctica. But a temporary mood of resentment could be detected in some of the diary entries made at this time.

Emergencies are never far away when exploring in the polar regions and a wireless message came through from Halley Bay on 17 September asking for immediate help. Robin Smart, the IGY leader, had fallen and diagnosed himself as having internal injuries. He was the IGY doctor but he could not treat his own internal injury. Thinking he might have broken a rib and this in turn might have damaged his liver, he needed the assistance of the TAE doctor, Allan Rogers.

All other plans were put on hold as the preparation of the Auster would now take priority. Gordon Haslop and Allan were soon in the air heading the 200 miles to Halley Bay. Unfortunately, they had over-flown the base as it was obscured by driving snow. What they were not sure of was by how much they had erred. Circling round for a while brought them no nearer to finding Halley. Rather than risk running out of fuel, Gordon set the Auster down near the ice edge. A quick signal to Shackleton notifying their base of the situation engendered another emergency effort. With the Otter still suffering from the snow and ice that had settled on her during the winter, Bunny organised a round-the-clock schedule to get the second plane airworthy. In the meantime he spoke with

Finn Ronne, the leader of the Americans at Ellsworth, to see if they could help find the missing Auster. Although the Americans sent their plane to Shackleton, it was never involved in the rescue but it did bring some drugs that were not available at Shackleton to treat the injured Robin Smart.

The Auster was equipped with some emergency rations and Gordon and Allan had to survive on these for the next 10 days or so. The first flight of the Otter was cut short due to low mist and cloud but eventually she managed to get into the air and, with the help of the SARAH beacon on the Auster, the two stranded men were soon located. The Auster was refuelled and Halley Bay was reached within half-an-hour. The Auster had over-shot by about 50 miles whilst circling around. Much to everyone's relief, Robin Smart had not injured himself as seriously as he had thought and he was able to continue with his duties as base superintendent.

The upside of all this activity was that now Bunny had two airworthy planes in action. The down side was that Jon Stephenson and Ken Blaiklock were kept waiting for two extra weeks at South Ice for their relief party to arrive. Here, too, the winter blues had set in and with some unsettling behaviour ensuing. Hal wrote in his diary that he felt that the other two were becoming slovenly and lazy; but this was a passing phase and no harsh words or feelings lingered to really spoil their rapport.

Having dealt with the medical emergency satisfactorily, Bunny probably felt vindicated in not allowing a fourth man to stay at South Ice. His choice would have rested between Gordon Haslop the second pilot and possibly George Lowe. If he had sent Gordon to South Ice then the rescue mission that had just been accomplished would not have been possible with only one pilot on hand at Shackleton Base.

Bunny's earlier plans were constantly being modified to suit the situation and after the medical emergency he requested and received the help of two men from Halley Bay with the preparations that were underway for the pioneering trip to South Ice and its relief. One of the two Halley Bay men, Fred Morris, was flown to South Ice with Allan Rogers to relieve Ken and Jon on 8 October and – at last – on the same day the reconnaissance party of one Sno-Cat and three Weasels left Shackleton for the route-finding mission to South Ice.

In addition to this sudden burst of activity a further exploratory trip was about to be set in motion: two teams of dogs and their handlers would be airlifted to the Shackleton Range and used to scout for a way through for the tractor team. It took two flights using the Otter to ferry the four men with their two teams of dogs and all the necessary supplies for at least four weeks to the selected site in the mountains. The four men were David Stratton and Ken Blaiklock as the two surveyors, Jon Stephenson as geologist, and George Lowe. George went along because his experience would help the others when they moved up into the mountains. The first flight left Shackleton on 11 October and after a delay for bad weather the second flight took off on 13 October. They anticipated having behavioural problems with the dogs but by strategically placing the dogs in such a way as to keep them separated with boxes and sledges, the dogs proved to be model passengers and in fact watched out of the windows most of the time the plane was in the air. After some initial geology work and surveying had been completed, the Auster arrived on 18 October bringing Taffy Williams to work alongside Jon because Bunny was recalling George Lowe so that he could carry on with the photographic record of the expedition – he couldn't miss the beginning.

As on previous occasions the radios the sledge parties carried could not be relied upon and the plan to use them to instigate a recall to a rendezvous point so that the plane could bring them back to Shackleton had to depend on the radios acting only as signalling devices with no two-way facility. With this communications problem Bunny might have needed to send the Auster out to the vicinity of the field party's last known position to try and make contact. In fact, on 28 October it became necessary to recall all four men to their original starting point where the plane could land safely. The Auster was sent out to look for them. Having located the survey team and seen the geology team from the air, the plane made a landing to tell both teams of the reason for their recall. It transpired that the Sno-Cat and surviving two Weasels were struggling with the surface conditions they were encountering on their journey to South Ice. Bunny was anxious to make available as many men as possible back at Shackleton Base to continue getting the final preparations completed for the assault on the traverse.

At this lonely spot in the approaches to the Shackleton Range the Auster was damaged, not irrevocably, but the tail skid was wrenched off as the plane slithered to a halt after failing to complete the take-off. It was obvious from its final resting place some assistance would be required to get it airborne again. At least the Auster's radio worked and soon the Otter was on its way from base with the requisite spare tail skid. Peter Weston, the aircraft mechanic, who was aboard the Otter, very quickly repaired the Auster and the plane was towed into a position from where it could get airborne.

The Otter spent the next two days fetching and carrying the four men and their equipment and the rock samples they had gathered back to either South Ice or Shackleton. Normality had been resumed at both bases by 1 November.

The surveying of the Shackleton Mountains had taken place at the same time as Bunny and his convoy progressed towards them, so to follow the events of the tractor convoy the story must now go back to 8 October.

Trial Run to South Ice –
and the Press Arrive

Problems continued to beset the reconnaissance party as it headed out from Shackleton to forge a way through to South Ice. Barely had it left base when one of the Weasels shed a track and caused an axle to get bent out of line. This occurred less than 8 miles into the journey. The only option open was for Roy Homard to limp back to camp with the injured vehicle, change the damaged shaft and try and catch up with Bunny and the other two vehicles. This was never achieved and the Weasel remained at Shackleton until the main foray began some weeks later. Meanwhile, Bunny and his fellow crew members were able from time to time to locate the black marker poles set up by Ken and Rainer the previous year showing where the safest path was to miss any crevasses.

Bunny was always in the leading vehicle, whether it was a Weasel as on this occasion or a Sno-Cat when the main journey took place. This he felt sure was where the leader should be, and so it was his dubious privilege to be the first to fall foul of a crevasse. His Weasel and sledge were hauled out using the extra power of the Sno-Cat that was following him. The other Weasel also had a mishap with a snow bridge collapsing under it, causing further delays. The convoy was now faced with a whole system of hidden crevasses and Bunny again called up the Auster to carry out an aerial search to see if there was a better way through the maze. At this juncture Bunny recalled Roy Homard to use his expertise with crevasse crossing that he had gained in Greenland. He was flown in on the Auster's next flight.

The report from the Auster confirmed Bunny's worst fears, there was no obvious way through and a U-turn had to be performed. Simple as this solution sounds, turning several twenty-four-foot sledges, each loaded with about two tons of fuel and other supplies, needed quite a lot of room for the turning circle, not easily found without the danger of falling into another crevasse. Eventually the manoeuvre was accomplished. They had brought along some rope with a 15-ton breaking strain and this was now attached to all the vehicles and the convoy started its retreat bound together.

They arrived back at the 50-mile depot late that night, two days after leaving it. At dawn on 14 October it was apparent that it would be folly to resume the advance with barely 100 yards visibility. Laying up for a day in the hope of a better tomorrow didn't help, as the next day was not much better. All these delays could not be tolerated for much longer so Bunny gave a cautious order to start out on the new course to swing round the crevassed area they had just left.

A broken pipe line to one of the Weasel's engines held them up for a while but soon they were on the move again, making a precious 25 miles before stopping for the night. Bunny could detect a strange noise coming from his Weasel's engine and a stop to swap most of the load from his sledge to one of the others in an attempt to take some of the strain off his engine lost them some time. But Bunny reckoned they still made 40 miles on 16 October. The engine problem turned out to be a bearing starting to collapse. They were now too far from any workshop, so the only way was onwards and upwards and fingers crossed.

Having spent most of 18 October carrying out maintenance on the vehicles and a seismic test for ice thickness, they pushed on for the rest of the afternoon travelling over hard sastrugi for a number of miles, only to find that this gave way to another area of crevasses. The crevasses had the last laugh that day and a sledge was left stranded on one side with its Weasel on the other and a collapsed snow bridge between them, which put paid to any further progress. Two days later the Auster returned to carry out another search of the way ahead, looking for a path through the crevassed area. Responding to this search the convoy back-tracked a few miles, changed direction onto a new route and resumed the journey to South Ice.

Shackleton Base camp meanwhile was alive with various activities. They had retrieved all the other vehicles from the snow drifts that had accumulated over them, but with only one of the two engineers, they were struggling to make further headway with running the motors up ready for trials. David Stratton had also been involved in the push to locate a path through to South Ice, being one of the party of four that had been flown down to the Shackleton Range for a surveying operation; but on his return to the base site he was now in charge of the effort there to complete preparations.

The tractor group were now approaching the Ice Wall that they had received information about from the two surveyors who had been looking for a way through the mountains. Bunny and his team still had a crevassed area to negotiate and their progress was painfully slow. John Lewis had flown in and took off with Bunny aboard to make yet another search ahead. This resulted in yet more delays as the column retreated for at least the third time to safer ground. Because the air reconnaissance was becoming so valuable a tool Bunny requested that an advance airstrip and aviation fuel dump should be located in the vicinity, so that the plane could be called upon at short notice to search for a safe passage ahead.

While this was being organised, Bunny had to try and push ahead because his original timetable was now so very far behind. They should have been at South Ice by 28 October but still had at least 150 miles to go. On 27 October the group were immersed once more in a whiteout. Knowing that crevasses lay ahead, Bunny left the vehicles and started probing ahead with poles to mark out a safe way through as soon as visibility cleared. It was around this time that he heard about the small accident with the Auster losing its tail skid but that was history and he could now rely on its services from the advanced airstrip. It took three days of probing to cover about 6 miles but this seemed to bring them through the crevassed area and now the route ahead looked reasonable.

Pressing on across a smooth, wind-swept surface, they approached a snow cairn that Ken Blaiklock and David Stratton had erected to mark the start of the route up the ice wall that they would have to negotiate to reach the pass through the mountains.

Bunny's Weasel was experiencing a loss of engine power with the gradual collapse of the bearing on what turned out to be the camshaft, so rather than abandon the vehicle, his last remaining sledge was hooked on to the back of the Sno-Cat. The climb up the route marked out by the earlier surveying party now made it possible to move ahead without too much probing, which had been so time-consuming during the preceding few days. They did take the precaution of skiing up the slope before committing the tractors to the climb and were rewarded with the sight of a dog team advancing towards them from the direction of the air base that had recently been set up.

This was a very wise decision to bring in the dogs because from now on the path ahead could be closely reconnoitred in advance of the tractors. After a short reunion the whole group headed up the ice wall and finally made camp at the top. David and Ken brought Bunny up-to-date with all the news of their survey trip to the mountains and how base camp was coping with the preparations for the next phase of the expedition, which Bunny hoped to start on 14 November. Bunny realised that the absence of the second engineer was proving a severe handicap to servicing the remaining vehicles. Now that the air base was available, he despatched Roy Homard back to Shackleton at the end of October to take charge of this important task.

The ailing Weasel finally gave up on 30 October and was abandoned together with a sledge that had become superfluous to requirements for the time being. They could be recovered when the main party came through at some time in the future. Their transport now consisted of one Weasel and the Sno-Cat, with still many miles to go; but at least they had the essential back-up of the dogs and the advanced air base.

The small convoy had to proceed with extreme caution for several days due to the discovery of more and more crevasses along their route. The main reason for the exposed crevasses was that the ambient temperature was rising with the advancing season and longer days and this was causing the snow bridges to soften and collapse.

After crossing the Shackleton Range and negotiating their way down to and across the Recovery Glacier, the route ahead was steadily uphill and as they finally approached South Ice they had climbed to over 4,000 feet above sea level. In doing so they had gained their first foothold on the Antarctic Plateau. Using the radio to contact South Ice, Bunny was able to advise them of his imminent arrival. Hal Lister skied out to meet them the next day. After 37 days, on 13 November they completed nearly 400 miles of hard slog from Shackleton Base. They had lost two Weasels on the way but hoped to recover one of them during the second trip to South Ice, which Bunny hoped to start on the day after they arrived at this southerly outpost. Bunny and his team of three men were flown back to their base in just a few hours, on 15 November. Bunny's problems were still not over before the big push.

The new start date for the crossing was set to be 24 November; this allowed just nine days of frantic work to complete all the necessary preparations. One of the unwanted side-effects of the long time it had taken to get to South Ice were the continual requests from the organising committee in London, the BBC and other press for updates about progress and anticipated future schedules. Bunny was not the most communicative person in the first place and his team often felt left out of any decision-making or even of being informed as to the next step, so they were naturally reticent about handling any of these enquiries while Bunny was absent from Shackleton, in case they said something of which their leader would not have approved. Radio communications between Shackleton and the convoy out on the ice were fragmentary at the best of times and this only added to the cagey replies that base camp sent back to England. Even those travelling with Bunny were acutely aware of the almost embarrassing silences that took place between the infrequent communiqués that were sent to the outside world, where people were becoming more and more aware that something exciting was starting to happen down in the Antarctic. The Expedition Committee had a contract with *The Times* newspaper for exclusive coverage of the expedition's progress but other papers were sniffing out news through different sources and this was becoming an embarrassment to the Committee. Scott Base, the eventual terminus for the expedition, had an excellent link with a radio station in New Zealand and a lot of telegraphic traffic was passing through it.

It was at this juncture that New Zealander Douglas McKenzie was invited to join Ed Hillary and his team as they started off from Depot 480 across the Antarctic Plateau to set up Depot 700. When they arrived at the site of Depot 700, he was flown back to and stayed at Scott Base for the duration and was privy to most of the communications that passed through it. He was a freelance reporter and his contacts allowed him to provide information that would not have been allowed if he had been channelling his stories through Shackleton. There was soon to be another reporter on the scene and he worked for the *Daily Mail* in London. Noel Barber was the overseas correspondent for the paper and he arrived at the American base of McMurdo Sound on the Ross Sea early in December 1957. He persuaded the very amenable Commander there, Admiral Dufek, to fly him to the Scott/Amundsen Base at the South Pole. It was from there that he gained first-hand information about the progress of the TAE. The Americans had granted Bunny and Ed Hillary permission to use their base radio as a link between the two halves of the expedition and they did not regard the messages as a security matter. Barber could tap into the signals passing from one half of the expedition to the other. This meant he could often get a scoop. These two reporters could therefore set the scene for one of the most controversial facets of the whole expedition, 'The Second Race to the Pole'.

Douglas McKenzie had been a bomber pilot during the Second World War and after being shot down and captured he was released at the war's end and spent a couple of years with the intelligence services, where he rose to the rank of Squadron Leader. He took up journalism in 1953.

Noel Barber was born in Yorkshire but spent most of his journalism career abroad as the *Daily Mail*'s foreign correspondent. He covered various hot spots for the newspaper including the

Hungarian Uprising of 1956, during which he was shot in the head by a Russian guard. He received stab wounds in Morocco during anti-French riots. He travelled extensively with his job but the Antarctic brief was totally new, even for him. He also found time later in life to become a television series presenter and finally a novelist.

Both men wrote of their experiences while covering the expedition. Noel Barber's *The White Desert* was published in 1958 and Douglas McKenzie brought out his book in 1963, *Opposite Poles*. They make interesting reading as both men wrote of how they saw the relationship between Bunny and Ed Hillary develop as they observed the expedition during the crossing period, even though they had almost no involvement with the actual crossing.

As 24 November approached so the activity at Shackleton became more and more frenetic, the men seldom getting to bed before the early hours of the morning. Up to the point when the pioneer party returned to base the manning level there was lower than the 16 men who were actually taking part in the expedition. Up to six were occupied getting the vehicles to South Ice, two were out with a dog team trying to help get the convoy through the crevassed areas, two more were at South Ice doing weather and related studies and three men were responsible for keeping the planes serviceable and manning the advanced air base that Bunny had requested. A total of 13 men were absent for these various reasons at various times during this crucial period. It wasn't until after 15 November that most of them were assembled at base to take on the final organising and loading operation that had to be done.

The most important link in the chain was the readiness of the transport, which consisted of three Sno-Cats, the two remaining Weasels, and one Muskeg tractor. The one surviving Ferguson tractor was not thought fit to take part in the final journey and was left behind. Spares for the range of vehicles going made it essential that every contingency was catered for. Could this have been simplified? The cost of one Sno-Cat was probably more than all the five Weasels put together. The Weasels were known to be temperamental beasts and shed tracks like a tree in autumn sheds leaves but they could pull a good payload and were more economical than the Cats. They had no heating system to speak of, however, and due to their shorter track length would be more susceptible to falling into crevasses. As mentioned earlier, another reason the Weasel was inferior to the big Cats was the footprint they left. Pound for pound, they exerted nearly twice as much pressure on the ground (ice) as the Cats and were therefore more likely to break through snow bridges. This analysis is easy to make, but when the important decisions had been made thousands of miles away, it was too late for regrets. With hindsight, the expedition was nearly three years in the planning and maybe more field trials would have shown up the Weasel's deficiencies. After all, look at what Ed Hillary achieved with the humble Ferguson tractor!

On the Starting Blocks

Having set in stone the departure date from Shackleton as 24 November 1957, Bunny forced the pace of the preparations by involving all the men in the final stages of checking stores and loading the sledges. Though it is not clear how involved the three RAF personnel were because on the day of departure George Lowe comments, 'They bestirred themselves to cook our final meal before departure.'

Bunny sent his final communiqué to Ed Hillary on the departure. It makes fascinating reading in the light of future developments:

Hillary
Owing to 39 days spent forcing route to South Ice our start delayed 10 days giving 200 miles to catch up to maintain 20MPD. This will be attempted. Distance run to South Ice 400 miles but will be 330 next time. Seismic Sno-Cat and one Weasel at South Ice. One Weasel abandoned one returned to Shackleton early on journey. Leaving 24th with 3 Sno-Cats 2 Weasels one Muskeg. Air recce to 84°S visibility to 85°S indicates Shackleton to South Ice most difficult section to Pole. Not certain 20 MPD can be maintained to South Ice but expect over 20 MPD thereafter. We could be up to fortnight late arriving Scott Base but will endeavour to reduce this though possibility remains we do not arrive till 9 March. Hope to improve this pessimistic statement on passage. If your conditions difficult we can accept intended D700 at D600 miles

but would then appreciate proportion of fuel you save in addition to twelve drums. Time so gained may be useful to you for your work on mountains. As it seems unlikely we can meet at D700 would appreciate guide from Plateau Depot if possible. Delighted you have vehicles on plateau and going well. Congratulations from all. ,

Bunny.

Bunny estimated that they covered 400 miles to get to South Ice on the reconnaissance journey and hoped to reduce this by at least 70 miles to 330 with a proportionate reduction in the days it took, down from 37 to nearer 30 days.

He gives Hillary advance warning of not being able to maintain the 20 miles per day he hoped to achieve and backs this up with information he has received from his pilots that the terrain between Shackleton and South Ice was probably the worst part of the route, certainly as far as South Ice. Bunny was hopeful of picking up some lost time once they got to South Ice, again citing the pilots' observations as they looked due south from their cockpit and observed what looked like better travelling conditions.

Despite the hopes he had of his party's progress and the prospect of getting back to a 20 miles per day average, Bunny felt it wise to inform Hillary that ETA at Scott Base could be as late as 9 March.

Of course Bunny had no idea at this juncture how Ed Hillary was progressing and probably still thought that the 700 depot was over-ambitious, so suggested that one be laid at 600 miles from Scott Base. This would suffice if that was the best Hillary could achieve, but if this was the case, he was then asked to leave some extra fuel at this new depot 600 to make up for the extra 100 miles Bunny would have to cover before refuelling his convoy. In addition to the suggestion of a modified depot position, Bunny says he would appreciate a sketch map of the route down from the Plateau should Hillary not be able to meet him and guide his party down from the plateau owing to the lateness of season.

On the day of Bunny's departure from Shackleton Ed Hillary was about to arrive at the spot chosen for Depot 480 and by

15 December he had reached Depot 700, so he was well placed to complete what he had thought possible from very early in the planning of the expedition, a run-through to the South Pole with the three tractors that had served his party so well up to this point.

The information now supplied to him by Bunny only added to his conviction that this final leg could be achieved without any inconvenience to the expedition as a whole – and in fact by carrying on southwards he could also survey the final 500 miles that Bunny would have to cover once he arrived at the Pole from South Ice.

There was to be a huge amount of press coverage as to the rights and wrongs of Ed Hillary's actions; even some of his own men felt he had carried out the 'South Pole Dash', as it became known, purely to satisfy his own ego.

Although Bunny completed the 2,200 mile trek in 99 days and did actually achieve just over 20 miles per day, it was a close-run thing and he also came in for a lot of criticism. The original schedule for a crossing time of 92 days would be missed by quite a margin.

On 24 November 1957 the convoy set out to the cheers of the RAF contingent of three and Taffy Williams. Also adding to the cheers was a small group of Argentine explorers who had arrived from their base a few miles away to see off the polar party.

The convoy consisted of three Sno-Cats, two Weasels and a Muskeg tractor. They had all been given names by their respective drivers; Bunny and David Stratton who were in the leading Sno-Cat, called theirs *Rock and Roll,* David Pratt one of the two engineers in the party and Ken Blaiklock who would later drive a dog team from South Ice to the South Pole, followed Bunny in *Able.* The third Sno-Cat was named *County of Kent* after the birthplace of the driver Roy Homard, who was accompanied by Ralph Lenton. They brought up the rear of the convoy. In front of them was the Muskeg tractor named *Hopalong* by its driver, the Australian Jon Stephenson. Jon would also drive a team of dogs with Ken Blaiklock from South Ice to the South Pole. Between the Muskeg and the two leading Sno-Cats came the two Weasels, the front one called *Rumble* driven by the team doctor Allan Rogers and the second Weasel driven by the expedition photographer George Lowe. He gave the name of *Wrack and Ruin* to his machine.

They were all heavily laden and towed sledge trailers also loaded up. Over 20 tons of stores, mainly fuel, with sufficient food for the section between Shackleton and South Ice and many sundry items including spare parts for the vehicles, were stacked and lashed onto the sledges. The plan was to keep the convoy supplied with extra items by utilising the Otter to fly in more of anything that they might need en route.

In an area where they thought they were relatively safe from crevasses, just a few miles after leaving their first overnight camp, the leading Sno-Cat slumped through a snow bridge and finished up wedged in a precarious position above a chasm some 60 feet deep. Bunny and David scrambled out to take stock. It took time to establish how the recovery would be expedited and the technicalities are beyond the scope of this book. Needless to say, it was a complicated procedure that involved all the other five vehicles being co-ordinated. Two were to hold the Sno-Cat from behind while the others took the strain from the front and as those at the rear inched forward the front ones moved slowly away from the lip of the crevasse and gently drew the stricken tractor unit out. Nearly half a day was lost.

Every time an occurrence like this took place a similar routine was employed and on each occasion precious time was being sacrificed – but no lives were lost nor for that matter did they lose any tractors into crevasses. The only ones that didn't make it to the South Pole suffered mechanical failure or were redundant.

Five days out from Shackleton they picked up the small depot that Ken and Jon had put down 50 miles out from their base camp during the first winter, when only the advance party were present at Shackleton. Bunny and his men had achieved those 50 miles in five days of very careful probing. Little niggling mechanical faults with the Weasels' radiators and tracks on all the vehicles had to be dealt with as they occurred. Bunny could not afford to lose any transport at this early stage.

Clearing that first area of crevasses was a great relief to the crews and the rate of progress changed gear from 10 miles a day to first 27 miles, then 41, followed by 65 miles on 3 December. The next obstacle was looming up, the Ice Wall and its attendant crevasses.

Despite knowing they were approaching a danger zone Bunny and his co-driver David were caught out and found themselves once more up-ended in a crevasse. This time there was considerable damage to one of the steering platforms. This had snapped and needed to be repaired before they could start off again.

While the repairs took place the other members of the party started to probe ahead for the safest route through the dangerous area that led up to the Ice Wall. Using long bamboo canes they thrust them into the snow to test for any weaknesses that would reveal hidden traps for the tractors and sledges as they threaded their way through the labyrinth.

The best part of two days passed before they could resume the trek and Bunny decided that the two Weasels should lead from now on, as he could not afford to lose a Sno-Cat at this early stage of the operation. The leading Weasel was now driven by Bunny as he held to the principle that only he should take on the onerous task of heading the convoy, not because he couldn't trust any of his men but merely because he felt incumbent upon himself to show that he was their leader and any immediate risks should be his.

The Weasels and the Muskeg had been fitted with suitably strong anchor points that enabled them to be hitched together with a strong tow rope so that in the event of a tumble into a hidden pitfall they would be held by the following tractor and extracting them might not be such a time-consuming act. The Sno-Cats did not have these anchor points as a result of there being insufficient time before they left base to weld them onto their chassis.

Despite this precaution it was to be the fate of the last Sno-Cat to be the next victim of a collapsed bridge. All the others had negotiated this particular crevasse and had probably weakened the crossing point, resulting in *Able* coming to grief. The main problem now facing the rest of the team was that they were all technically speaking on the wrong side of the crevasse to facilitate an immediate rescue. The Sno-Cat had plunged in head-first with her front pontoons resting against one side of the gaping trench while the back of the cabin had come to rest against the other side, leaving the rear pontoons dangling in space above the void beneath.

Anticipating something of this nature occurring they had brought with them some aluminium bridging trestles. Roping up for safety, two of the men were lowered into the crevasse and by cutting away at the walls they created ledges to enable them to position the trestles across the gap and slide them under the trapped tractor. By a system of ropes attached to the Sno-Cat and tied onto the other Sno-Cats they managed yet again to retrieve one of their most important assets. All the sledges had been unhitched and left where they were, to enable the other vehicles to take part in the rescue operation. Now they were coupled up again to their respective tractors and the convoy resumed its faltering progress.

John Lewis flew out to meet them with some spare parts for the tracks and a replacement pontoon for the damaged unit on *Rock and Roll*. He circled the area around the tractor units and made a landing in no more than 100 yards. The tractor crews were looking for a safe way forward and hurried back to meet the two men as they climbed down from the plane. After a short reunion and an exchange of news, John and his companion climbed back on board and returned to Shackleton in a take-off that was executed over an even shorter distance than the landing.

The way now seemed relatively clear to carry on up to the Ice Wall, which was reached at the end of a long day of careful travelling on 10 December. Over the next two days they skied and probed a route to the top of the Ice Wall marking it out with flags. Meanwhile, the two engineers fitted the replacement pontoon to the Sno-Cat.

Of relevance at this juncture is how the Americans based at Ellsworth experienced very similar scenarios. John Behrendt, who was responsible for the seismic work, carried out on their own transit of the Ronne Ice Shelf, writes about the difficulties they encountered in his book, *Innocents on the Ice*. They were active on the Filchner Ice Shelf at the same time as Bunny and his expedition were heading towards South Ice on their reconnaissance. The five Americans involved in the surface exploration set out on 28 October 1957 from their base camp in two Sno-Cats of the same design as the ones used by the TAE. One was equipped with all the seismic gear and the other tended to be used for eating, resting and most importantly rescue in the event of the other becoming ensnared by any crevasses.

Following an aerial reconnaissance of the planned route, they soon realised that crevasses were going to be a major obstacle. The two machines were in contact through portable radios. Another safety aid was a device mounted to the front of the leading Sno-Cat. This feature projected some 15 feet or so out in front and, by means of signals bounced off the surface, gave an indication of weaknesses in the surface that indicated the presence of crevasses. It had its limitations and gave rise to a false sense of security: inevitably a Sno-Cat went down into a crevasse. Like Bunny, they had no experience of how to retrieve the downed vehicle and it was by trial and error that they succeeded in salvaging it.

Instead of carrying huge quantities of tractor fuel on trailers, the Americans relied on deliveries coming in from Ellsworth by an Otter aircraft. The plane could also keep them stocked up with provisions. They had a far more varied diet than the TAE men could hope to obtain. And the aircraft could also be used as a route finder. Their fuel drums weighed as much as 350lbs each, but several years later, when the author was again down in the Antarctic, the Americans had developed rolling drums which could hold 500 gallons and later still, the Hercules aircraft that serviced their depots came equipped with detachable wing tanks of even greater capacity. Despite localised problems with their radios, they were able to listen to various overseas broadcasts from other countries. On 4 November they heard from a BBC broadcast that Ed Hillary and his crew had reached the Polar Plateau.

November saw their apprenticeship in Sno-Cat retrieval begin. The leading Cat had just about crossed a crevasse when the trailer it was pulling capsized sideways through the snow bridge and dragged the vehicle backwards towards the chasm. Fortunately, the Cat had only dropped its rear end pontoons into the crevasse so in this instance the rescue went ahead in a straightforward manner. In fact, getting the five heavy fuel drums off the sledge before retrieval could begin was the most difficult part of the operation. Needless to say, there were three very shaken-up occupants.

Another shaky moment occurred on 15 November early in the morning. Their supply plane had just landed at its second attempt and took two of the survey men up for a look ahead at the path they would need to take. On its return the other three on the ground watched it come down. One of them started running towards the plane where it had come to rest and suddenly disappeared. John Behrendt ran for some rope and very shortly was being lowered down to the fortunately uninjured man, who was wedged some 20 feet down the crevasse. They managed to extricate him after about 10 minutes but it was a nasty experience while it lasted. The only casualty appears to have been his movie camera. Although they went back down on a rope to look for it there was no sign.

Later that day as they set off to complete navigating through the crevassed area via the route indicated by the pilot they again had a Sno-Cat stranded halfway across a crevasse. The detection device mounted on the front of the vehicle had failed to do its job. The Cat was straddling the gap but with both the front and rear pontoons tilted down the sides of the crevasse. Dragging the trapped Cat out resulted in some damage to the drive shaft of the front pontoon. They were now stranded. Unlike the TAE, the spare parts for this type of breakdown were held at base camp, Ellsworth, and as the weather had clamped down on them the plane was unable to fly the parts in.

They spent the time waiting for the plane in scouting the way forward but the situation was getting critical, the route ahead looked dangerous but the way back could turn out to be equally undesirable. The plane was delayed for a week and in the meantime an inspection of the belts on the Cat's pontoons revealed some undetected damage that would require welding. It wasn't until 26 November that the repairs could be carried out and they were again able to move forward, 11 days after damaging the caterpillar. At least the TAE party never got held up for more than a day during the whole trip across Antarctica, despite all the mechanical breakdowns and incidents involving crevasses.

On 12 December Bunny and his team were set to ascend the Ice Wall for the second time and estimated that after starting out from Shackleton on 24 November they were now three days ahead of the 20 days it had taken them to reach this same spot during the pioneering run.

The convoy reached the top of the Ice Wall without mishap and soon arrived at the Weasel they had been forced to abandon back in October. The camshaft had been damaged by the broken bearing and was impossible to repair without wasting several days, so Roy and David salvaged all the useful parts and they moved on.

Crevasses continued to dog their advance and at one stage the leading Weasel fell sideways into a large rift that collapsed under it. The lurch threw Hal Lister from his perch on the vehicle's cab roof where he had been acting as lookout. Luck was with them that day as he only suffered some torn clothing, a cut to his leg and a damaged ego.

They had started travelling at night to take advantage of the lower temperatures when the sun was lower in the sky. Although progress was still laborious, Bunny claimed that by 19 November they were nine days ahead of the previous run. Care still had to be exercised but they appeared to have passed the worst. They even stopped for a few hours of geology work at the Whichaway Nunataks that Jon Stephenson had briefly explored with Ken the previous year.

They pulled into South Ice on 22 December 1957 with all the vehicles that had left Shackleton Base 29 days earlier, though they had left behind the Weasel abandoned during the earlier sortie near Recovery Glacier. The original pioneering trip had taken 39 days according to Bunny so they had bettered that by about 10 days and had trimmed an estimated 60 miles off the distance covered. Some of this improvement was attributable to the fact that he had three Sno-Cats that were already proving their worth, with a greater reliability record and being able to negotiate the crevassed areas with more confidence in the knowledge that a Sno-Cat in a crevasse could be extricated with the assistance of the other two machines just as easily as a Weasel.

Calling Ed Hillary,
Over and Out!

The next day Bunny contacted Ed Hillary by cable stating his arrival at South Ice and gave a quick résumé of the plan he had in mind for the next step to the South Pole – but by this time Ed Hillary was already on his way to the South Pole.

There was no direct line of communication between Bunny and Ed, all the radio communications were routed through either the American Base at the South Pole, Scott Base on the Ross Sea, or sometimes both. The consequence of this was that when one man sent off a cable to the other in response to an earlier message received, several days would have elapsed; and so it was when Bunny sent his update to Ed Hillary on 22 December. Hillary had already cabled Bunny with his decision to set off from Depot 700 ostensibly to check the route farther south by 100 miles or so. His cable was in the form of a request, asking if Bunny wanted him to lay an additional depot even nearer the Pole than Depot 700. But because he did not receive an answer one way or the other, he decided that no harm would come of the probe southwards anyway. By the time Bunny answered asking for an extra depot of fuel to be laid, Ed Hillary was out of radio contact and pushing hard for the Pole. When Hillary finally received another message about this proposed extra depot he sent a cable back saying that he was now too far south to turn back and comply with the belated request and owing to his own fuel supply he could only go on south and not return to Depot 700.

Ed Hillary had established the Depot 700 well in advance of the timetable and with Bunny running several weeks behind his schedule, it would have meant sitting around at the depot for several weeks, which a man of Hillary's temperament was not likely to do. The temptation to carry out this manoeuvre seems to have been uppermost in his mind for a long time. He had persevered with getting the tractors up onto the plateau and optimising their performance. The Beaver plane had flown in a surplus of tractor fuel to Depot 700 for their requirements and time was on his side. The only negative was the fact that their main supply-plane, the Beaver, was not capable of reaching any party travelling beyond Depot 700 when flying out from Scott Base, Should the polar party get into trouble then it could prove very difficult to extricate them. To obviate this problem John Claydon had had the foresight to establish a refuelling depot several hundred miles farther south than Scott Base. He placed a dump of aviation fuel with two men to look after it in case the plane ever needed to make an emergency landing following a breakdown in the weather at either end of its flight path to or from Scott, or the tractor party out on the plateau.

The New Zealand Committee through their chairman Charles Bowden had also tried to contact Ed Hillary and dissuade him from what appeared to be an unnecessary undertaking. He stressed that Hillary's function and contractual agreement as laid down before the expedition's departure from New Zealand specifically stated that the Ross Sea party were to lay depots as far south as 700 miles from Scott Base and meet Bunny as he journeyed north from the Pole to guide him safely through any obstacles to Scott Base. Any variations from this path could only be carried out with the express permission of the expedition's overall leader, Bunny Fuchs. In the eyes of Charles Bowden, Hillary was exceeding his remit. Again, the time lapse between sending and receiving messages meant that Ed Hillary had not received the latest communiqué and had carried out what he perceived to be a legitimate exercise; rather than sit around at the depot waiting, he took the initiative and moved out.

The delay in passing on messages was to have a profound effect on the relationship between Ed Hillary and most of the other participants in the expedition. It had been widely known that he would have a shot at getting to the Pole, and let's face it – which of us wouldn't, given the circumstances? Or perhaps more accurately, who wouldn't go for it if they happened to be the first man to the summit of Mount Everest? Hillary now had a once-in-a-lifetime chance of doing something that was last achieved by Robert Falcon Scott over 40 years before. It really wasn't what he did that ruffled so many feathers – it was the way he went about it. Was it really necessary? It wasn't part of his contract. Was he taking a huge unknown risk not only with his own life but of the four others who went with him? Why hadn't he been more open about his scheme? If he failed, would that have affected the outcome of the whole expedition by his not being at Depot 700 to guide Bunny and his men down off the Plateau? These questions and many others would be a talking point for years to come. It was almost a rerun of the Cooke/Peary controversy about which one of them actually got to the North Pole, if either of them did.

The source of the news that broke on the world scene seems to have been a conversation between Noel Barber, the *Daily Mail* overseas correspondent and John Claydon, the New Zealand pilot. Barber had temporarily returned to the American Base at McMurdo Sound from the Scott/Amundsen Base at the South Pole. The American base was only a couple of miles away across the ice from Scott Base and Barber had walked over to talk to the men stationed there. According to Barber's recollection of the event in *The White Desert*, he and Claydon were talking about how the two halves of the expedition were faring and what Ed Hillary might do once Depot 700 was established. After a number of probing questions, Barber asked if Claydon had a personal opinion on the matter and Claydon ventured that he thought Ed Hillary would push on from 700 to the Pole. With a promise not to quote John as having given this information officially but merely as his own opinion, Barber sent out a message to the effect that he, Barber, thought Hillary was racing Bunny to the Pole. Barber felt this was the best story he had ever sent from the Antarctic. The news of Ed Hillary's move towards the Pole now became common knowledge.

The exact whereabouts of Bunny's column was often uncertain but the last message from him to Hillary seemed to indicate that he might get to the Pole between Christmas and the New Year, precisely the same arrival date that Hillary was hoping for. So the race was on!

Both parties had about 500 miles to travel to reach the Pole and the leak of Ed Hillary's intention and the long silences on Bunny's side fuelled the speculation. An example of the time lag between sending a message and the other party receiving it can be seen from a cable sent to Ed Hillary on 24 December, which he read on 28 December. This message took up the offer of an additional dump about 100 miles farther south from Depot 700. Bunny planned to abandon vehicles as and when they either broke down irretrievably or became surplus to requirements. This would restrict his ability to carry any excess fuel. Of course once Bunny reached the Pole, then fuel would have been available from the Americans; but the expedition had a contract with British Petroleum to use their supply exclusively, according to the sponsorship deal. Bunny seemed at this late stage to have concerns for his fuel stocks and acknowledged in his message that now he was aware of Ed Hillary's desire to proceed to the Pole, he was sorry if this request for an extra depot would put an end to the New Zealander's capers. The cable had come too late for Ed Hillary to be of any personal assistance unless he did as Bunny suggested and turned back to await a fresh supply of fuel to be flown in from Scott Base. He was at the half-way point towards the Pole and this first option was just possible; or he could get Bob Miller and George Marsh to return early from their surveying trip to the Beardmore Glacier. Whichever way he wanted to help, some men would be required at Depot 700 to help unload the fuel drums from the plane. When Miller and Marsh heard how he had considered their recall, they were extremely angry to think that he would sacrifice an important surveying expedition in order to pursue his personal goal of reaching the Pole with no benefits, except to his own ego.

Dwelling on the issue of messages that had been delayed, *The Times* printed an article from their Special Correspondent entitled 'Sir E. Hillary asked to plan Depot 800', with a subtitle of 'N.Z. Committee reaffirms full support for expedition'. This was dated 8 January 1958. It appears that the London Committee had received a cable from Charles Bowden in New Zealand about Ed Hillary pressing on south from Depot 700. Sir John Slessor, the Chairman of the London Committee, had sent a cable on 6 January to Charles Bowden stressing the need to ensure that Hillary completed his duty to the expedition and support Bunny as far as humanly possible to get him and his team to Scott Base. Bowden replied that the New Zealand committee were keeping a close eye on developments with Bunny's squadron and would contact Hillary with regard to the request from Bunny to lay in an additional depot 100 miles nearer the Pole, Depot 800.

The New Zealand Committee had received news that Ed Hillary had stocked Depot 700 and had reached the Pole on 3 January. They had initially thought Hillary was moving south from Depot 700 to create Depot 800 as Bunny had requested, not realising that Hillary had not received this request until he was too far into his journey to the Pole to be of any immediate assistance.

We know that Hillary had set his heart on getting to the Pole if he had even half a chance and the delay in him getting the request from Bunny had come at a fortuitous moment for him. He now played on the situation to his full advantage, probably sensing that his Pole run would be frowned upon by the powers that be but using the delayed message to cover his actions.

Charles Bowden, concerned at the rash of publicity about the 'Race to the Pole', and the fact that the London Committee were coming down hard on him to keep a strict eye on Hillary, had contacted the New Zealand Prime Minister Nash, requesting him to issue a statement reaffirming the full co-operation of New Zealand and in particular of Ed Hillary's part in the stocking of any depots that Bunny might require. Nash also tried to pour oil on the troubled, icy waters between Ed Hillary and Bunny over the New Zealander's suggestion that the main party should concentrate on getting to the Pole and then return next season to complete the crossing. He affirmed that Ed Hillary had been misunderstood and had merely been concerned with the main party's continued problems in keeping up with a schedule that would get them to the Pole with sufficient time to complete the crossing safely.

The London Committee sent Bunny a cable fully supporting his decisions whatever they might be, as he was the field commander and any change of plan could only be carried out with his consent. Ed Hillary was unrepentant and felt he had acted with the expedition's welfare at heart in his suggestion of an interrupted journey.

The rights and wrongs of the two team leaders' points of view are woven into the fabric of missed radio communications and press speculation and must be seen in a historic context. Nobody will ever be quite sure who held the moral high ground.

South Ice to the South Pole – the Worst Is Yet to Come

The story resumes as we find Bunny arriving at South Ice to be reunited with Hannes la Grange and Geoff Pratt, who had been keeping a continuous weather record and looking after the two teams of huskies that were about to start on their historic journey to the South Pole, the first such undertaking since Roald Amundsen in 1911.

The reunited group were not to be together for very long. The plan was for Ken Blaiklock and Jon Stephenson to set out for the Pole on 23 December 1957, just one day after Bunny's team arrived at the South Ice encampment. Their brief was to check out the route ahead of the tractor party as it made its ponderous way further south and, if possible, mark any obstacles that they could locate with flags mounted on poles. The dog teams had a two-day start on the mechanised convoy and they were now a vital part of the strategy to get to the Pole in as short a time as possible.

The main group, which would now include the two hermits, Hannes and Geoff from South Ice, would follow a couple of days behind. It was a big demand on the dog teams to keep ahead of the tractors because once they reached a good surface the tractors would be able to cover many more miles a day than the pair of sledgers could. However, every 200 miles the tractors needed to be serviced and this took at least a day. Breakdowns could also occur and frequently did and most important of all, the scientific element of the expedition had to be attended to, namely the time-consuming one of seismic testing to determine the thickness of the ice cap. This procedure was carried out every 20–30 miles right through to the South Pole. The idea was to help determine whether the continent was all one land mass or, as some thought, two or more separate giant islands.

The dogs maintained a superb average of about 20 miles a day all the way to the Pole and even when they were eventually caught up they still managed to keep going long enough each day to keep company with the tractor group.

On 25 December after a Christmas lunch and listening to the Queen's Christmas Day broadcast, the vehicles began the second leg of their historic journey. The convoy now comprised four Sno-Cats, two Weasels and the sole Muskeg tractor. Each unit pulled two sledge-based trailers with a combined total of 20 tons of supplies that would have to last them until they reached Depot 700, more than 1,000 miles away on the other side of the South Pole.

The convoy would attempt to keep to the shortest possible route on this the next leg of the journey. An average of 20 miles a day was the original target and they were already well behind this schedule after the problems that had beset them on the way from base to the outpost at South Ice. They hoped fervently that now they were on the Plateau the only obstacles in their way would be crevasses – which they now knew how to deal with – and the weather. Having coped with the Theron Mountains and the Shackleton Range to get to the South Ice encampment, they had climbed to well over 4,000 feet above sea level. Their route now lay along Latitude 29° East.

A reminder of the seven vehicles in the convoy. The leading Sno-Cat *Rock and Roll* was driven most of the way by Bunny and his deputy David Stratton. This was followed by *Haywire*, so-called because Ralph Lenton the wireless operator used the name as his call sign when trying to connect to base camp. *Haywire* was not only the radio link to the outside world but it carried all the seismic testing gear and in that sense was probably the most important Sno-Cat that the expedition possessed. With them were Roy Homard's Sno-Cat *County of Kent* and David Pratt's *Able*. These two men were key to keeping the vehicles on the road. There were two Weasels left out of a total of four brought out from the UK and these would be left out on the Plateau before the crossing was completed. *Wrack and Ruin*'s name probably accurately reflected the overall condition of the vehicle, and *Rumble* indicated the noise that had to be endured as the second Weasel tracked over the rough sastrugi that they encountered from time to time. Last but by no means least was the only Bombardier Muskeg tractor, *Hopalong*. Jon Stephenson had cut his driving teeth on this when the party left Shackleton Base for South Ice and it would appear that letting the clutch in over-vigorously became a feature of his efforts, resulting in a characteristic kangaroo start.

The dogs were raring to go and for the first mile or so Jon Stephenson later recalled he needed the assistance of three of the tractor men to help control the dogs' exuberance. Several times the sledges keeled over as a result of the uneven surface and as the two dog teams were some distance apart, each man had to cope as best he could in righting them.

The two men managed 15 miles in the first day's travel and at every 5 miles they cut snow blocks and stacked them with flags on top in the traditional way of polar explorers, to show the way forward in case the wind obliterated their tracks before the tractors came along. Some of these monoliths were architecturally impressive and became known as snow henges.

Bunny's strategy was to stop every 30 miles or so and allow Geoffrey Pratt to carry out his seismology tests. These tests were time-consuming and they did not always go to plan, in which case they were repeated. Additional time was lost when any stops were made to repair vehicles and a system of preventative maintenance was carried out every 200 miles to obviate or at least minimise breakdowns. Coinciding seismic tests with routine maintenance made sense.

Ken Blaiklock and Jon Stephenson radioed in at the end of their second day to report that they had not discovered any major problems by the time they covered 32 miles. The biggest problem that the following army of tractors faced was the extremely hard sastrugi, most of them seemed to lie across their path and the constant shaking up and down played havoc with the caterpillar units, not to mention the unpleasant experience for the drivers, especially of the three smaller units. The sastrugi zone was hopefully not going to last forever and at least Bunny and his team were on their way.

After a tentative start of about 15 miles the convoy camped for a few hours rest, but when the resumption was made there was a whiteout. This caused a delay which lasted until the afternoon and even then great care had to be exercised to avoid any mishaps.

Despite repeated efforts, Ralph Lenton failed to make contact with their old base at Shackleton, Halley Bay the IGY base, or Ellsmere, the American station. The radios being used by the expedition as a whole had been unsatisfactory and this must have been so frustrating. One of the Weasels had experienced a breakdown and the fourth Sno-cat stayed behind with it as a back-up while the others pressed on to the next overnight stop. By the time the main party were ready to resume their journey the next morning, the two vehicles had still not caught up. Due to that lack of radio contact Bunny had to send the Muskeg back to determine the problem. In the end all was well and having changed yet another radiator, the two back markers were about to set off in pursuit.

Despite all the familiar set-backs, by day five Bunny could record that they had covered a fairly satisfactory 100 miles, not enough to make any inroads into the low daily mileage up to South Ice but at least a promising start.

There had been numerous occasions in the run-up to the departure date from South Ice when George Lowe had been very critical in his diary of the apparent lack of cohesion in the expedition's planning. He noted especially the failure of Bunny and David Stratton to bring other expedition members into meaningful discussions. It should be remembered that George probably noticed this more acutely than the others in the party. His function was primarily that of the official photographer and when not occupied with his brief he willingly set to and helped other members with their official duties. This brought him into contact in a more intimate way with the others and much as a barber listens to his clients opening up about their frustrations in life, he performed the same role in this expedition. He also shared a cubicle with Bunny Fuchs and would have been privy to what was being planned at the earliest possible stage – but was not able to pass this information on.

A small group of people forced together soon learn who they can confide in and George acted as a confidant and a go-between. However, now that the tractors were rolling he could again pursue his official role and he found that he was able to shed the depression that had crept over him and start to enjoy the unique experience of being once again free to be his own boss, much as he had done when he and Ed Hillary were pitted against the elements high on the roof of the world as they strove to overcome the challenge of conquering Mount Everest.

The two dog sledge teams do not appear to have experienced the whiteout that hampered the tractors and instead reported some excellent weather conditions. They were eventually caught up by 29 December and it gave the two parties a few short hours to compare notes and then away went the dogs again, leaving the engineers to carry out welding repairs to the tractor and sledge tow bars that had taken so much punishment crossing the sastrugi.

Ken Blaiklock who was driving the leading sledge navigated with the use of a sun compass. Ken obviously had a proprietary sun compass but the simplest form of this is an analogue watch. This can be used to determine due north or south, provided of course the sun is visible and you have a watch that is telling the correct time. In the southern hemisphere hold the watch horizontally and point the 12 o'clock position on the dial directly towards the sun (irrespective of where the sun is in the sky) and holding the watch still, draw an imaginary line that bisects the angle formed between the hour hand and the 12 o'clock position. This will give true north and by deduction true south must lie in the opposite direction. By this simple method the pair was able to maintain a true south direction. A magnetic compass would not have been so effective. This scouting of the route took a lot of the navigational strain away from Bunny and David Stratton in the leading vehicle, but no doubt they checked every so often that all was well. Bunny mentions a sun compass being mounted on the leading Sno-Cat so they obviously could check from time to time on the path they were taking but he at no time found it necessary to correct their route, despite detours to avoid obstacles.

Although the dog teams experienced capsizing problems they still managed to maintain an excellent daily mileage. The convoy following them found the sastrugi gave them an extremely uncomfortable ride and the strain exerted on the tow bars as the sledges came crashing down from the tops of the ridges onto the back end of the tractors resulted in numerous stoppages to re-weld the broken tow hitches. This unpleasant situation continued for many miles and it didn't improve until they were only a couple of days drive from the South Pole.

Another problem they had to deal with was a totally unexplained bout of sickness that overtook each member of the expedition. Even the two dog team drivers eventually caught the bug and Ken Blaiklock actually collapsed while driving his dogs and had to be helped into one of the Weasels until he could recover. George Lowe took over his team and David Stratton drove Jon Stephenson's for the next three days until both men had recovered enough to continue with their teams.

Trans-Antarctic Flight –
Touch and Go

South Ice Base camp was now officially closed down but would be used just once more by the four aircrew, as they attempted the first ever flight across Antarctica in a single engine plane. The Otter was far too valuable an asset to be abandoned by the expedition at Shackleton and could not be saved except by this audacious flight, planned to take place before the weather started to deteriorate. John Lewis, Gordon Haslop, Peter Weston and Taffy Williams formed the crew of the Otter, which had been fitted with an extra fuel tank to give it the range to reach Scott Base. The plane could not afford to land anywhere on the high Polar Plateau as the rarefied air would not give the plane's engine sufficient oxygen for it to take off again. The working ceiling for this type of plane was unlikely to exceed 12,000 feet and it was quite possible that the flight would have to be carried out at this maximum altitude to cross the mountains in their path, which rose to an uncomfortably adjacent 11,000 feet.

The traversing ground party were supposed to advise them of weather conditions likely to be met to the south of South Ice but a radio schedule set for six o'clock on the evening of 29 December failed to materialise. The weather at South Ice where the four intrepid airmen waited was perfect for the flight but they needed confirmation of a good report from farther south. Their chance came when the American station at the South Pole came on the air to give the news that apart from some cloud cover there shouldn't be any problems. The Americans also confirmed that the weather at McMurdo Sound looked good.

At 10.30 pm on 29 December they lifted off having taken the best part of half-a-mile to gain the necessary speed to get the heavily laden machine into the sky. The flight was due to take an estimated 12 hours and the two pilots would be able to take over from one another as they flew first south to the Pole and then, of course, due North.

From the air they could see the tracks that the seven vehicles were leaving as they ploughed across the snow and ice in the same direction. About an hour into the flight the ground party were spotted as they camped for the night. The crew tried to make radio contact but Bunny and his radio operator had switched off for the night! According to Bunny, 'They had had a long day and were safely tucked up in their sleeping bags.'

Further south an ominous cloud formation was observed and this thickened until they lost sight of the ground. They had reached about 10,000 feet but this was no guarantee of safety so as the cloud thickened they had no choice but to head back to South Ice and hope they could find what would be a speck in a vast, icy expanse. The return journey was going to be a nail-biting 400 miles of flying with no guarantee that they could land safely.

Making for the Whichaway Nunataks as a landmark from where they could work out a flight path directly to South Ice, the relief must have been enormous when a break in the clouds allowed them to do what lost air crews have always done – follow a railway line to its destination to locate themselves. Not exactly a railway line, but good enough. As the clouds cleared there below them were the remains of the tracks made by the tractor party a couple of days before. After seven long hours John Lewis who was at the controls of the Otter brought the plane safely back to South Ice.

They were now faced with a dilemma, their stock of fuel was insufficient to try and repeat the flight. There was a cache of four drums of fuel sitting at Shackleton Base but to retrieve these four drums would entail a return flight of about six hours and that would consume most of what was at Shackleton, so they had to think of another solution.

The situation was solved as a result of a conversation over the radio between Taffy Williams and his counterpart at the American IGY base of Ellsworth, 40 miles or so along the coast from Shackleton. The Americans offered to pick up these four drums of fuel and ferry them up to South Ice in the next couple of days once the weather had cleared up.

Waiting for the weather to improve seemed to take forever and there was nothing to do. On 6 January 1958 the longed-for improvement came and with it the four drums of aviation fuel kindly brought in by Major Jim Lassiter. This was just one of the many occasions when the TAE had good reason to be thankful for the fact that in the background all the time was the reassuring presence of the Americans and their air cover.

The scheduled contacts with firstly the crossing team and then the Pole station confirmed a settled period in the weather, so all seemed set for another attempt to fly across the continent. Taffy informed Bunny's squadron and the Pole station that they would try to get airborne around 11.30 pm that same day. The Otter lifted off just before midnight, although of course it was still daylight. They again passed over the tractor convoy but still failed to raise them on the radio, which was strange as you would have thought that the convoy would want to know how they were getting on and would have had their radio on, listening out for progress reports. Bunny blames this missed opportunity to talk with the fliers on a lack of a confirmation by the Pole station that take-off had actually been achieved and again, they were safely tucked up in their sleeping bags. The Otter flew on towards their next target, the South Pole, and at about 4.30 in the morning the plane picked up a radio signal that indicated they were approaching the Pole itself. Without attempting to land at the Pole they circled it a couple of times as a salute and changed course for the Beardmore Glacier, which would lead the flyers down off the Plateau to the Ross Ice Shelf and then across that to the New Zealand base on McMurdo Sound. The flight passed over all the old familiar named landmarks which had been so important to Scott, Shackleton and their men when they had occupied the now empty and ice-filled huts at Discovery Point and Hut Point. Geographical locations such as the Cloudmaker

Mountain, Mount Hope, Mount Discovery, Minna Bluff, Black and White Islands and finally Mounts Erebus and Terror passed beneath their wings as they ticked off the last few miles to the end of their unique and record-breaking flight. A couple of American planes buzzed them as they lined themselves up for the approach to Scott Base's landing strip.

The flight had taken 11 hours and had covered a distance of just under 1,500 miles, if the first attempt is ignored. There was little press coverage of the achievement, as all eyes were on the drama that was taking place out on the Plateau. *The Times* covered the event in less than 700 words and the article was from 'Our Special Correspondent', whoever that was.

Another Controversy – and Bunny Reaches the Pole

By New Year's Eve the Muskeg tractor in Bunny's convoy had to be left behind. It was proving too slow over the better surface they were experiencing and to speed up their progress, they rearranged the load it was towing and left the vehicle behind. The sting in the tail came just the next day, when one of the Weasels broke a track for which there were now no more spares.

Two men were delegated to return to the last campsite and bring back the Muskeg. The soft going caused the Muskeg to fall behind again; but by relieving her of the second trailer she managed to keep up a speed of 5mph, sufficient to stay in touch for the next few days.

The average mileage was creeping up towards the magic 20 miles a day. Bunny estimated that as they approached an even more severe section of sastrugi on 13 January, the distance still to go before the Pole was reached had now dropped below 200 miles. Steady if restricted progress was maintained over the next three days but the surface was proving very difficult for all the smaller vehicles because it was a combination of hard sastrugi ridges with soft snow lying in between the peaks.

On 17 January they finally drove onto a smoother surface and this was to continue all the way to the South Pole, much to everyone's relief. On this same day the encampment was buzzed by two Neptune aircraft from the American base at the Pole. On 19 January Bunny and his men knew they were getting close and the first sign of the Scott, Amundsen base camp came into view as they topped a rise about 8 miles out on the Plateau. They scanned the horizon standing on the tractor cab roofs and there it was, a few black shapes on the horizon. The first and probably the worst half of the journey was nearly completed.

Communications with the New Zealand half of the expedition had never been very good and were still having to be carried out over the relay system they had devised through the American base at the South Pole. Contact had been briefly established directly with Scott Base during this period and through this link Bunny learnt that Hillary had reached the South Pole on 3 January (due to time zone differences this was actually the 4th on Ed's calendar but the 3rd on Bunny's).

What followed would provide another round of press speculation. Ed Hillary had sent a cable to the Ross Sea committee in New Zealand through Scott Base informing Bunny that he had reached his controversial target, the South Pole, and followed this up with his view of the situation as he saw it. He started with, 'I am very concerned about the serious delay in your plans.' He goes on to stress that the distance still to be covered by Bunny and his team when the Pole was finally reached would be a further 1,250 miles to Scott Base and from Depot 700 north the going would only start to deteriorate due to the lateness of the season. Hillary's mechanics had expressed their concerns about working on broken-down vehicles in worsening temperature and weather conditions, which could lead to the whole convoy getting stranded out on the Plateau with winter upon them. Even if the Americans could drop supplies to them and some sort of suitable shelter so that they could survive until the next travelling season, Hillary realistically saw a situation developing where lives could be at stake. His suggestion to Bunny was to get to the Pole and then be flown out and return the following summer. Hillary, aware how much farther Bunny still had to go before getting to the Pole, informed him that he and three of his men were being evacuated from the Pole by the Americans back to Scott Base to await further developments. He proposed that if Bunny decided to press on, he would fly to Depot 700 and guide him for the remainder of the journey from there. A set of guidance instructions from the Pole northwards to Depot 700, where Hillary would arrange for extra fuel to be flown in, would be left with Peter Mulgrew, Hillary's radio operator, who was remaining at the Pole for the time being to ensure that the two halves of the expedition could keep in touch more readily.

The next day Bunny composed the following cable in answer to Ed's suggested course of action: 'Appreciate your concern, but there can be no question of abandoning journey at this stage.' Bunny said he had no intention of carrying out a two-part crossing. He was confident that his Sno-Cats could operate at 60° below but felt that these temperatures would not be reached even in March. With regard to asking personnel to stay on so long that they might not get evacuated from the Antarctic before winter set in, he fully understood their situation and was prepared to release any man wishing to return to New Zealand at the end of their contract – including Ed Hillary.

In other words, 'You do as you see fit and I'll complete this with or without your help.' Bunny gave their position as 84° 43′ South, 7,000 feet above sea level.

Bunny informed his team of the exchange of messages and reassured them that even Scott had not reached the Pole until 18 January and 'We have transport and a proven route to the north.'

Meanwhile, this exchange of views had been picked up by various members of the press due to a breach of security by the Ross Sea Committee. The newspapers were eagerly looking for any titbits with which to fill their columns now that Ed had 'beaten' Bunny to the Pole. The fact that a subordinate officer should have the audacity to suggest that the expedition be more or less abandoned at this critical stage, especially as the idea was coming from a mere colonial to the leader of a British Expedition, was tantamount to insubordination in the eyes of the press. The Trans-Antarctic Expedition was and always had been Bunny's idea and the last thing he wanted was somebody telling him what he should do. The press had a field day.

On 17 January 1958 two American Neptune aircraft circled over their encampment. Radio messages were exchanged to the effect that all was ready to receive the explorers. On board the planes were a number of reporters together with Admiral Dufek and Ed Hillary. John Lewis one of the two Otter pilots who had successfully navigated the single-engine plane across the continent was also on board.

The final mile or so had been flagged as the way in to the Pole Station to avoid any disturbance of an area that the Americans were eager not to be contaminated with anything, as they were carrying out sensitive environmental experiments on the snow surface there.

By arriving on 19 January they had actually achieved the 20 miles a day target that Bunny had set for this part of the crossing. The dog teams that by now had been caught up still managed to keep pace with the tractors and arrived at the Pole on the same day. Their fate was now in the hands of the Americans who had very generously offered to fly them out to Scott Base. There was now no longer any need for them to try and keep ahead of the mechanised column for reconnaissance purposes and provisionally they were to be used for more exploration nearer to Scott Base at McMurdo Sound the following season by Jon Stephenson and Ken Blaiklock, who had made plans to return for further field work. As it turned out, this option never materialised. Some of them were culled, much to the anguish of Ken and Jon, before the two men returned to Scott Base. But the remainder were probably kept by the New Zealanders who were staying at the base for the winter and they probably used them the following year for the continuation of their exploratory travels. No one seems to have recorded their final fate.

The reception at the Pole that the Americans extended to Bunny and his men was wonderful. Nothing was too much trouble, showers, hot food, clean beds and a chance to relax after their 16-hour days must have seemed like heaven to the weary travellers.

After all the speculation in the press as to how Bunny and Ed Hillary would react to one another, the encounter seemed to pass off with relatively little drama. There was the obligatory hand shake with Ed Hillary, repeated a number of times so that all the press men who had assembled at the Pole could film the historic moment. This was followed by the introduction of Bunny firstly to Admiral Dufek, the McMurdo Sound Base leader who had organised the flight into the South Pole station for Ed Hillary, then to the two men responsible for the running of the American station at the South Pole, Lieutenant Verne Houk and Major Mogesson. There followed a short press conference to bring everybody up to date with Bunny's future plans.

The Americans generously offered their workshop facilities for Bunny's two mechanics to do some essential maintenance on the overworked vehicles. The group spent four days recuperating and, with the sun still circling round the sky every 24 hours, they set out on 24 January for the final leg across the continent.

Ed Hillary returned to Scott Base with a promise to meet them at Depot 700 as originally planned. The path to the Pole for Hillary had been a long one and at times a very fraught one. His intentions had always been honourable but his methods had come in for a great deal of scrutiny over the last few weeks of December 1957 and the beginning of January 1958. Despite all the fuss that had been kicked up, the fact remained that he had led a very successful expedition in its own right and landed an extraordinary double that no other man could ever achieve – getting to the summit of Everest first and reaching the South Pole.

Hillary and His Team
Plan Their Strategy

It had all started with the initial trip down to the Antarctic aboard the *Theron* in January 1956. It was as part of this advance party that Ed Hillary became aware of how the organisation of all the expedition's functions needed to be analysed, checked and verified before committing any act that might jeopardise the smooth running of the project. Watching the mistakes that were made at the expedition's base on the Filchner Ice Shelf, Ed Hillary was determined to not repeat them when he led his team down to the McMurdo Sound the next season at the start of the New Zealand side of the enterprise.

On his return from the *Theron* voyage after the setting up of Shackleton in the Weddell Sea, Ed Hillary made a list of priorities for his own expedition. He organised the loading of the ship so that the unloading would bring out the most important items first, such as shelter ashore for the men to cook, sleep and work on breakdowns under cover. The tractors and sledges were to be moved onto the landing area quickly to rapidly move stores away from the ice edge to a place of safety, the Beaver assembled for aerial reconnaissance, the hut site selected and the huts built by experienced manpower brought down specifically for the job, these men returning with the ship when she sailed back to New Zealand at the end of that first short summer season. Finally, those staying would get as much driving experience as possible on the Weasels lent to them by the Americans, and their own Ferguson tractors.

As mentioned earlier, New Zealanders were sent down to the Antarctic as a precursor to the main expedition being mounted on 21 December 1956. The three men involved in this exercise had brought back much useful information relating to the area chosen for the base camp and a possible route onto the Plateau.

The original idea was to travel across the Ross Ice Shelf, up the Ferrar Glacier and across the Plateau to establish the depots required by the crossing party by dog sledge to find suitable sites for the supply dumps, and then these were to be stocked up using the Beaver aircraft. The Ferguson tractors had only been supplied to move stores from the ship's side to the chosen base site and any local movement in the general area of the main base. However, after seeing for himself the performance of these tractors when they were trialled in Norway, Hillary was convinced that they could take on a far greater role in the expedition. The New Zealand half of the expedition was equipped with five of these tractors and by modifying them to be driven by caterpillars instead of conventional wheels, apart from in very deep, soft snow, they could cope very well. Sledges were designed to carry the requisite supplies for long-distance travel and the tractors were fitted with a canvas cover mounted on a tubular steel frame to give some protection to the driver. Although tents were to be the main accommodation, Hillary had one of the sledges modified to form a shelter for the men in the event of seriously bad weather. They called the covered wagon a caboose. In this they could cook, work if required and use the radios and most importantly of all, rest in relative comfort.

This change of plan didn't mean the abandonment of the dogs, they were still an integral part of the transport system and to this end he took on two experienced Englishmen to help him train his fellow explorers in the art of dog handling. Dr George Marsh was no stranger to the Antarctic wastes; he had cut his polar teeth with FIDS at Hope Bay on the Graham Land Peninsula for two seasons as medical officer and during that period he had become very proficient at handling dog teams, so he had two good reasons for being selected by Ed Hillary, not to mention Bunny's recommendation. Lt Commander Richard Brooke RN had been to Greenland with the British North Greenland Expedition a couple of years before and had gained all the necessary experience to handle teams of huskies in polar conditions. Richard Brooke was a trained surveyor and an experienced mountaineer. Dr Marsh became the expedition's chief medical officer. They both became key members of the subsequent exploration that took place after the establishment of the polar depots. Despite being English on a mainly New Zealand expedition, they were both held in high esteem by the men they worked closely with and they carried out some very important work during their stay on the continent.

Once he arrived back in New Zealand, Ed Hillary started his preparations for the expedition by setting up a training camp in the Southern Alps of New Zealand's South Island. The Southern Alps provided excellent ski training facilities for all the men and it was here that most of them gained their first experience of dog handling. Stocking the training camp by air proved a useful exercise for the two pilots. This site proved an excellent place to practise aerial drops and also landing and taking off from frozen surfaces. These functions were performed now and throughout the expedition by Squadron Leader John Claydon (the same John Claydon who was to start the furore about the 'Race to the Pole') and Flying Officer Bill Cranfield. Not only did the participants in the training session benefit but some of the equipment had a fairly good field trial that revealed a number of shortcomings, including problems with the landing gear of the Auster.

The reassessment with regard to the equipment being taken down meant a new design for the hut, or rather huts, as there would be six main ones and three for scientific work, some on the magnetic field that needed to be away from metal items. Each hut was constructed on a pattern developed by the Australians. They were built using insulated panels that locked together without the need for fiddly nuts and bolts. The cost proved to be a stumbling block but eventually the New Zealand Committee saw the advantages and the Government stumped up the extra money. The main advantage was the speed with which each hut could be erected and by taking down extra personnel who were competent in construction the expedition members would have a safe place to sleep and work very quickly; unlike the Shackleton Base hut, which was never really completed until nearly 12 months after it was started.

As the stores began to be assembled for loading into the expedition ship the *Endeavour*, she had just completed the crossing from England with stores that could not be procured in New Zealand. Upon inspection a large proportion of the cargo in the lower part of the hold had been spoilt by the ingress of water during the voyage. There were last-minute requests for replacements to be flown out. Some items that had been specially made for the expedition could not be replaced in time and a frantic search was undertaken to try and find local alternatives.

By the middle of December 1956 the ship was ready to sail and she was given a hearty send off from Wellington. Working her way down the coast towards Lyttelton, Captain Kirkwood had to make several stops so that more supporters could say their farewells and possibly raise a few extra funds for the expedition. On 17 December His Royal Highness Prince Philip hosted a last official engagement aboard the royal yacht *Britannia* and the *Endeavour* was ready to sail. Then one more last-minute frustration: as she eased away from the quay somebody had forgotten to release a mooring cable and this swung the *Endeavour* sideways against another ship moored ahead of her. Of the two aircraft on board, the Beagle was snugly crated but the Auster sat securely anchored on the after deck ready for action. This proved to be its undoing. As the *Endeavour* swung sideways, the Auster's right-hand wing collided with the other ship.

The wing was so severely damaged that even though the departure was delayed for a couple of days no spares could be found. The final solution was to source a wing and ask the American Military to fly it down to their base on McMurdo Sound when convenient. The repair was straightforward enough when it took place but the delay meant that 'the eyes in the sky' at the crucial stage when the ship met the ice had to be sacrificed. This accident was the second one to the Auster. The first happened during the training period. She was being flown up to the Southern Alps with the idea of testing an experimental undercarriage that was a combination of skis with wheels mounted in the middle of each ski. As the plane skimmed in to land on the snow slope, the wheels snagged on the snow and this catapulted the plane onto her back, damaging the tail fin and the propeller. The repairs were successfully carried out on the mountainside, all good practice for the main event.

Four days before Christmas 1956, the men who were to take part in the depot-laying journey had their last sight of New Zealand for the next two years and more. They finally returned home on 17 March 1958.

The New Zealand team consisted of four separate groups. There would be those who would carry out the establishment of the depots up on the Polar Plateau. They would be supported by the airmen drafted in from the New Zealand Air Force who were delegated the task of reconnoitring the way onto the Plateau and once the depot sites had been chosen by the team on the ground, airlift supplies to the selected areas. A third group of five men, all scientists, would carry out New Zealand's contribution to the IGY experiments. The final party of men involved were the skilled tradesmen who, after they had completed the base construction, would return to New Zealand. A total of nearly 40 men went down in the *Endeavour* plus her crew, and 23 were to remain for the duration of the expedition.

We have met some of the group earlier in this narrative: Ed Hillary (leader), Bob Miller (deputy leader), George Marsh (doctor), Richard Brooke (surveyor), Harry Ayers (mountaineer), the four RNZAF men – John Claydon, Bill Cranfield, Wally Tarr and Pete Tate – Bernie Gunn (mountaineer), Peter Mulgrew (radio operator) and Trevor Hatherton (IGY party leader). When Ed Hillary set out from Depot 700 towards the South Pole he had four companions. Murray Ellis was one of Ed Hillary's principal mechanics and came from Dunedin where his father ran a business that produced a range of sleeping bags used on the successful Mount Everest expedition and on this one as well. Jim Bates was one of the two mechanics responsible for the maintenance of all the tractor units (he was a trained engineer) and after TAE he went on to become a very successful inventor and development engineer. In fact, he could turn his hand to all sorts of useful work, including carpentry. Peter Mulgrew, the party's radio operator, learnt his radio skills while serving with the New Zealand Navy. Like Hillary he loved mountaineering and during one climb several years after the TAE had been completed, he lost toes on both feet due to severe frostbite whilst climbing in the Himalayas. He replaced Ed Hillary on the New Zealand tourist flight to the Antarctic that crashed into Mount Erebus, killing all 257 people on board in 1979. Ed Hillary married Peter Mulgrew's widow when he in turn lost his first wife and a daughter in a plane crash as it took off from an airfield at Katmandu in Nepal. The last member of the polar party was Derek Wright, originally taken on as the official film maker for the New Zealand half of the expedition. He had returned to New Zealand after the first summer but following a request from Ed Hillary and with the help of Admiral Dufek at McMurdo Sound he was flown back to Antarctica to take part in the leg of the journey between Depots 480 and 700 driving one of the Fergusons, following injuries to Murray Ellis and Peter Mulgrew, two of the regular tractor drivers.

The IGY contingent was under the leadership of Dr Trevor Hatherton. Vernon Gerard was a trained geophysicist who spent the first full year working around the base where he was tasked with looking after magnetic readings taken from instruments placed in one of the special huts. This entailed having to walk some distance to the hut in all sorts of weather conditions and doing it continually right through the year, in darkness, blizzard or dazzling sunshine. Herb Orr had worked on seismic exploration connected with the oil industry for several years in the early 1950s, he continued in this vein during the IGY year of 1957 taking seismic and magnetic observations in co-operation with Vernon Gerard. Before joining the expedition Peter MacDonald had been employed looking for minerals but his job in Antarctica was chiefly looking into radiation. Radio specialist Neil Sandford occupied his time experimenting with the effects of auroral displays on radio transmissions, of which very little was known at the time. Dr Ron Balham studied meteorology during the expedition but was also a trained biologist/zoologist. He returned several times after the TAE to the Antarctic to study the Dry Valleys first discovered during Scott's expedition of 1912 by Griffiths Taylor.

No expedition can survive long without food and the culinary expert was Selwyn Bucknell. His background prior to selection was as a trained machinist working in the railway workshops in Hutt in New Zealand. He was a competent skier but had moved on to take charge of a research centre dealing with wildlife. His cookery training came courtesy of a crash course with the Army Cookery School. One of the fittest members of the group was Roy Carlyon, a keen sportsman who excelled at rowing, swimming and athletics. He had been trained as a surveyor at Canterbury University. Another Canterbury University graduate was Guyon Warren, the same age as Roy Carlyon, so they probably knew one another. Guyon was taken on for his geological qualifications, his other skills included surveying, photography – and he could cook.

Originally due to be in the Antarctic for the first season to help setting up Scott base, Ed Hillary had formed such a high opinion of Murray Douglas that he was persuaded to stay for the duration of the expedition. He had mountaineering experience and was competent on skis.

Radio communications were going to be of crucial importance so it became incumbent upon the organisers to recruit experts in that field. Ted Gawn fitted the bill exactly. He had spent several years of his life at sea, starting during the Second World War on hospital ships and finally working aboard a merchant ferry service vessel as its radio operator. He had also worked for the New Zealand Broadcasting organisation, a useful experience.

A few days into the voyage as things started to settle down Ed Hillary had time on his hands and during those moments he mulled over the team that had been selected and the use to which they could be put. There was already a nominal plan in place once Scott Base was up and running, but Hillary was always looking for ways to adapt it. These changes came as a result of last-minute alterations in the expedition's circumstances.

As the *Endeavour* finally got underway she was accompanied by two frigates that the New Zealand Navy despatched to escort her down as far as the first ice. This manoeuvre was mainly as an insurance against the heavily laden expedition ship getting into rough weather and needing assistance, something that many earlier expeditions would have been jealous of as the seas between New Zealand and the Ross Sea are notorious for storms. Because Antarctica is surrounded by oceans, the prevailing wind has little to stop it building up into a hurricane force, driving the waters into a maelstrom with waves 30 and 40 feet high. An overloaded ship such as the *Endeavour* could easily founder with catastrophic consequences. She was not even a modern ship and had already proved she could leak badly during the passage from England, when precious cargo was damaged by the water that had penetrated her holds.

The first serious ice came into view on 27 December and late in the afternoon the two naval vessels, the *Hawea* and the *Pukaki*, signalled their intentions to return to New Zealand. Three rousing cheers came across the darkening Antarctic Ocean from the two consorts as they wheeled away towards home.

Now on her own and faced with some foggy weather and the proximity of the ice, Captain Kirkwood slowed down the *Endeavour*, much to Ed Hillary's frustration and eventually after several days of this slow progress Hillary's temper finally snapped with an out-and-out row with the skipper. It is of course the captain's responsibility to command his ship; not for the first time in history do we find the leader of an expedition chafing at the bit to push on despite the hazards that lay ahead.

The confrontation soured the atmosphere for a couple of days but Captain Kirkwood seems to have been prodded in the right direction because the *Endeavour* was soon making reasonable headway again by pushing hard through medium pack ice that was being softened by the continuous sunshine they were experiencing. The prospects for a quick passage were starting to look good but then progress came to an abrupt halt on 1 January as the *Endeavour* rode out a storm that seemed to come out of nowhere. On 3 January an enormous wave swept across the deck and some of the dog's crates were dislodged releasing some of the animals. Crew members quickly spotted the danger they were in and caught the bedraggled animals, restoring them to a safe place for the duration of the onslaught. The ship resumed her journey late on 3 January 1957 as the storm abated, and the two beacons of the Antarctic continent hove into view. Mounts Erebus and Terror were sighted. Now it seemed the great adventure could begin in earnest.

The next day was the start of a period of frustration for the ship's complement. Hillary had gathered all the men together in the mess room for an informal talk about his plans for landing and establishing the base but the ice halted all further progress to their preferred anchorage. They had hoped to land at Butter Point, so named by Scott's expedition because a cache of supplies was placed there that included a large quantity of butter. This hoped-for landfall was still many miles away across the pack ice and the *Endeavour* could not cope on her own. Not for the first or last time, Ed Hillary contacted the American base commander Admiral Dufek to ask for the assistance of an ice breaker known to be moored at the American base on McMurdo Sound.

The ice breaker *Glacier* forged through the ice and soon both ships were making positive progress towards Butter Point. The *Endeavour* came to rest moored against the American ship at the solid ice edge, still about 8 miles from Butter Point; but at least it seemed possible to start the unloading process.

The damaged Auster was still awaiting her replacement wing and the Beaver was also out of commission because it had been stowed away in crates to await assembly. The Americans very kindly took Ed Hillary and his deputy Bob Miller, together with Captain Kirkwood, up in one of their helicopters for an initial survey of their surroundings. There appeared to be a considerable amount of melting taking place on the ice surface, which, if it deteriorated further, would prove extremely difficult to negotiate with the Ferguson tractors and their accompanying trailers loaded with expedition supplies. Returning to the *Endeavour* a start was made on getting the tractors out onto the ice and carrying out a ground survey of the 7–8 miles they would have to cover. Ed Hillary had seen from the helicopter that the way across the ice would be difficult so, with Ron Balham, Peter Mulgrew and Arthur Helm, he drove one of the tractors towards Butter Point, the other three flagging the route as they went. Arthur Helm spent this first summer helping to set up the base camp but he was later to be the liaison officer back in New Zealand for the duration of the expedition. He co-authored a book written about the New Zealand side of the expedition with Bob Miller, the deputy leader, called *Antarctica*. Together they had an in-depth knowledge of the whole enterprise and access to many expedition papers etc. that were invaluable to their account.

The sun proved to be too intense and it was making the surface unmanageable, so after only a mile or so they returned to the ship with a decision made to set off as the sun dipped, giving them cooler conditions. This ploy helped and now using two tractors, a route was staked out to within a couple of miles of Butter Point. While they were away Ed Hillary had left instructions for seven trailers to be loaded with supplies to be taken across the ice. They were to be accompanied by three dog teams. On the tractor party's return, a convoy of four Fergusons and their trailers and the three dog teams were readied to try and push across the ice to reach Butter Point the next night.

Now that the tractors were pulling loaded trailers, several times they slipped into melt pools where they had to wait for another one to pull them out. Hillary's tractor split its track. Eventually all the party reached the furthest point of the reconnaissance of the previous day and they camped for the next few hours while the sun continued to burn down. Sleep was a luxury they could not afford and the journey was becoming more and more difficult. During a short stop the radio crackled into life and John Claydon aboard the *Endeavour* sent a message that the Americans had suggested a new base site, close to their own station on Ross Island. They again offered to ferry Ed Hillary by helicopter to have a look at the potential. This generous offer was readily accepted and soon Hillary was being landed at Pram Point. After a quick look round the benefits of the site became obvious and although the distance to the *Endeavour*, now anchored at Ross Island, was still 8 miles, the way across the ice shelf was far easier than the route to Butter Point. Decision made, Hillary immediately ordered all tractors and dog teams back to the *Endeavour* ready for what was to prove a welcome escape from their predicament.

The new site at Pram Point was given the name of Scott Base in memory of Robert Falcon Scott, just as the Weddell Sea side of the expedition had christened their base after Sir Ernest Shackleton. Scott Base was only a couple of miles from the huge American base that was known after the branch of the Ross Sea on which it was sited, McMurdo Sound. It was from here that the Scott/Amundsen Base at the South Pole had been established. Giant Globemaster planes of the American Air Force were flown from an air base on the South Island of New Zealand to land on an ice runway that had been levelled for them on the Ross Ice Shelf before refuelling and flying over the Plateau to reach the South Pole where they discharged their cargo by parachute, together with the requisite number of personnel to build their IGY station. None of the heroics of sledging in the old-fashioned way for the Americans, this was done with military precision and the least possible inconvenience. The Antarctic had never seen such a huge logistical exercise. It even outstripped those expeditions carried out by Admiral Byrd when he came down to Antarctica and established the various 'Little America' stations before the war.

It was essential that building work should start as soon as possible. Ed Hillary did not want a repeat of the debacle at Shackleton 12 months earlier. It was now 10 January and the unloading had yet to begin. Eight miles along an ice road was likely to cause some unforeseen problems. The Americans had brought down a good proportion of the New Zealand expedition's stores in one of their ships because the *Endeavour* had a very limited capacity. The hut sections were the main focus of attention as it was essential to get them up and the expedition functioning as quickly as possible.

As explained earlier the cost of the new hut design caused some feathers to be ruffled, both Ed Hillary and Bunny expressing dismay at the extra financial burden these items put on an already strapped budget. £36,000 was the cost against an estimate of about a quarter of that for the original style. In the end the New Zealand committee felt it would be money well spent as they had an eye on future exploration in their sector of the continent extending into the foreseeable future.

Instead of one large hut and a few smaller ones for scientific work, the Pram Point site would accommodate six huts –all built to a similar design. There were eight men brought down specifically to build them and they had already practised putting up a hut back in New Zealand. Apart from a re-siting of the scientific huts, the original layout was adopted. Once the first sections started to arrive at Pram Point and the site had been levelled by an American bulldozer, work could commence. Hut 'A' was completed by 14 January. Any large items for installing into the huts had to be placed on the floor before the walls were built because there was not enough room to get them through the doorways.

Not everything was going to plan. On the next day Ed Hillary received news from George Marsh, who had sent a message from near Butter Point where he was examining the Ferrar Glacier. The melt water and the crevasses would rule out the use of the glacier as a route onto the Plateau.

Change of Plan for New Zealand Plateau Route

With the damaged Auster still to receive its spare wing, a concerted effort was put in by Wally Tarr and several helpers to rebuild the Beaver aircraft that had come down as deck cargo on the *Endeavour*. The assembly required not only the wings to be fitted but the tail plane, elevators and rudder, which that had all been stripped off to save space. After a sustained effort she was completed and test-flown the next day. The two pilots, John Claydon and Bill Cranfield, pronounced her airworthy. Ed Hillary quickly made use of his new tool and was flown directly to Butter Pont to see for himself the extent of the barriers to progress up on the glacier. It didn't take very long to confirm the news that Marsh had sent; the Ferrar would be a no-go.

Captain Kirkwood was contacted to arrange for the evacuation of the dog teams from the vicinity of Butter Point using the *Endeavour* and a new plan would have to be prepared to explore alternatives. Ed Hillary really wanted to establish this important route before winter set in and armed with some information that Bernie Gunn had brought back from the 1956 reconnaissance trip about another feasible route, this using the Skelton Glacier further inland, he set about organising a party to fly out and start exploring.

Having dismissed Butter Point and the Ferrar Glacier as a way up onto the Polar Plateau, two aerial sorties up to and around the Skelton Glacier area confirmed Gunn's brief report and, on returning to Scott Base, Hillary organised for three teams of dogs to be readied to go and ascertain the Skelton's suitability for the ascent and to determine a way onto the Plateau.

It had to be reached using the route taken all those years before by Scott and Shackleton, across the Ross Ice Shelf from Pram Point, allowing the explorers to skirt White and Black Islands then swing back south towards Minna Bluff; but not too close, so as to avoid the crevassed area created by the Bluff interfering with the flow of the ice shelf as it passes its end. Finally, leaving the not that well-trodden path laid down by the earlier explorers, the route turned to the east to arrive at the Skelton Glacier where it discharged onto the Ross Ice Shelf.

The main drawback to the new route was the extra miles to reach the Skelton Glacier. Fortunately, each time they needed to move stores for the depots they hoped to lay down for the crossing party they could enlist the help of the Beaver. This meant it was only really necessary to drive the tractors with their attendant sledges just the once to get them to the point where the main journey could commence and the plane could do the rest of the ferrying of the stores.

George Marsh, the expedition's doctor; Richard Brooke, the Greenland expert; Harry Ayers, Ed Hillary's long-time climbing companion, and Peter Mulgrew, the radio operator sent to check the effectiveness of the portable radios they had brought down with them, set out on 19 January with the dog teams to reconnoitre the way through to the Skelton. On 22 January an emergency occurred that put the plans into reverse. Miller who was in his tent at Scott Base heard an urgent shout, which was then repeated several times and after emerging from his tent he was shocked to see Richard Brooke and Peter Mulgrew pulled up with their team, bringing the news that George Marsh needed immediate medical help. The radio had failed and contact with base camp was impossible so they had raced back 32 miles to raise the alarm. The Beaver was dispatched immediately and George Marsh was airlifted back to base camp, accompanied by Dr John Findlay. The Americans insisted he be evacuated to the medical facilities aboard USS *Curtiss*. The illness was far more serious than immediately thought. It turned out to be diphtheria. Surprisingly perhaps, a full recovery was possible without having to evacuate him to New Zealand. Dr Findlay had only gone down for the first summer and he returned to New Zealand on the *Endeavour* at the end of that season.

This setback had increased the pressure on the surveying parties to the point where Hillary now made one of those swift changes of plan that were characteristic of his approach to all problems. The new strategy was to split the survey into two, with one dog team investigating the approaches to the Skelton Glacier from Scott Base while the second team were flown to the glacier itself and could then climb it to find a passable route for the tractors up to the plateau. The second group would need sufficient supplies for a stay of several weeks. The Auster was still out of commission so the plan had its risks. If the Beaver was damaged in any way, then it would seriously jeopardise the whole operation and possibly the expedition. This plane was the only means of transporting large quantities of fuel and rations to stock up the depots they were there to lay. The dangers of landing any aircraft on an untested surface were what Hillary had to weigh up before committing to the venture. His mind must have flashed back to the episode in the Southern Alps training session, when the Auster came to grief trying to land with an experimental undercarriage.

Despite all the uncertainties the plane lifted off on the proving flight at midday on 25 January. On board were Ed Hillary and Richard Brooke, with John Claydon as the pilot. From the air most surfaces looked promising to land on but as the plane descended they could see out of the cockpit window areas rippled with sastrugi. The problem with this feature of the vast, weather-beaten surface was that the ridges could be relatively low and soft, or, as was the case in this instance, higher and frozen to a hard crust. At the point of impact they discovered which type they had to cope with as the plane skimmed into the first sastrugi with an almighty crunch, followed by a couple more severe jolts while the pilot fought to bring the plane's nose up and accelerate away from the danger. John Claydon's reactions saved the day but the three of them were shaken by the experience. A short time later another attempt couldn't have been simpler, the plane floated down to a text-book landing. They were now just short of the glacier's junction with the ice shelf and about one hour's flying time back to Scott Base.

Richard Brooke now took over as leader of the glacier party in place of the incapacitated George Marsh. The party would consist of two dog teams and the three remaining members of the original group, Murray Ellis, Harry Ayers and Murray Douglas. After depositing the four men and all their gear and dogs at the base of the Skelton Glacier the plane continued a shuttle service bringing in enough fuel and other supplies to form what turned out to be the final depot for the crossing party, which was still a year away from completing its historical journey.

Brooke's party made steady progress up the glacier and after eight days they were rewarded with the sight of a possible way up through the mountains that promised to bring them out onto the Polar Plateau. New peaks came into view at every stop they made when visibility allowed. Wind and snow drift reduced visibility so that at times it became impossible to know exactly where they were – but the inclination of the surface indicated the top could not be too far off.

Ed Hillary had told Richard Brooke that he would despatch the plane at some stage to try to locate them in case of another radio failure and sure enough, despite the poor visibility, the group of men gathered near the tents heard the drone of an aircraft engine. Ed Hillary had come to see for himself what progress they had made but could not talk to the men on the ground. He could, however, hear some communication from them but was unable to reply. What he did hear persuaded him that the surface was too difficult for a landing by the Auster. He returned to Scott Base, meaning to make a second attempt within the next couple of days.

Late in the day on 9 February 1957 the Beaver was heard and spotted from the ground, looking for the tents. As luck would have it the surface nearby proved to be an ideal landing strip. After the first successful landing of a single engine plane on the Polar Plateau, there followed a whole stream of flights to establish what was to become known as the Plateau Depot. That first landing established the important fact that the plane could take off from this higher altitude, which boded well for the supply dumps they would need to establish further out on the highest and coldest plateau in the world.

They were now an estimated 300 miles from their base and with the new depot fully stocked the party turned back down the Skelton Glacier to fill in the details of the survey that had been left unfinished on the way up due to poor visibility. They expected to rendezvous with the party that had started out from Scott at the same time as they were dropped onto the Skelton. This group was being led by the expedition's deputy, Bob Miller. He was basically given the task of updating the route initially proven all those years ago by the explorers of the Golden Age. His real challenge would come once he headed off that track towards the Skelton Inlet, where the glacier disgorged its ancient frozen contents onto the ice shelf. Bob was accompanied by Roy Carlyon. Both had only limited experience with handling dogs, especially dogs that had been mooching around the base camp and were so full of vim that the best the two men could do was to hang on for dear life as they set out at top speed. All went well and on 11 February they passed White and Black Islands and Minna Bluff.

Now instead of continuing on due south as the older generation of explorers had done they turned westwards to strike out towards the glacier terminus, which would lead them to a rendezvous with the glacier party and the depot set up a couple of weeks before by the first flights of the Beaver.

Locating the fuel depot took a whole day but when they arrived at it they settled down to await the others coming down from the glacier, or the arrival of the plane to airlift them out. What they didn't expect was a visit from Bernie Gunn with two comrades, Guyon Warren and one of the summer-only men, Arnold Heine. They spent several hours swapping stories about their adventures and it transpired that the three arrivals had been airlifted in to the glacier to do some geology fieldwork but due to a shortage of dogs had come equipped with just a man-hauled sledge. This had actually simplified their task and one of the highlights of their trip was an ascent of Mount Harmsworth, which at just over 9,000 feet was the highest peak yet climbed on the Antarctic mainland.

It took them well over a day to carry out the feat but three happier men it would be hard to find. Mount Harmsworth was first seen by members of Scott's 1902 expedition and named after Lord Harmsworth, the publisher who was a major sponsor of Scott's expedition.

Most of the clothing the men were issued with had come from the UK in the *Endeavour* and, as with the advance party at Shackleton, there were some shortcomings. The material that the anoraks were made from was proving too flimsy and tore easily, the hoods could not be drawn close to the face to exclude drifting snow and the wind, and the gloves were for the most part too tight a fit, which made it extremely difficult for them to be put back on quickly, resulting in a few frozen fingers.

One notable feature of the depot site was the incessant wind that they had to endure every time they went out of their tent. This was caused by the rush of cold air draining down the glacier from the Polar Plateau above. Called a Katabatic wind, it is caused by a flow of warmer air being drawn in from lower latitudes pushing the cold air at the surface (being heavier) down the glacier due to gravity, its line of least resistance to exit the Plateau. As the air current moved downwards so it got colder, heavier and gained impetus, resulting in the continuous gale force current. Douglas Mawson had experienced a similar wind during his Australian expedition to Adélie Land in 1913. His book about this expedition was called *The Home of the Blizzard*.

The surveying parties were reunited at the Skelton Depot on 23 February and there they found a message from Ed Hillary telling them to wait until 10 March before attempting to trek back to Scott Base if the Beaver had not picked them up earlier. The weather held them in their tents for the following five days and they were just trying to decide should they stay longer at the depot or start on the two weeks sledging trip back to Scott Base when the Beaver circled them a couple of times and came in to land. The first man to be repatriated was Harry Ayres with his gear and dogs. Within a few hours the plane with Bill Cranfield at the controls was back, this time removing Bob Miller and his dogs. Later that same day the other three men, Roy Carlyon, Murray Douglas and

Richard Brooke with the last of the dogs and as much of their equipment as could be crammed into the remaining space took off for the final recovery flight. The last day of February 1957 brought the wintering group together once more at Scott Base. To some of the men who had been away since 29 January, when only a couple of the huts had been built, this return to 'civilization' was a shock. Now all the six main huts and three smaller ones for scientific work were completed and a churned-up snowfield had become a small settlement. A network of covered walkways had been erected between the various huts to provide shelter and improve access from one unit to another in bad weather.

Each hut was given a letter of the alphabet:

'Hut A' was for the mess room, galley, radio and Ed Hillary's accommodation.
'Hut B' housed the laboratory and darkroom.
'Hut C' was a 14-bed dormitory.
'Hut D' held the sick room and an additional six-bed dormitory.
'Hut E' provided for the men's ablutions and housed one of the generators.
'Hut F' had additional generators combined with a workshop.
'Huts G, H and J' provided cover for all the scientific equipment that needed to be screened from other activities.

Only one of these nine huts now stands and has been designated a Building of Historical Interest. This is Hut A, Ed Hillary's old bunkhouse and the expedition's mess room.

The omission seems to have been the lack of a workshop big enough to house a vehicle where the engineers could carry out any major repairs or modifications. Bates and Ellis were up to the challenge and out of discarded packing cases and other spare materials they soon constructed a very passable shanty that was to be in constant use throughout the winter.

Transferring the stores from the *Endeavour* and the American ship the *Towle* to Scott Base had been carried on throughout the greater part of January and the last loads were despatched by 29 January. In total nearly 1,000 tons of supplies and fuel had been unloaded, the majority of it transported across 9 miles of frozen ocean by the ever-willing Ferguson tractors and two Weasels that had been lent to them by Admiral Dufek.

The *Endeavour* let go her ice anchors on 24 February and swung out into McMurdo Sound for the long journey back to New Zealand following a party on the 20th attended by the expedition members at the base camp and the returning workmen, together with Admiral Dufek and a contingent from the US base. Several scientific staff who had only been posted down for the summer season were also present, as were the members of the ship's crew and Captain Kirkwood.

Now that all the travellers were back from exploring the route up the Skelton Glacier and the *Endeavour* had sailed with the remainder of the men back to New Zealand, the expedition could start to settle down to the task in hand. All the stores were organised so that even if they were submerged in snow drifts they could be located without too much difficulty. The generators were up and running, supplying all the power that the camp needed and a routine was starting to establish itself.

Very early in February 1957 radio contact had been established between Scott Base and the Awarua radio station in New Zealand that would, for the duration of the expedition, handle all the news being sent back from Antarctica by the expedition. Situated on the southern end of South Island was a large tract of very flat, marshy ground that had become the location of a long-distance radio station. The site's remoteness from any other sources of radio signals and the wetness of the ground provided perfect ground conductivity essential to the radio signals being sent and received. The station became operational in 1913, just before the outbreak of the First World War. The work to build the station was carried out by the German communication company Telefunken and at the time there was considerable concern that the Germans would make use of the facilities for their own military purposes, but this never came about. Awarua stayed open for business until 1991 and during its lifetime handled most of the ship-to-shore radio traffic for shipping in and around New Zealand right the way down to Antarctica.

Following the successful contact with New Zealand, the two radio operators at Scott Base tried other wave lengths and, to their surprise, received an answer from a station in Greenland. Reception was excellent. It took until 5 March to make a direct radio link through to Shackleton Base and arrangements were made to try to maintain at least a weekly scheduled communication between the two bases. During this first exchange of news Ed Hillary was told of the comings and goings of the Shackleton team. He learned they had established South Ice using the aircraft and completed their base ready for the winter but had not had time to carry out any surveying towards the interior, as he had succeeded in doing with his sledging parties and was about to attempt with the tractors. He felt that this lack of preparation for the would-be drivers of both tractors and dogs and the failure to explore the overland route to South Ice would mean that all that would have to be accomplished at the beginning of the next travelling season, when they set out for South Ice on the first proving run.

Hillary's Future Agenda

Now Ed Hillary began to put into operation several other ideas he had been mulling over before the darkness of winter finally put an end to exploring until the next season.

Most readers of polar history would be familiar with a journey undertaken by three of Scott's men to Cape Crozier to bring back some emperor penguin eggs, which Dr Edward Wilson hoped would prove to be a biological link with prehistoric bird-like creatures. The journey was written about by one of the three men, Apsley Cherry-Garrard, in *The Worst Journey in the World*. It has become a classic in polar literature. The three men were away for five weeks of the most horrific weather that any man could be asked to travel in and on their return, the other members of the expedition barely recognised them.

Ed Hillary wasn't about to replicate this horrendous journey but he did plan to travel to Cape Crozier on a proving run for the tractors. The engineers had fitted two of the tractors with canvas hoods that would protect the drivers from the worst of the weather. Each of these two Fergusons was to tow two sledges loaded with fuel, camping equipment, food supplies and field radio sets that they planned to test. These last items had really fallen below expectations and had to be put right. There might not be another chance and a failure now could only be rectified by ordering a complete set of new units from New Zealand in time for the *Endeavour* to bring them down the next summer. Even then it might be too late. Peter

Mulgrew accompanied Hillary as the radio operator and Ted Gawn stayed at the base to man the receiver. Murray Ellis and Jim Bates, the two mechanics, made up the foursome. The distance was nearly 50 miles and Ed hoped to make the trip in a lot less time than it took Wilson, Bowers and Cherry-Garrard.

A period of intemperate weather inevitably caused a delay before the exploring party could set off but on 19 March 1957 the little convoy set out towards Cape Crozier on the first real proving run for the tractors. Of course they had been shuttling backwards and forwards between the base and the ship, hauling heavy sledge-loads of supplies, but the route was a proven one across the relatively flat ice shelf. The next 45–50 miles would soon winkle out any shortcomings that the tractors had. Indeed, the collapse of a snow bridge under the exuberant Ed Hillary as he raced away from the station nearly ended the trip before it had begun. The second tractor was soon on the scene and helped to haul the stricken tractor to safer ground. A chastening start that was duly noted and progress was at a more controlled rate from then on. The first day's travel found them 12 miles from base and the second day in grim conditions got them another 12 miles nearer their target. Soft snow gave them the foretaste of how the tractors might struggle on such a surface but cope they did and this was reassuring to the men. On the third day the surface improved significantly and off they went at an estimated 6 miles an hour. By the end of the third day they had reached a feature in the landscape called the Knoll, this location would have put them within striking distance of the stone igloo that Scott's three men had built while they searched for a way down off the cliff top to reach the Emperor penguin colony they knew could be found out on the sea ice 800 feet below them. Ed Hillary and his three companions now tried to find any remnants of the walls of the igloo that might have survived from all those years ago.

Cherry-Garrard had practised constructing a stone igloo near their base at Hut Point prior to setting out and the roof would have consisted of a rubberised, waterproof sheet supported on an upturned sledge with large stones tied to the edges of the sheet to keep it in place. Wilson and his two friends were trapped for two days in this structure as a ferocious storm whipped across the high cliff and in the process tore the roofing off the stone walls leaving the trio shivering and nearly dead under the only covers they had left, their sleeping bags. As the storm abated they ventured outside to find that any gear they had left lying around had been swept away by the violent wind. To their horror the one article they could not afford to lose was the tent and without this they knew they were doomed because the return journey was likely to take many days and without the shelter that the tent would provide they had little or no hope of surviving. They split up and searched the surrounding area finding all sorts of articles wedged under stones where they had been driven by the wind and to their enormous joy a few hundred yards from the igloo they came across the tent still in one piece.

Cherry-Garrard:

The horror of the nineteen days it took us to travel from Cape Evans to Cape Crozier would have to be re-experienced to be appreciated; any one of us would be a fool who went again; it is not possible to describe it. The weeks which followed them were comparative bliss, not because later conditions were better – they were far worse – but because we were callous. I for one had come to the point of suffering at which I did not really care if only I could die without much pain. They talk of the heroism of the dying – they little know – it would be so easy to die, a dose of morphine, a friendly crevasse and a blissful sleep. The trouble is to go on.

The tractor party having searched an area that might contain the igloo's remnants were getting to the point where they thought all evidence of it had been obliterated when Hillary suddenly spotted something sticking above the surrounding snow. Upon investigation he realised he had found an old sledge wedged with rocks into an upright position and surrounding it were the remnants of the stone work that had formed the igloo. As they dug through the accumulated snow, a whole collection of items came to light. These were carefully eased out of the snow and ice and just as carefully consigned to one of the sledges for repatriation to a better place.

The relics found had obviously been left behind as surplus to requirements by the three desperate men in their bid to reduce the weight they would have to pull on their return journey. The hoard included such diverse items as a pick axe, thermos flask, canvas bag, Nitric acid, sample test tubes with corks, a thermometer still working, envelopes with the Terra Nova crest and three rolls of unexposed film still in their containers. In total over 50 items were found and with the later permission of Apsley Cherry-Garrard, who was the last surviving member of the trio, all the finds were sent to New Zealand for preservation in a museum.

The climb down to the ice shelf that Edward Wilson and his two friends undertook to retrieve penguin eggs for later analysis was deemed too difficult and hazardous by the newcomers and reluctantly they returned to their tractors, loaded up the camping equipment and started for home. The weather and surface conditions proved so good that by the end of the day they were pulling up outside the huts at Scott Base after a near perfect 45 miles of driving that had taken just over 12 hours. They had been away from Scott Base for five days. The exercise was as good a test as they could hope to carry out with the tractors and it had given the four men a crucial chance to test their driving skills. Peter Mulgrew, Murray Ellis and Jim Bates had accompanied Ed Hillary on this proving run and it was to be these three men plus Derek Wright that Hillary turned to when he set off towards the Pole from Depot 700 after completing the task set for the New Zealand team to support the crossing party under Bunny Fuchs. As suspected, the radio sets proved to be inadequate so a request was sent to New Zealand for replacements to be sent with the *Endeavour* when she came down again at the start of the next season. The new sets of a different make were received in time to use during the remainder of the expedition and turned out to be much better.

Now that the sledging operations were over for the foreseeable future, a systematic overhaul of all the sledging gear was implemented. All the tractors were fitted with the same canvas cabs that had been used on the Cape Crozier run and one of the tractor trailers was adapted to be used as a caboose. Great care was taken over the rations that would be taken by the exploring parties. It was found that by repacking certain foods into plastic bags the metal containers could be done away with, realising a saving of 8lbs for each ration box and allowing the equivalent weight in extra food to be taken along.

The ration boxes held a good selection of food and the exploring parties could expect to find items such as bacon, dried soups and milk powder, tea, coffee and Horlicks plus Marmite for spreading on biscuits together with butter and jam as alternatives. There were oats for making the obligatory porridge and sugar to add to it plus raisins if required. Pemmican of course made up the bulk of their rations and could be flavoured with curry powder but the men often added all sorts of other ingredients to it to make what most sledgers called Hoosh. An average calorific intake of 4,800 calories per day was the standard rate for Ed Hillary's journeys and this was comparable with other expeditions such as Sir Ernest Shackleton's attempt to reach the South Pole in 1908, who worked out his daily ration to be 4,300 calories per day. Shackleton had experienced the onset of scurvy when he accompanied Scott on the Discovery Expedition in 1902 and he had determined that this was not going to happen to his men. Common sense dictates that a man travelling on a mechanised form of transport would need significantly less than one hauling a sledge for many miles. Sir Ranulph Fiennes and his companion Dr Michael Stroud attempted to cross the continent unaided and on foot in 1992. They followed a course not so very different from the TAE expedition and very nearly came to grief. Attempting to cross from the Filchner Ice Shelf to the Ross Sea via the South Pole, a distance of 1,700 miles, they failed to complete the last 350 miles of the Ross Ice Shelf. They had walked 1,350 miles completely unsupported and it was the longest ever such walk in the history of polar exploration up to then. Man-hauling takes about 6500 calories a day but Mike Stroud estimated afterwards that in reality they should have been consuming nearer 10,000 calories. The calories required per day for the various means of travelling in polar regions can be approximated: driving a dog sledge, 5,000; sitting on a tractor or skidoo, 3350; and work around the base camp, 2750. Most of the older expeditions supplemented their rations by slaughtering seals and penguins for fresh meat for use as an anti-scorbutic. Today's explorers to Antarctica are not allowed to catch, let alone eat, any of the wildlife following various amendments to the Antarctic Treaty.

Ed Hillary gives an example of a menu put together by himself and Harry Ayres as mess stewards for the week at Scott Base. The cook was relieved of this duty every Sunday and the two helpers had to step up to the mark for the day.

Breakfast	Cereals and apricots followed by bacon and scrambled egg.
Lunch	Cold roast lamb, mashed potatoes and potato salad followed by a pudding of tinned, fruit salad.
Dinner	Game soup then roast beef and Yorkshire pudding accompanied by parsnips, onion, mashed potatoes and tinned, green beans, boiled pudding and custard.

He goes on to say that George Marsh was the best cook they had, producing culinary delights that would have done credit to any restaurant.

The Ross Sea committee were keeping abreast of the expedition's plans and was concerned to learn that Hillary was planning a number of subsidiary journeys that they felt were beyond his remit. To support the crossing party was his primary objective. They were particularly worried that his plan to venture farther south than Depot 700, even to attempt to get to the Pole itself, could jeopardise the whole expedition. Hillary also planned to send a team to visit the coast of Victoria Land to the north of Scott Base. Additionally, he had plans for exploring a region to the east of the Skelton Glacier which included the Mulock, Darwin and Barne Glaciers. Further exploration he wanted to attempt was around the great Beardmore Glacier and he hoped some of his men could investigate this area after establishing Depot 700. He even contemplated trying to locate the South Magnetic Pole where the Russians were hoping to build their IGY base.

The committee back in New Zealand were justifiably concerned that this over-ambitious programme would stretch the groups resources so thinly that in the event of any accidents occurring, especially if they involved the Beaver aircraft, lives would be put at risk and reputations would be lost in the eyes of a press that was always ready to criticise. Ed Hillary's response to all this apparent timidity was a veiled contempt for what he saw as meddling in *his* expedition.

Initially he acquiesced and contacted Bunny to talk over the options as he saw them. Depot 480 would be established as planned. The Beardmore Glacier trip was modified. Now Ed Hillary suggested that Depot 700 could be used as a fuel dump for the crossing party but that could only be supplemented with fuel if the Beaver had a refuelling station at the foot of the Beardmore Glacier. The plan agreed with Bunny to place fuel drums at a depot to be established at 83° South (Depot 700) seemed to placate the committee for the time being and as there was no more mention at this stage of a push to the Pole, the whole matter appeared to have been resolved.

In *The Crossing of Antarctica* by Bunny Fuchs and Ed Hillary there is no record of the conversation mentioned above between the two of them relating to any changes to the plans for laying in Depot 700, nor the phone call between Bowden and Ed Hillary. In his own book, Hillary does refer to this exchange of views about the proposed push to the Pole and its implications, as seen by Bowden and the New Zealand Committee. There is more information about the New Zealand Committee's concerns when another telephone call is received on 9 May 1957 from Charles Bowden, during which misgivings about Hillary's over-ambitious plans for the next season are expressed. Again there is no reference to this conversation in the book he co-wrote with Bunny. Arthur Helm and Bob Miller transcribed the various messages that took place between Ed Hillary and Charles Bowden in their book *Antarctica* but even they have no record of anything being exchanged in March or April, so maybe Ed Hillary has discreetly adjusted the calendar or his notes have been misinterpreted regarding this point. From other sources it would appear that Hillary's diary reveals his reaction to the phone call he received from Charles Bowden. The reference, however, is dated 9 April, not 9 March as in Ed's book.

*Above: Thero*n berthed at South Georgia. (George Lowe courtesy of Mrs Mary Lowe)

Below: Preparing to unload the Auster at South Georgia. (Ralph Lenton courtesy of Mrs Helen Lenton)

Getting ready to trial the Auster fitted with floats. (The Sir Edmund Hillary Collection, courtesy of Peter and Sarah Hillary and the Auckland War Memorial Museum)

The 16 men of the advance party aboard the *Theron*. Back row, left to right: David Stratton, Vivian Fuchs, Keith Blaiklock, Ralph Lenton, Taffy Williams, Tony Stewart, Derek Williams, Hannes la Grange, Rainer Goldsmith. Front row, left to right: Gordon Haslop, Peter Weston. John Lewis, David Pratt, John Claydon, Peter Jeffries, Roy Homard. (George Lowe courtesy of Mrs Mary Lowe)

Above: The eight men of the pioneer group for the first 12 months. Back row, left to right: Rainer Goldsmith, Peter Jeffries, Ken Blaiklock, Roy Homard. Front row, left to right: Ralph Lenton, Taffy Williams, Hannes la Grange, Tony Stewart. (Ralph Lenton courtesy of Mrs Helen Lenton)

Below: An American icebreaker, USS *Glacier*, assisted the New Zealand group. (The Sir Edmund Hillary Collection, courtesy of Peter and Sarah Hillary and the Auckland War Memorial Museum)

Above: Stores hastily unloaded from *Theron*. (The Sir Edmund Hillary Collection, courtesy of Peter and Sarah Hillary and the Auckland War Memorial Museum)

Left: The pioneer party wave goodbye as *Theron* departs for home. (The Sir Edmund Hillary Collection, courtesy of Peter and Sarah Hillary and the Auckland War Memorial Museum)

Below left: Another shot of the Magnificent Eight, alone at Shackleton base for the first year. Back row, left to right: Ralph Lenton, Ken Blaiklock, Peter Jeffries, Tony Stewart, Rainer Goldsmith. Front row, left to right: Taffy Williams, Roy Homard, Hannes la Grange. (The Sir Edmund Hillary Collection, courtesy of Peter and Sarah Hillary and the Auckland War Memorial Museum)

Shackleton base hut under construction. (Dr Rainer Goldsmith)

Snow engulfing Shackleton hut. (Hannes la Grange)

The *Magga Dan* arriving at South Georgia on her way south. (George Lowe courtesy of Mrs Mary Lowe)

Above: *Magga Dan* berthed at the ice edge near IGY base at Halley Bay. (George Lowe courtesy of Mrs Mary Lowe)

Below: Sno-cat unloaded at Shackleton base from *Magga Dan*. (Dr Alan Rogers)

Fitting a wing to the Otter at Shackleton base. (George Lowe courtesy of Mrs Mary Lowe)

Workshop erected at the beginning of the second season. (George Lowe courtesy of Mrs Mary Lowe)

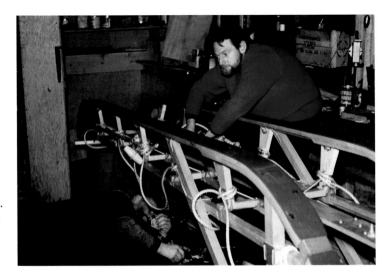

Fitting Tufnol linings to sledge runners. (George Lowe courtesy of Mrs Mary Lowe)

Above: Trying to start Sno-cats after a blizzard. (George Lowe courtesy of Mrs Mary Lowe)

Left: Transferring fuel to a Sno-cat. (George Lowe courtesy of Mrs Mary Lowe)

Above: Auster on reconnaissance near the Theron Mountains. (Dr Philp Jon Stephenson)

Below: The Otter transferring a dog team to the mountains for survey work. (George Lowe courtesy of Mrs Mary Lowe)

Top: Both expedition planes bringing in supplies. (George Lowe courtesy of Mrs Mary Lowe)

Above: Sno-cat *Rock 'n Roll* teetering on the edge of a crevasse. (George Lowe courtesy of Mrs Mary Lowe)

Left: Probing for hidden crevasses to find a safe route for the vehicles. (Dr Philp Jon Stephenson)

Setting up a seismic test shot. (George Lowe courtesy of Mrs Mary Lowe)

Firing the explosives used in the seismic tests. (George Lowe courtesy of Mrs Mary Lowe)

Rock 'n Roll towing sledges laden with fuel drums. (George Lowe courtesy of Mrs Mary Lowe)

Camping out as the convoy closes on the mountains ahead. (George Lowe courtesy of Mrs Mary Lowe)

Waking up to another covering of snow. (George Lowe courtesy of Mrs Mary Lowe)

'Snow henges' set up by dog handlers for the vehicles to follow. (Hannes la Grange)

Mobile workshop in use on the Polar Plateau. (George Lowe courtesy of Mrs Mary Lowe)

USAF Neptune on a visit as the crossing party approaches the Pole. (George Lowe courtesy of Mrs Mary Lowe)

David Pratt's Sno-cat at the South Pole. (Dr David Pratt CBE)

Twelve happy men reach the South Pole. Back row, left to right: David Pratt, Hal Lister, Ralph Lenton, Ken Blaiklock, George Lowe. Front row, left to right: Bunny Fuchs, Dr Alan Rogers, Geoff Pratt, David Stratton, Jon Stephenson, Hannes la Grange, Roy Homard. (George Lowe courtesy of Mrs Mary Lowe)

Above: Otter bringing in more fuel. (George Lowe courtesy of Mrs Mary Lowe)

Left: Camping in a blizzard. (George Lowe courtesy of Mrs Mary Lowe)

Below left: Clearing snow from tents during a blizzard. (George Lowe courtesy of Mrs Mary Lowe)

Attending to Ferguson tractor at Scott Base. (The Sir Edmund Hillary Collection, courtesy of Peter and Sarah Hillary and the Auckland War Memorial Museum)

Caboose hitched behind a tractor. (The Sir Edmund Hillary Collection, courtesy of Peter and Sarah Hillary and the Auckland War Memorial Museum)

New Zealand team heading south from Scott base. (The Sir Edmund Hillary Collection, courtesy of Peter and Sarah Hillary and the Auckland War Memorial Museum)

Loaded sledges being hauled towards Skelton Glacier depot. (The Sir Edmund Hillary Collection, courtesy of Peter and Sarah Hillary and the Auckland War Memorial Museum)

New Zealand dog teams on the trail to a new depot. (The Sir Edmund Hillary Collection, courtesy of Peter and Sarah Hillary and the Auckland War Memorial Museum)

None of this appears relevant except to point out that Hillary up to this moment was only supposed to go as far as Depot 480 and it was an afterthought that he and one of his exploring parties could make use of an extra depot 200 or so miles nearer to the South Pole, Depot 700. If it was a late decision, he must have planned the extra depot once he became convinced that the tractors could accomplish a lot more than they had been given credit for. He would certainly not have attempted to get to the Pole using dogs alone.

Ed Hillary sent a long telegram to Charles Bowden on 10 May with his reformed plans for the depot laying and other activities he hoped to perform but discreetly fails to mention any further plans for a push to the Pole. Depot 700 now definitely features in this modified plan. Charles Bowden replied on 22 May accepting in principle the main proposals that Ed Hillary put forward with the proviso that the party left at Scott Base should not be depleted to the point where any rescue that might have to be mounted would be jeopardised by lack of suitable personnel.

It is impossible to follow all the messages that crossed between Scott Base and Awarua radio station and there may have been some relevant to this episode that are not on record. History has cast a shadow over these events and the facts as they stand would indicate that Ed Hillary had made up his mind that he would ultimately carry out his long-held dream of pressing on to the Pole once he had completed the lines of support that the crossing party needed.

The darkest days of winter were still ahead of them and the prospect of the returning sun and all the blessings that it would bring to Scott Base were still a long way off. No part of Antarctica is immune from storms and in the middle of all the internal wrangling between the committee and Ed Hillary, they experienced one that left them with huge drifts of snow that had been driven by violent winds making outside work impossible. Wind speeds of nearly 100mph were recorded and, as is not unusual, the local temperature rose to give the warmest spell of the winter, about 10°F.

The snow had drifted to such a height that the Auster could only be identified by the tip of the tail plane and the hump in the snow where it had been tethered for the winter. It required a concerted effort on the part of all the members of the expedition to 'un-earth' the plane and even then more work was required to scrape out the snow that had infiltrated into all the cracks and crevasses where the wind had driven it.

A milestone in the calendar was mid-winter's day, which was celebrated in the usual fashion with the mess hut being decorated in flags and bunting, a slap-up meal, small gifts to be opened and the main highlight, messages received from and sent to friends and relatives in New Zealand.

The men not directly involved in the day-to-day scientific activities that went on right through the shut-down period were encouraged to use their spare time helping where they could. To promote a further sense of taking part in the practical side of the expedition, talks by the relevant experts were given every Tuesday afternoon. They included one on the aerodynamics of planes and how they actually fly, another was one on fishing techniques. The talk about earthquakes was particularly interesting, as seismology was to be studied by the IGY scientists. Many hundreds of shock waves were recorded by the scientists during their stay at Scott Base and these could be traced to the exact spot on the Earth's surface where the quake took place. One such quake occurred in Wellington in New Zealand and was detected 7 minutes later at the base hut.

One very important subject that Ed Hillary felt was extremely relevant for those men going out as members of exploring parties was navigation. There were three surveyors on the expedition and should any of these men be disabled or worse, then other members in that party would need to know at least the basic skills of navigation to get everyone home safely. Maps and charts on their own can begin to look meaningless in such a landscape, when applied to the few visual markers available. The landmarks of the Ross Ice Shelf could be mountains many miles away and the distance to them could be so distorted due to miraging – or the clarity of the air making them seem much closer than they really were – that the sightings of them would be virtually useless.

Compasses tended to be badly affected by the proximity of the

South Magnetic Pole. Sun compasses, theodolites and sextants relied on the operator being able to see the sun or stars to locate positions on charts – and so the list goes on. Dead reckoning could help but it relied on a magnetic bearing, a known starting position, a means of measuring the distance travelled, and usually a chart. To complicate the matter still further, the student should be able to perform various calculations using navigation tables and trigonometry; all this to be carried out whilst suffering the inconvenience of frozen fingers and a storm-force wind blowing snow and ice crystals into instruments and faces. The students persevered under the expert tutelage of Bob Miller, backed up by Richard Brooke and Roy Carlyon.

Ed Hillary was to come in for some scathing criticism regarding navigation when it came to siting the depots out on the Polar Plateau. Both Bob Miller and George Marsh complained of his 'approximate' navigational skills that led to the depots not being put where it had been agreed they should be. If a depot was put down at a point that had not been agreed, then during bad visibility it would be easy for a tired and desperate party to fail to locate one of these crucial dumps and wander round for hours. Ken Blaiklock and Jon Stephenson experienced a similar scenario while they were exploring some Nunataks about 30 miles from South Ice hut. The weather had prevented the plane from picking them up at the agreed rendezvous and after waiting for a number of days to be collected, as they were getting low on supplies they set out for South Ice in near whiteout conditions. Ken was an experienced navigator and although the two men were heading in about the right direction, they had no means of checking the distances they were covering each march. With food getting desperately low their survival finally depended on the timely arrival of the plane just as the weather cleared. In four days they had barely covered half the distance to get them to safety.

One of the outstanding problems the expedition faced was the poor performance of the field radio sets. Ed Hillary had fresh ones brought down from New Zealand before the main journeys took place. The replacement radios were brought down by an American plane which also acted as postman, bringing the first mail the men had received for nearly seven months. Bunny had no resupply to fall back on and in the end had to make the best of a bad job.

All the expedition members due to go on spring journeys were making sure they had completed the overhaul of their rations and equipment. The first to get away were George Marsh and Guyon Warren bound for the Ferrar Glacier, where they were scheduled to meet up with Bob Miller and Roy Carlyon. This foursome with their dog teams spent some time checking for a route up the glacier but at each point they reached, the answer was the same, unpassable for sledge teams. Covering over 170 miles all told, they completed the last 30 or so in about seven hours having been tent-bound for two days due to a blizzard.

Ed Hillary took out the three untried but modified tractors, crewed by his faithful band of drivers, Bates, Ellis and Mulgrew. They took with them, for the experience, Herb Orr, who would later look after the seismic experiments that were part of the IGY studies. They crossed over McMurdo Sound to Butter Point to establish several dumps for the future use of the Northern exploring party that would be travelling along the coast of Victoria Land later in the season. The tractors performed so well that they completed the total journey of 160 miles in a very creditable eight days. This was just the encouraging result that was needed to bolster their confidence for the forthcoming trials they were about to experience.

One other trek of note was to be the repeat of the famous 'Worst Journey in the World'. A party of four men and two dog teams were hoping to actually reach the Emperor penguin colony down on the ice at Cape Crozier just as Edward Wilson and his two stalwart companions had done back in 1911. This time Harry Ayres, Murray Douglas, Ron Balham and Neil Sandford were going to travel to Cape Crozier in the middle of September and not as Scott's men had done, in the heart of winter. They succeeded in their mission and even brought back some penguin eggs and several dead chicks in an attempt to examine them and establish the development of the fledglings.

When Apsley Cherry-Garrard returned to England he carried with him the eggs that he had looked after from the time when he and Edward Wilson with Birdie Bowers had struggled under such horrendous conditions to collect them from this same colony. Apsley's two companions had perished on their return from the Pole and he felt it his duty to see that the eggs were safely delivered to the Natural History Museum in London. Back in England Cherry (that was his nickname throughout the expedition) delivered the three surviving eggs and was snubbed by a junior assistant. Persevering, he finally saw a more senior member of staff but even then was given a pretty frosty reception. A further visit some weeks later to see how the project was progressing resulted in another rebuff; he was told there was no record of the eggs having been received. They were eventually examined by Dr C W Parsons but his official report several years later stated that there did not appear to be any link to prehistoric birds, as Dr Wilson had hoped.

Scott and Shackleton's huts were also visited but they were found to be quite badly iced up and after an attempt to clear some of the ice debris out of the two buildings the men returned to base.

The New Zealand Team
Move Out

Both Scott and Amundsen had been thwarted by the low temperatures that prevailed in September and into October and the New Zealanders had been exceptionally lucky to get their early spring journeys completed without suffering too much discomfort.

When Roald Amundsen reached Antarctica in 1911 he chose as his landing place an area called the Bay of Whales. This was an embayment of the Ross Ice Shelf that both Scott and Shackleton had found when visiting the area for the purpose of selecting a base site for the 1902 and 1907 expeditions. On his visit in 1907 Shackleton had promised Scott that he would not choose an area that Scott regarded as his own preserve, the area around Ross Island. When he inspected the Bay of Whales he concluded that the Bay had increased dramatically in size due to a rupture of the ice shelf and he felt that it would not be prudent to set up his base there in case of another calving. He subsequently reneged on his promise and reverted to the vicinity of Scott's old base but only after all other options were looked at. Time was pressing before the season was too far gone and he lost his opportunity to establish his expedition base before the onset of winter. The Bay of Whales gained its name from the number of whales desporting there.

Amundsen obviously took the gamble and it paid off but in a further couple of years the Bay of Whales had gone. This site had a great advantage over McMurdo Sound in that it was a full degree of latitude further south, that means 60 miles nearer the Pole.

As we know, Amundsen had put his trust in sledges drawn by teams of dogs and Scott had an range of transport, using tractors, ponies, dogs and man-hauling. Amundsen was determined to beat Scott to the Pole and managed to establish three depots, one each at 80°S, 81°S and 82°S. In the first season Scott could only manage one major depot and that was just short of 80°S. A large proportion of the supplies at the three depots Amundsen set up were made up of seal meat for the dogs. Scott had laid great store on the Manchurian ponies getting him well on the way towards the Pole and a lot of his sledge loads consisted of the fodder for them, which was very bulky and precluded him taking other vital supplies as far south as he would have liked. His dogs were never really part of the equation for his attempt on the Pole and he knew that man-hauling would provide the main thrust of his transport system.

The following spring both leaders were anxious to get started. Amundsen could not contain his impatience and thought he could get away really early in the season. His first attempt was to have been on 24 August 1911 but even he realised that was too early. The second date was 8 September, which very nearly ended in disaster with temperatures down to minus 56°C. The dogs' feet started to freeze and he nearly lost a lot of them. He finally got away on 20 October and as we know, beat Scott to the Pole by five weeks. By the end of January 1912 Amundsen and his expedition were on their way home, each man weighing more than when they set out three months earlier, so good had been the depot laying. Captain Scott's mixed convoy began on 24 October 1911 with the two tractors leading the way. They were followed by the ponies a few days later and the dogs brought up the rear nearly a week after the tractors. The tractors were abandoned after the first 50 miles and the four men with them had to resort to man-hauling. Many theories have been put forward as to why one expedition was so successful and the other led to the tragic death of all five members of the polar party. A lot of books have been written on this subject but in the end that one degree of latitude nearer the pole was probably the most telling feature.

So in comparison, Ed Hillary was extremely lucky to have achieved his spring journeys in September. The date of his tractor teams' departure from Scott Base was 14 October, and on 18 October the plane took the first two men to the Skelton Depot with their team of dogs.

The plan that Ed Hillary now adopted was to get the three Ferguson tractors and the Weasel up the Skelton Glacier and use them as the workhorses of the expedition. The dog teams could then go on ahead of the mechanised transport and reconnoitre the surfaces, just as Bunny would do over on the other side of the continent. This didn't always work to plan, as we shall see when the glacier was actually scaled, but it was a sound idea.

The decision to use the Skelton Glacier rather that the badly crevassed Ferrar Glacier had already been taken and the opportunity of pioneering a way to get to the foot of the Skelton had been accomplished the previous season, but it entailed a very circuitous one. The previous autumn several teams had been flown into the area of the Skelton Glacier and checked out its pros and cons as a route to the Plateau. Not only had the expedition's plans been changed, so had the site of their base camp. This was now at Pram Point on Ross Island, not Butter Point. Reference to a map would help to understand the situation Ed Hillary and his team now faced. By heading south from their base they could follow the tried and tested path of the previous expeditions but by the time they had gone past Black and White Islands, swung south and finally west around Minna Bluff to reach the bottom of the Skelton Glacier, they would have covered 180 miles. The Skelton depot was in fact only 10 miles farther south than Scott Base but overall it turned out to be a far better choice of route than the original Ferrar Glacier. Scott and Shackleton both used the Beardmore Glacier to reach the Plateau, which was 125 miles long, compared to the 40 miles of the Skelton. There were some spectacular ice falls on the Beardmore that the Skelton did not have, making life far easier for the expedition.

On 14 October 1957 the advance from Scott Base with the tractors began. It should have been very straightforward as the route had been tackled the previous season. But just a few miles after setting out the drivers had no sooner settled down when a crevasse opened up under the sledge that Ed Hillary was towing and it canted over at an alarming angle, bringing the tractor to an abrupt halt. Manoeuvring the other three vehicles across the grinning slot in the ice they set about retrieving the partly submerged sledge. The sledge was carrying 12 drums of fuel, each weighing 350lbs. Releasing them from the straps that held them in place was difficult. The sheer weight meant that each drum had to be secured to one of the tractors before the slings holding it could be released and then the drum could be hauled to the surface. Once all the drums had been safely retrieved then the tractor that had been holding the sledge was reversed and slowly the sledge was also brought to the top of the crevasse, reloaded, and the convoy could proceed. The first day's progress was barely 8 miles; but at least they were underway.

The weather that had threatened to break up the day before, now promised to be fair on the following morning. Breaking camp was a routine that was to become very familiar to all of them over the coming months. Everybody had several duties to perform and this enabled them to get underway quite quickly. The only surface to really test the Fergusons was soft snow and they had that in abundance on the second day. The Weasel fortunately coped very well with this type of surface and so the convoy kept moving, if at times intermittently. To ease the weight being carried they jettisoned eight drums of fuel and shared the remainder between the sledges so that each vehicle had a similar load to haul.

On the following day the Weasel that had been such a boon the day before now had an iced-up radiator that had to be drained before a resumption of the journey. A further hold-up was nothing to do with the surface or the equipment but a fleeting visit by an American plane bringing some dignitaries to see how the column was getting on.

The next stage of the journey would prove a testing time for everybody – and for the tractors. White Island had the effect of stretching the ice shelf as it was forced past the island on its steady creep towards the Ross Sea. This stress zone inevitably meant more and longer crevasses of unpredictable sizes. The dog teams of the trips the previous season had found that the crevasses reached much farther out into the ice shelf than had been previously thought, but as they had not been marked out the tractor crews were being extra vigilant to look out for them following the incident with Ed Hillary's tractor two days before.

They camped just after 8.00 pm having covered 30 miles and had not seen any crevasses. The next morning looked very promising for a good run on the new, more southerly course, but more trouble with the radiator of the Weasel held them in camp for several hours. They then had a good two-hour run before a mist slowed them down but they pressed on at a reduced speed using an astro-compass to navigate by. Towards the end of the day another 30 miles had been accomplished.

The following morning was clear and bright, revealing Minna Bluff far away to the west. Not far from this spot lay a small depot that had been left by one of the dog teams that had passed through on its way back to Scott Base. It had been marked with a five-foot-high snow cairn surmounted by a bamboo pole. Only the pole could now be seen, an indication of the snow accumulation over one winter.

By the time they camped on the 18th they had covered more than 100 miles. Later that evening the camp was buzzed by the expedition's Beaver and over the radio Ed Hillary learned that the first two men and their dogs had been transported to the base of the Skelton Glacier on schedule. Another good days travelling brought them to within 50 miles of the Skelton Depot and the awaiting dog team but the next morning the Weasel failed to start, this time the problem lay in the distributor. After a lengthy delay, Hillary decided to try and make up for lost time and so they set off to get as close to the depot as possible, where great care would be required to negotiate a path through the jumble of ice that had formed at the junction of the Skelton Glacier with the ice shelf. Hillary had noted from the several trips he had made in the aircraft that there was a way through, but it would take some careful navigation to locate this track from the ground. After the late start and with the constant worry of hidden crevasses and the mechanical recalcitrance displayed by the Weasel, a tired man could very easily make a crucial mistake; but all went well and when they spotted the black mark that indicated the tent erected near the depot, the end of the first leg of their journey was in sight. They bumped along over the hardened sastrugi and as they drew nearer to the encampment they could distinguish more of the separate elements of it. They were noisily greeted by all the dogs and the three men, George Marsh, Bob Miller and Jim Bates, who had just been flown in by the Beaver on one of its supply runs. They had been detained at Scott Base on account of the delayed arrival of Jim Bates' replacement, who was being flown in from New Zealand.

The tractor party had just completed 24 hours of non-stop driving and after such a long day, the men were desperate for respite. But the defective distributor in the Weasel needed fixing and this involved removing the engine.

Reflections on Shackleton's 1914 Expedition

In 1914 Sir Ernest Shackleton was determined to carry out a feat of endurance that would once and for all put the name of Great Britain firmly on the map of Antarctica. Comparisons with the TAE are irresistible.

Once the South Pole had been conquered, it would seem that another attempt at getting to the South Pole by a British expedition would be difficult to justify, let alone finance, so he set about organising what he saw as the last great journey on the planet, to cross Antarctica from one side to the other. There was no shortage of volunteers to take part in any enterprise that Shackleton put his name to; his problem was money. After appealing for funds he found a major sponsor in Sir James Caird. Sir James was a well-known philanthropist who had made his fortune from the jute industry in Dundee. Several other private sponsors came forward in time to save the expedition from extinction. Shackleton's plan, as is well known, was to start off from the Weddell Sea and finish up near his and Scott's old huts on McMurdo Sound. The expedition ended in failure but the matter does not rest there. Twelve men were landed by the *Aurora* on Ross Island in January 1915. They had been set the task of doing what Ed Hillary and his team were about to carry out in 1957. Shackleton had the same need as Bunny and that was a series of depots to replenish his expedition's supplies on the final leg of their journey across Antarctica, once they had passed the

South Pole. To this end, the landing party surmounted unbelievable odds to complete the depot laying – but with tragic consequences.

They had set out from New Zealand just before Christmas 1914 and landed on the Antarctic continent on 16 January 1915. After exploring the prospect of landing near Scott's Terra Nova hut, the *Aurora* was sailed farther south to Hut Point. An exploratory trip across the sea ice by a small team led by the *Aurora's* skipper Joseph Stenhouse and Ernest Joyce with dogs and a sledge brought them eventually to the old hut. The place was completely iced-up and entry had to be forced through one of the windows. Several of the party had experienced dunkings through the rotten sea ice and they took advantage of the refuge the hut offered to dry out and heat their meagre food ration. A storm kept them indoors for the next day but after collecting some useful spare clothes, boots and a variety of preserved foodstuffs they headed back to the *Aurora*. The Hut Point site was obviously not suitable to unload the stores destined for Shackleton's support depot. The ship retraced her way back to Cape Evans and the unloading began in earnest. The use of radio was not far enough developed at this time and the set they had taken with them proved inadequate for the conditions under which it needed to perform, so the party had to work on the assumption that Shackleton would make a successful landing in the Weddell Sea and would start his plan to cross the continent immediately. There was no time to lose before the depots might be needed.

The Ross Sea party of Ernest Shackleton's expedition concentrated all their efforts on getting the supplies ashore that were required for the stocking of the depots. The sledges were loaded and sent on their way south as quickly as possible. They would be able to deal with their own requirements of food, clothing, fuel and other essential stores to see them through the winter once they had set up the depots out on the Ice Shelf.

The leader of the landing party was Aeneas Mackintosh. He had been with the Shackleton's expedition in 1907 during the attempt to reach the South Pole that ended about 100 miles short of its target. He had sustained a bad injury whilst helping to unload the ship, the consequence of which was the loss of one of his eyes after being hit by an unloading hook swinging out of control and hitting him full in the face. He was evacuated back to New Zealand when the expedition ship, the *Nimrod*, returned for the winter and he did not take an active role in the journey south. Although Mackintosh was a man who was known to take risks, Shackleton appears to have taken a liking to him and entrusted him with the leadership of the support party.

Depots were planned for 79°, 80°, 81° and 82° South. Mackintosh's plan was to split his team, himself and 11 men, into four groups of three and, working in relays, move the stores steadily across the Ross Ice Shelf. In this first season it would only be possible to reach 80° South and then, if Shackleton didn't arrive that year, they would have to push farther south and lay in the last two depots reaching right down to the Beardmore Glacier.

The route south would be from the hut at Cape Evans, Scott's second and last expedition hut, across the sea ice to Hut Point where his first expedition hut was situated and on to the Ross Ice Shelf. This route, not marked on any map but known to be the way to go, then passed to the east of two islands imbedded in the ice shelf called Black Island and White Island. Keeping well out to the east of these to avoid a known crevassed area, they would then swing directly south for about 60 miles to pass Minna Bluff and establish the first major depot of the trip. This was called Bluff Depot, just as it was for the earlier expeditions and it stood at Latitude 79°S.

Ed Hillary and his tractors would also pass very close to where these supplies had been left before he and his team could turn west towards the Skelton Glacier. Many feet of snow accumulation would have occurred in the intervening years to cover any traces of earlier depots even if they were in the same vicinity and had not drifted north with the movement of the ice.

The first team to get started was led by Ernest Joyce and he was accompanied by Keith Jack and Irvine Gaze. Joyce had also been with Shackleton in 1907 and was the only man in this party with any sledging experience, Jack and Gaze had been taken on in Australia and were last-minute recruits but had not been given any specific roles apart from helping set down the various depots that would be required. The three men left on 24 January with the sledge being pulled by a team of dogs that as yet had not had any team work instilled into them, and as they had only been off the ship for a few days, they were extremely lively and difficult to handle.

The next team was led by Aeneas Mackintosh with Arnold Spencer-Smith and Ernest Wild to assist him. They got away two days later with their dog team. Spencer-Smith had recently gained a degree at Cambridge and gone on to be ordained whilst Wild was the younger brother of Frank Wild, a key member of Shackleton's Weddell Sea party. They were followed on 31 January by the other two groups.

John Cope together with Alexander Stevens and Victor Haywood were teamed up. Cope had been a student at Cambridge and took the post of biologist. He also became the team doctor in the absence of any other suitably qualified physician. Hayward had charge of the dogs based on his experience of using dogs on a farm. Finally the party using the motorised tractor consisted of Howard Ninnis, motor mechanic; Dick Richards, an Australian with a qualification in sciences who became the party's physicist; and Lionel Hooke, responsible for the radio and its operation.

The make-up of the teams was to be modified several times with various personnel exchanging with one another as circumstances dictated. These 12 men formed the shore party and Joseph Stenhouse was left in charge of *Aurora* and her destiny.

Joyce's group took on more stores that they found at Scott's Discovery hut and were soon re-laying the load as the surface conditions deteriorated. They had lost a dog following a fight during the stop-over at the hut and this had reduced their pulling power. The soft going and the re-laying forced them to camp out on the sea ice.

Mackintosh had been similarly caught out by the bad conditions and before he could reach Hut Point and its relative safety, he and his two companions found themselves with no alternative but to stop and camp for some much needed rest. When they resumed their trek, Mackintosh and his two companions became disorientated: their compass was swinging wildly, the chronometer had stopped because they had forgotten to wind it, and the perpetual light left them with no sense of passing time. In the deteriorating conditions their sledge meter was all they could rely on and although it indicated they had more than covered the distance required to get to Hut Point there was still no sign of it. After a second night spent out on the ice they picked out a landmark and realised they had been going too far south and would have missed the hut. They finished up travelling twice the actual distance that was needed. Once back on course the two leading parties met and consulted with one another about the best way forward. But instead of making a united team they seem to have entered into a foolish rivalry to see which team could get to the site of the Bluff Depot first.

Meanwhile, the other two groups had set out from Cape Evans. One was using a depleted team of five serviceable dogs, the other the experimental motor sledge. It was a tale very reminiscent of Scott's failed motor sledges. The machine started well enough but although the sledge had been trialled in Norway and Switzerland, it would soon prove inadequate for the task. The only way forward was in first gear and this set up such a vibration that the tank holding the cooling water soon cracked and leaking water found its way onto the ignition system causing an engine failure after about one mile. Patching up the water leak, the group headed by Ninnis carried on. Then they found that the extreme vibration was handing out even more severe punishment in the form of a broken oil pipe and a slipping clutch. With no load the machine had performed with some promise, but under load it proved to be a disaster. Eventually, the last two teams joined forces and set about man-hauling towards their goal, leaving the tractor to its fate. Mackintosh's outfit was continually struggling to get the best out of their dogs and he was to realise too late that the one pound of dog biscuit per day per dog he had planned on was too little and herein lay the problem; not the dogs but the master. Less than two weeks after setting off he was down to only four serviceable animals and the pulling power of their human companions would be sorely tested in the near future. There was a long, long way still to go before the depot could be cached.

Joyce had received a ducking by falling through some slushy ice and without the speedy action of his two companions would certainly have died. He took several days to recover and at one point he thought it might be the onset of scurvy. As he recovered, so too did the weather and at last a decent mileage was recorded. They covered an estimated 18 miles in a single day. They had been away from the *Aurora* for two weeks and were still about 30 miles short of the proposed depot site but they persevered, pressing on towards their target. The first two teams were still acting separately but in a friendly rivalry to see who could get to the designated place to put down the depot before the others. It was to be Joyce's team that arrived first and even then he had to depot his rations short of the mark because he was now desperately low on food for the return trip. Mackintosh arrived the next day, 11 February, and had already made up his mind to swap Spencer–Smith over with Joyce because the Padre, as he was known, had badly damaged his feet as a result of poor footwear and frost bite and would be a handicap for the next leg of the operation. Mackintosh planned to continue on with his two strongest companions and get to 80° South and place there as much as they could spare and then make a dash back to the *Aurora*.

The trip out and back to the first major depot was supposed to have taken about 20 days and already the two leading parties had been on the road south for nearly all of that time just to get to 79° South. This was one of the reasons why the Bluff Depot was put down short of its intended position by a few miles. Joyce knew he had only just enough rations to see his team safely back to base and they were already behind schedule.

The newly arranged team turning for home was sent on its way with Spencer-Smith in charge. The Padre was to proceed with all speed to Hut Point and attempt to meet up with the motor party.

Not only was Spencer-Smith badly hindered by his sore feet but Mackintosh also took the best dogs leaving only four weaker ones for their sledge. Lack of decent footwear had caused the sore feet in the first place, this was due to a shortage of snow shoes in their supplies. The shortage had been made up by scavenging some leather boots left behind in Scott's hut by an earlier expedition but some of these had proved to be unsuitable for the job. Their original stock of footwear had missed the sailing of the *Aurora* from New Zealand.

Before Mackintosh and his men could begin the next leg of the journey to put a depot at 80°S they were kept in their tent by a blizzard that raged for over a day, however when they did manage to start the going improved allowing them to make good mileages. They covered the final 12 miles to reach the position for the 80^0 depot on 20 February. The original plan was to put down 220 pounds of stores but the difficulties encountered during the journey meant they could only spare about 130 pounds. Amundsen-style, they laid out satellite markers to the east and west of the depot to help Shackleton locate the cairn marking where the stores had been laid down.

Spencer-Smith with the two Australians Keith Jack and Irvine Gaze were down to the last of their provisions when they saw the now motorless party coming towards them. This fortunate meeting enabled the three men and dogs to get some food inside them. It was decided that Keith Jack would turn south again and replace the struggling Alex Stevens. He had been reduced in strength by the diet and was having difficulty holding down his rations.

The two groups parted company the next day and two days later Spencer-Smith's group arrived at the Barrier's edge leaving about 8 miles to cross over worsening ice to reach the relative safety of the Discovery Hut. The three men had no option but to attempt the crossing of the ice and reached the hut and relative safety. They knew the hut held little attraction for a prolonged stay due to its filthy and frozen interior but at least it represented safety for now. There was no sign of the *Aurora* and within a couple of days the sea-ice began to break up. They had arrived just in time; the other parties would find it extremely difficult to work their way round by Hut Point Peninsula and would have to negotiate some very difficult sloping ice to reach the hut.

Out on the ice the six men who now made up the final group, which included the motor tractor detachment, were in trouble; the loads they had been attempting to pull were proving unrealistic and two of the party, Ninnis and Richards, were well below par. After a discussion it was decided to depot a good quantity of supplies and send back the two weakened men with Lionel Hooke to help. In this way, Ninnis would be able to devote some time to repairing the tractor, Hooke could be useful working on the wireless on *Aurora* and Richards' rupture would have time to heal before the next shuttle of stores to the south after the winter had passed. They never succeeded in getting the radio or the tractor to work.

This left John Cope in charge of Keith Jack and Victor Hayward with the remaining dogs to carry on south to meet up with Aeneas MacIntosh and his two companions who were still out on the Ice Barrier.

The returning trio under Richards' leadership made steady progress back north. They had taken only seven days' food. Within four days they had reached the barrier's edge only to find the ice that had supported Spencer-Smith's men had broken up, leaving no alternative but to trek round the barrier's edge and climb the steep ice slope where they could camp and rest. The following day they made it safely to the hut to be reunited with the first three men. Spencer-Smith and his two companions made the newcomers a welcome meal of porridge, sardines and coffee. They now had to wait until the *Aurora* picked them up, or the other two groups of depot layers returned from the trip south.

Captain Stenhouse had been given orders to find a suitable winter quarters for the ship and after trying several locations he made up his mind on 2 March to drop anchor at Cape Evans. It was close to one of the huts and the stores could be discharged onto the shore if required.

Nine days later, on 9 March, the weather deteriorated and the next day the ship dragged her anchors and was steadily forced away from Cape Evans to finish up many miles to the north. The storm had been a mixed blessing because as the *Aurora* steamed back towards Cape Evans it became clear that the ice near Hut Point had also been forced out by the southerly blizzard. This was the same ice that Spencer-Smith and his two friends had used to cross over from the Barrier to reach the safety of Hut Point.

It can be imagined with what relief the six men at the hut felt when a week after the second trio had arrived, the expedition ship made a very welcome appearance. The storm that took place between 6 and 9 March had cleared the ice from around Hut Point and allowed *Aurora* to get close enough to the shore. On 11 March, after several attempts, the ship's boat was lowered and picked up the six men. They fell upon a meal of seal steak stew, soup, plum pudding and pancakes after what had been a very hard eight weeks on sledging rations and the rigours of the trail.

Also on 11 March, the southern depot-laying party under the command of Aeneas Mackintosh reached the Bluff Depot on their return journey and coincidentally John Cope and his two men arrived at the Barrier edge to find all the ice gone. They had missed being seen by the crew of the *Aurora* by a matter of hours and they would have to make their way overland to the hut that had just been vacated by Spencer-Smith and the other five men. When they arrived at the hut another mighty blizzard kept them inside for many days and when it finally abated they managed to retrieve their sledge and gear that had been abandoned in the rush to get to the refuge. A poignant moment occurred the day after the blizzard when Hayward and Jack, Cope's two companions, sighted the last three members of the expedition under the leadership of Mackintosh making their way back across the Barrier. The two men had climbed to the top of a nearby hill and looking south detected something out on the ice. At first they could only see a black spot but gradually it became several and finally the two waiting men knew that their three companions were near to completing the depot-laying journey and would soon be safe.

Having picked up the six men from the Discovery Hut the *Aurora* headed for Cape Evans to find another suitable anchorage to overwinter. Wherever they looked the problems were the same. She would be exposed either from the north or south, with storms from the south and ice being driven in from the north. They finally dropped anchor again off Cape Evans using the protection of Glacier Tongue to the south. This was a projection of ice that jutted out from Ross Island. They thought that the problem was at last solved but the wind had other ideas. It shifted around and brought back in all the ice that had so recently been blown out of McMurdo Sound and the ship was once more threatened. The *Aurora* was being assailed from one side by the incoming ice and threatened by the ice tongue of the nearby glacier on the other – and with so much force that her stern post and rudder were damaged beyond repair. The ship was again carried out to sea towards Beaufort Island 40 miles to the north. Stenhouse feared the worst and ordered his crew to be prepared to abandon ship but by mid-day they found themselves amongst pancake ice, which has a tendency to placate the sea, and they could begin the long haul back to Cape Evans.

All this manoeuvring was eating into the ship's stock of coal which would be crucial for her getting out of the ice and back to civilisation the following year. The original plan had been for *Aurora* to return to New Zealand for the winter but Shackleton had changed his mind in the interests of economy and had decided that she was to stay in the Antarctic for the winter.

Mackintosh's group started back from the depot they had managed to lay just short of the 80th parallel on 24 February, but they were held up for several days in a blizzard, so they went back to the depot and took some further rations to see them safely through to Hut Point.

Their next problem was the condition of the dogs. They had been sadly underfed since day one and had now reached the end of their endurance. Of the eight only one was now capable of pulling, so the others were untied and allowed to curl up where they fell. None of them recovered.

Problem after problem was heaped upon them; the loss of the dogs, the days lost due to blizzards, the dropping temperatures leading to frostbitten extremities and frozen sleeping bags denying them a good night's sleep. Rations were halved and the only surviving dog succumbed to the same fate as the others. They were now dependent on one another.

Slowly they headed north and when they reached the edge of the Barrier ice they were faced with open sea and the prospect of a trek over unknown ground to safety. By the time they reached the Discovery hut they had taken 28 days to accomplish a journey that had been done in just 19 days on the outbound trip.

Although the hut was a welcome refuge, the conditions were grim. The blubber used as a means of light and heat had covered everything with a layer of soot and grease and their health had deteriorated. John Cope now had three severely weakened men to treat and with only the very basics of a medical kit which he wasn't even medically trained to use. With a diet that now included fresh seal meat, all six men started to recuperate and by May they were approaching some level of fitness.

Fuel for cooking became an issue as their only source of this was seals, of which there was a scarcity. Just in time, several were located on the nearby beach and dispatched to form a welcome addition to their rations as well as supplying them with the blubber they needed for fuel. Trapped by the lack of sea ice to provide a bridge on the next leg back to Scott's hut at Cape Evans and thence to the *Aurora*, they were unaware of the drama unfolding there.

Spencer-Smith, Stevens, Gaze and Richards, four of the men rescued by *Aurora*, had decided to live ashore in the Cape Evans Hut leaving Ninnis and Hooke on board the ship. As the *Aurora* lay secured by seven cables and anchor chains at Cape Evans the sea started to freeze, holding her to the shore. But a wind blowing up from the south forced the ice against the chains. Between 7 and 25 April, four of the chains broke.

A storm on 6 May late at night forced all the ice out of the bay and drove it to the north of Cape Evans and with it went the *Aurora*. Imagine the scene, the ship's boilers had been shut down for several weeks to conserve coal and were not thought to be needed again before next summer. Now they were adrift with no power available and all the sails furled and stowed for the winter.

Once the crew realised they were adrift and being carried north with the ice still encasing them Joseph Stenhouse ordered the boilers to be relit and steam to be raised. This was going to take many hours but it was the only means by which they could claw their way back to Cape Evans. The ice was being steadily driven against one side of the ship giving her a distinct list to port and with the wind blasting her continuously, it looked at one point as if they might have to abandon her. Preparations were soon put in hand with the ship's boats readied and sledges loaded with supplies. The crew were divided into watches.

At that time of year there is only about two hours of twilight and as the sky lightened the next day the crew were able to gain some idea of how far they had been forced away from Cape Evans. They appeared to be nearly 20 miles out to sea and out of immediate danger. The four men at the hut were blissfully unaware of the problems being faced by the master and crew of the ship. It took most of the day to get up steam but then the ice that had relented for a few hours had them in its grip again.

When the four at the hut discovered the ship was missing they thought that she would make it back to them in a day or so but had no idea what had become of her and later in the day they were assailed by a tremendous blizzard that lasted for three days with 100mph winds. Their greatest fear now was that the ship would go down and as they had no contact with the outside world, who would know of their plight until maybe it was too late?

This same blizzard travelled north and caught the *Aurora* driving her farther and farther away. As the worst passed and the ship was still in one piece, Stenhouse had to gather his crew together and appraise their situation. Still trapped in the ice and being carried away from land, the only chance they had was that if they were not crushed first and eventually broke free, they could make for New Zealand – they were never going to be able to reach Cape Evans again. The ice still held them and with no immediate prospect of any future sailing, to conserve their precious supply of coal they let the fires go out and sat back hoping for something positive to happen.

As the original plan was to land the forthcoming years' supplies for the shore party as near to Hut Point as possible, many of the essentials were still aboard the ship. (The Discovery Hut at Hut Point lay 20 miles farther south than the Cape Evans Hut across unsafe ice). Clothing in particular was in short supply for the shore party, they had virtually no spare change of weatherproof garments. Their food would be horribly limited in amount and variety, and would have to be supplemented with seals and penguins when they returned after the winter and any supplies they could scavenge from the two huts.

As the *Aurora* drifted with the ice farther and farther north the ice pressing in against her hull her timbers groaned and creaked alarmingly. The rudder was smashed beyond repair and it looked for some time as though she would succumb to the forces of nature. Not being able to sleep because of the noise the ice was making, the men lay awake in their bunks fully dressed waiting for the call to abandon ship. They had already placed the sledges and supplies on deck in anticipation of a disaster; but *Aurora* held together and the immediate danger subsided. Meanwhile, Mackintosh and the other five at Discovery Hut whiled away the days playing games or just walking around outside to keep fit. The ice kept trying to form in the bay but before it was safe, another strong wind would break it up and the waiting game would have to start over again. Finally, on the morning of 2 June they got their first chance. They set out as early as possible because they knew that to complete the journey it would take them until nightfall and the moon could provide sufficient light to cover the 20 miles they would have to travel in one go to reach safety. Successfully negotiating the hummocky surface they reached the Cape Evans Hut late in the evening, having found a rope ladder that the other team of men had strung up at the best point to get up off the sea ice. Reunited, the 10 men spent the next three months reflecting on their past efforts and planning a better strategy for the forthcoming sledging season. With only six dogs left and a big question mark hanging over the tractor, it would be down to the men to supply most of the muscle.

Aurora continued her drift northwards and it was well into March 1916, nine months after being forced out of her anchorage at Cape Evans, that she finally broke into fully open water and headed under her own power back towards New Zealand. Nine months! Even at this late stage there had been talk of trying to return to the isolated men at Cape Evans but in the end the knowledge that coal was desperately low and they could not afford to get ice-bound again persuaded them to make for New Zealand.

The ship, remember, had no functioning rudder following the damage caused by the ice and the jury one that had been rigged failed to work satisfactorily. She was assisted by a friendly southerly wind that allowed Stenhouse to reduce steam and use just the sails. This helped to conserve coal for the final leg to New Zealand and safety.

On 2 April 1916 the *Aurora* took a very welcome tow from the tug *Dunedin* to complete the journey. As she approached the harbour at Otago she was met by several smaller craft bringing the pilot to help steer her in to safety. He was accompanied by a doctor, a customs officer and a reporter from the *Daily Telegraph* that had exclusive rights to the expedition. In another launch came several dignitaries including the mayor, but they were not allowed on board in case of a publicity leak.

Between the beginning of September 1915 and Christmas Day Mackintosh, Spencer-Stevens, Joyce, Cope and the other six men left at Cape Evans, together with the last few dogs, made strenuous efforts to complete the series of depots down as far as 82⁰ South. They guessed that Shackleton had not been able to attempt the crossing in the first season so this final effort should enable them not only to stock up the existing depots but also place two more supply dumps at 81⁰ and 82⁰ South. Maybe right down to where the greatest glacier on the planet, the Beardmore, discharged its ice onto the Barrier at 83⁰ South.

Nine men were to form the sledging team, leaving Stevens alone at the hut just in case the *Aurora* returned. Once the depot at 80°S was stocked up with more provisions, three of the men could be sent back leaving the other six to continue on to the next depot, where a further three would turn for home. This plan was loosely based on a similar format to the one that Scott and other explorers had adopted when setting out to reach a certain point by turning back support groups at predetermined points. In this case John Cope was delegated to return to Hut Point with Keith Jack and Irvine Gaze. John Cope was chosen to lead the trio and no thought seems to have been given to the fact that he was the only member of the nine men taking part who had any medical experience – and at this stage both he and his two companions were probably fitter than either Mackintosh or Spencer-Smith. Even Richards had at one stage been having a problem with a suspected rupture earlier in the expedition. When Cope reached Cape Evans he would ask Stenhouse on the *Aurora*, if she had returned, for help. Hopefully

Stenhouse would be able to send out a back-up team of fresh men. On their arrival at Cape Evans, where Stevens had been enduring a lonely vigil, there was no ship.

Mackintosh with Spencer-Smith and Wild, and Joyce with Hayward and Richards went on to complete laying the next two depots. Cooking became a problem as one of their two remaining primus stoves had developed large holes in the perforated gauze that kept the flame trimmed and cooking for six men with only one operational cooker slowed down the camp routine considerably. The next depot at 81° was completed on 12 January and the original plan was for three men to return from this point but, because of the cooker problem, the stage to the next depot would have to be tackled by all six men and the four dogs – otherwise one group would not have a serviceable cooker.

Both Spencer-Smith and the leader Mackintosh were suffering from scurvy. The last time any of Mackintosh's men had tasted fresh seal meat was when they had left the Discovery hut on 29 October over 10 weeks earlier. Scurvy was beginning to show in all of the men.

By the time the new depot at 82° South was laid on 18 January 1916 a major decision had to be taken. How could they get even further south for one final dump of provisions with at least two of the group incapacitated due to the advanced effects of scurvy? On 22 January Spencer-Smith declared he could go no further and he was left behind in a tent until the others could get back to him. A final stock of provisions was put down near Mount Hope, first seen by Shackleton in 1909. This was the farthest south they were to reach but under the circumstances, what a truly heroic achievement it had been. Now for the return journey.

It would be a race against time. With no medical man in the team, Cope had been sent back earlier, they would have to rely on common sense and the few basic medical supplies they had to see them through. The Padre was now a complete invalid and he would have to be put on one of the sledges and pulled by the others. Ernest Joyce was delegated to make any decisions as Mackintosh's debilitating scurvy would soon force him to be a passenger as well. They decided to jettison all surplus gear and as the weather held they made good progress back north arriving at the 80⁰ depot on 11 February.

Mackintosh had managed by sheer willpower to keep up with the others but had not been able to assist in any way with the work. A blizzard trapped them for several days and it looked as though the disaster that had overtaken Scott might yet be repeated again. After a consultation the decision was made for Wild to stay behind and look after the two invalids while Joyce, Hayward and Richards were to try a forced march to the next depot for much needed food for themselves and their four dogs and to return as quickly as possible with food for the three men left behind.

Joyce and his two companions missed a route marker laid down on the way south so it would be touch and go as to whether they were even near their outward bound route. Luckily, Richards had taken the trouble to note down a series of bearings during the journey south and now these were to prove their real worth. Using the wind's direction and maintaining a straight course for two days, they eventually came across a cairn that confirmed their whereabouts, but not yet the depot's. As they camped that night in a tent that was threatening to disintegrate around them another blizzard struck leaving them stuck for a whole day.

Even as the wind abated the snow started to fall in ever greater quantities making it almost impossible to see where they were going. As they plodded on, hopefully towards safety and food but without really being able to see more than a few yards ahead, the dogs seemed to sense something and started to pull more strongly. Sure enough, they had picked out the depot and were now headed towards it.

The total distance covered since the two groups had parted was not much more than 10 miles but it had taken three days. All three men were showing symptomatic signs of the dreaded scurvy with swollen limbs and blackened gums. Having recovered a little and been able to give the dogs several good feeds they gathered their belongings and readied themselves for the journey back to rescue their comrades. The only sledge they had was now supplemented by a second one they found at the depot. This extra sledge would be needed to carry Mackintosh, who they guessed would be an invalid by now if still alive.

They made it back to the three anxious men awaiting them. Wild heard the dogs start to bark as the sledge and the three men approached the camp. His appearance in the tent entrance was a huge relief to the rescuing party. The first priority was to see to the immediate needs of the three men there and without waiting to rest, they all then turned for home. Progress was slow but determined and they arrived at the Bluff depot on 1 March 1916. From this depot they took on board what they hoped would be sufficient stores to get them back to Hut Point. Rigging up a sail they managed to utilise a strong southerly wind and this assisted them over what turned out to be a difficult stretch of recently fallen soft snow. Even when the wind turned into a blizzard the fitter men – Richards, Wild and Joyce – pressed on knowing that it was a small window in which to get the invalids back to safety. Spencer-Smith had now been invalided for 40 days and had spent all that time being pulled by his faithful companions.

At this juncture Hayward also needed help, so the dogs became even more important. It became apparent that a drastic plan of action was called for and with their dwindling strength they decided to leave Mackintosh with adequate supplies and one of the tents so that all their efforts could be brought to bear to get Spencer-Smith and Hayward back to Hut Point and then return for Mackintosh in a few days. Spencer-Smith was by now so weak that for most of the time he was hallucinating and unconscious, so this was a last desperate attempt to save his life. Two days after leaving Mackintosh, Spencer-Smith finally succumbed to his illness and passed away. They buried him still in his sleeping bag, placing a cairn over the shallow icy grave and marking the spot with a crudely constructed cross. They were only a day away from their destination and Spencer-Smith's possible survival.

Spencer-Smith had written a very poignant letter to his parents just before setting out in September and it summed up a premonition he seems to have had. In the event that he failed to return safely or should illness overcome him, then in very simple terms he says his goodbye. He bids farewell to his beloved parents and expresses sadness that he has not been able to comfort them in time of war. His faith shines through in the lines he penned, assuring his mother and father that whatever the outcome of the difficulties he found himself facing and, should the worst come to the worst, he was confident they could be proud of the fact that he faced his death as cheerfully as he could, right up to his end. He went on to express his certainty that they would eventually be re-united in a better world. This letter can be found in *Polar Castaways*, the book Richard McElrea and David Harrowfield co-wrote about the Ross Sea party.

The four men reached the Discovery Hut and immediately feasted on fresh seal meat for the next few days so as to build up their strength for the trek back south to retrieve their skipper, Mackintosh. Eight days had elapsed before the rescue party finally made it back to the lonely tent with Mackintosh in it. Despite his ordeal he had managed to stagger out of the tent as the rescuers approached. They had brought a selection of essential foods for him to help with his recovery and they were soon on the march again, pulling him along on the now lightened sledge.

In 170 days of sledging they had covered over 1,500 miles to achieve, against all odds, the task set them by Shackleton. Ernest Joyce, Ernest Wild and Dick Richards would, after the expedition returned to civilisation, receive the Albert Medal for the part they played in rescuing their companions. Hayward's medal was awarded posthumously.

So Mackintosh and his four surviving companions were back at the Discovery Hut by 18 March. At Cape Evans the other four men were anxiously awaiting the return of the depot-laying party and also by this time Shackleton and his Trans-Antarctic team, who were due to make an appearance towards the end of March at the latest. While all the drama was taking place in the Antarctic the *Aurora* was slowly but surely making her way under her own power towards New Zealand.

No group was aware of what had become of the others and it can only be imagined the stresses it must have placed on all of them. Where was the ship? Had she foundered? How would they be rescued? It is fair to say that several of the men were not coping well with the situation, but with support from their comrades somehow they had got this far.

The Discovery Hut men were being held up by persistent open water between them and the other four at the Cape Evans Hut. Mackintosh and Hayward, the two worst affected by scurvy, were making good progress and all five tried to keep fit by exercising near the hut. Time dragged on and Mackintosh was getting impatient to try out the new ice that was forming to see if a crossing could be attempted. There was a new moon due in the middle of May and if the ice continued to harden, then an attempt might be made utilising its light.

Not wishing to wait that long and in case the ice was again driven out, Mackintosh, together with Hayward, set out on 8 May in the afternoon. The others tried to persuade them to wait another week. A storm could be seen brewing away to the south and it came on to blow very hard a few hours after the two men set out. They were never seen again. Searching later the others found footsteps leading north but they disappeared at the ice edge. The three survivors must have felt devastated to know that despite the terrible struggle they had gone through to get these two men to safety after their physical collapse, all had been for nought.

The May full moon came and went, as did the one in June. Finally, on 15 July, the ice held long enough for the surviving trio to cross to the security of the hut at Cape Evans and once more be with their comrades. Of course reaching the safety of Cape Evans only brought into perspective their real plight: would anybody know where to look for these seven men? Unbeknownst to the forlorn group at Cape Evans, the *Aurora* had in fact made it through to New Zealand and the rescue of the survivors could now be organised. Who was going to organise it and who would foot the bill?

Shackleton too had escaped the freezing clutches of the ice in the Weddell Sea and returned to a world embroiled in the Great War. He had achieved the rescue of his own half of the expedition and now wanted to do the same for the others. There were no funds left and a large debt hung over him. He was sidelined in any case and only allowed to travel down aboard *Aurora* as a supernumerary with no authority. Even Joseph Stenhouse, who had captained the *Aurora* during her epic escape from the Ross

Sea, found himself superseded by John Davis as Captain of the refitted ship. The governments of Great Britain, Australia and New Zealand, having had to dip into their exchequers, stamped their authority on the enterprise and dictated who was to run it and all the other details.

The ship made an excellent passage through the ice to reach Shackleton's old hut at Cape Royds by 10 January 1916. Shackleton was allowed to lead the landing party only to find no sign of any occupation. As they returned to the ship Captain Davis was informed of an observation by the ship's lookout. His sharp and experienced eyes had picked out a moving black dot far away across the ice towards Cape Evans. As the others turned their focus of attention in the same direction it gradually became clear that the look-out had in fact sighted what could only be a small group of men coming towards the ship. Gradually the survivors drew closer to the ship and Sir Ernest Shackleton and his two companions who by now had regained the ship after their fruitless trek over to his old hut were once more dispatched across the ice to meet up with the advancing dog sledge and the men driving it.

Captain Davis suggested to Shackleton that by lying down on the ice the three rescuers could indicate from a distance to those on board the ship how many men had lost their lives. The two groups met whilst still some distance from the safety of the *Aurora* and just after the initial meeting Shackleton, Morton Moyes and Frederick Middleton lay down and the message was seen by those watching aboard the ship with their binoculars. It was understood that there would only be seven survivors.

There was a dignified but emotional reunion as the six men reached the ship and revealed that the seventh man was too weak to attempt the journey out on to the ice. Cope had stayed in the hut as he was not robust enough to travel across the ice. After some equipment and scientific records had been retrieved from the hut the *Aurora's* bow was turned for home.

Of course one cannot directly compare the Ross Sea party's exploits with that of Bunny Fuchs' TAE. On the one hand you have a poorly fitted-out group of men, most of whom knew very little about the difficulties of travelling across the icy wastes of the remotest landscape in the world, led by a man who at times took unnecessary chances. On the other hand the TAE had been organised down to the last detail and was equipped with all the latest technology to move the men and their equipment with relative ease across the same forbidding continent. An example is the relative ease with which Ed Hillary and his four tracked vehicles reached the base of the Skelton Glacier, a journey of over 180 miles, in seven days. Aeneas Mackintosh and the first two groups who set out to establish the depot at 80°S were away from their hut for 47 days. That was 19 days travelling out to the depot they laid and 28 days to get back to the hut. They had covered a total of about 230 miles.

Weather was another factor that the two expeditions found so different. Ed Hillary had set out in October. This was early in the season when the surfaces were probably at their best and the summer had not had a chance to open up the crevasses. Mackintosh did not even reach the continent until the middle of January and this gave him only a few weeks of summertime to accomplish his depot laying. The sea ice they had to negotiate at the beginning of their journey had already begun to break up, they were soon very short of dogs and the tractor failed during the first day's run.

Mackintosh and his group would have been amazed by the two planes available to Ed Hillary, not to mention that indispensable aid, the wireless, for calling in the plane when supplies were required or for ferrying men and dogs to strategic points along the way to the Pole. What had been required by Shackleton was carried out in the old-fashioned way and until the task was almost complete there had been no loss of life – apart from most of the dogs.

New Zealand Striving for the Plateau and Beyond

The second stage of the depot laying that Ed Hillary and his team would have to perform meant scaling the Skelton Glacier and establishing a supply dump somewhere near the glacier's roots high up on the Polar Plateau. The Weasel that had limped into camp on 20 October had been duly stripped of its engine to facilitate the repair to the distributor drive shaft, the engine had been replaced and the vehicle tested and declared ready for the next leg of the journey.

Marsh and Miller, the two dog drivers, set off two days later on 22 October. The going was some of the most difficult that they would experience during the whole expedition. The sastrugi were so hard that the sledges capsized frequently and with only two men to put them back on their runners and with full loads to contend with tempers became frayed, not only with the problem but also with one another. It was extremely difficult to go to your friend's assistance and keep an eye on your own team at the same time but equally frustrating for one driver to see the other negotiating an obstacle and find that his own sledge had been capsized by that same difficulty. Creditably they made 18 miles on the first run and were settling into camp when the first of the tractors rolled in. Ed Hillary driving the lead tractor of the four vehicle convoy pulled up alongside the tent of Marsh and Miller just over four hours after leaving the depot at the foot of the Skelton. The Weasel had performed well.

A day here was lost to swirling snow and mist but on the 24th off the dogs went, to be followed shortly by the four tractors. The snow became more intense and forced the two dog teams to call a halt and wait for the others; but the conditions did not hold up the tractors and they soon passed the dog teams without even seeing them. Hillary became aware that the dogs would probably have struggled in the present conditions and halted to see if they were going to catch up. Not wishing the tractor engines to get too cold, he signalled for the convoy to proceed and they travelled on to complete 19 miles for the day. This brought them to the zone they had named the 'Lower Staircase'. Another tough day lay ahead as the Staircase lived up to its name, with slopes of varying degrees of difficulty that caused them to resort to re-laying the sledges from one terrace to the next. Each ramp caused the tractors to dig into the surface and start to flounder before another tractor could come to its aid. The four men persevered and reached the 'Landing', another appropriately named feature that had been discovered the previous season. Camping at the 'Landing ' meant they had brought forward their loads 12 miles at the expense of probably four times that in tractor miles. The motorised group would wait here for the dogs to catch up. Each dog sledge carried some 650 pounds of gear and to their credit they arrived about a day after the tractors. Both Miller and Marsh were very pleased with the dogs' progress over the first two stretches of the Skelton. Ahead of the travellers was another series of steep slopes and shallower ramps that again had attracted a moniker. The 'Upper Staircase' was to prove a far greater test for the tractors in particular. There were times when it required two of the tractors to drag the sledges higher. Another difficulty the drivers had was that the tracks made by the dogs were being constantly obliterated by the drifting snow, leading to them losing the safest way through the ever-present crevasses. The dog teams were meant to pioneer the route but of course this did not always work out in practice due to the obliteration of their tracks.

Once the two groups were re-united for a few hours they had time to plan the next stage of the ascent. This would entail traversing an area of névé. (On a glacier there are distinct layers as the snow changes from one state to the next to form the solid ice which glaciers mainly consist of. Névé is the top layer consisting of recently fallen snow which is starting to coalesce into the first stages of ice.)

The surface should have been relatively easy but it would be an uphill grind and the wind had now increased in velocity whipping up any loose snow, and for the dogs at least it would be a day in camp. After their superb effort so far this would not go amiss, but Ed Hillary was determined to force the pace and despite some reservations amongst members of his party he proposed that the tractors would at least attempt to make some progress. The reservations were all about hidden crevasses. If more crevasses were met with in the conditions that now prevailed, would the tractor party be as lucky as on the earlier traverses of the Upper and Lower Staircases?

They set their sights on the depot at the top of the Skelton Glacier. The weather was getting worse and the bitterly cold wind blowing down off the Polar Plateau was driving loose snow particles into everyone's eyes. Ed Hillary and his team of four vehicles were fairly well protected behind their makeshift canvas screens and so he decided to force a path up the remainder of the glacier and wait for the two dog teams to follow on when they could. This would entail a journey of about 20 miles, which was about as far as the dogs could manage in one day's travel.

Unbeknown to Miller and Marsh, there was a change of plan after the two halves of the party separated. This was brought about by John Claydon, the pilot flying the Beaver that was to meet up with the ground party. He reported that he was unable to land near the proposed depot site and told Hillary where he could bring the plane in safely. His cargo on this trip consisted of two more teams of dogs and their handlers, Harry Ayers and Roy Carlyon. Later, he would bring a substantial amount of stores and fuel to this depot to service Bunny Fuchs' crossing party. It became known as the Plateau Depot.

So Miller and Marsh sat out the wind-driven snow in their tent for two days and as the wind abated they broke camp and moved off in pursuit of the tractors. The date was now 31 October, nine days into the Skelton Glacier climb.

An agreed rendezvous some 20 miles from their present camp site had been arranged but when Miller and Marsh arrived, the tractors were nowhere to be seen and their tracks had been obliterated by the driving snow. Realising that there had been some misunderstanding or change of circumstances the two teams drove on for an additional 2 miles but with still no sign of Ed Hillary and his tractors they decided to camp, feed the dogs and themselves and have a well-earned sleep.

Ed Hillary could not let Miller and Marsh know about the change in the depot's location due to a radio malfunction and had to rely on them picking up his trail to follow him to the new site.

With Claydon's information, the three Ferguson tractors and the Weasel now changed course slightly to bring them onto a bearing that would lead them to the site of the new depot. Ayres and Carlyon were already in residence when they got there but of Miller and Marsh there was still no news. They arrived two days later feeling distinctly disgruntled. It turned out that they had eventually picked up the tractor trail and followed it, between bouts of bad weather, to the newly positioned Plateau Depot. As the new depot took shape Bob Miller with the help of two other men took one of the tractor units and its sledge back to the original site and brought all the stores that were there to this new location.

The party now stationed up on the Plateau consisted of Ed Hillary, Bob Miller, George Marsh, Ron Balham, Peter Mulgrew, Murray Ellis, Jim Bates and the two newcomers Ayers and Carlyon. Ed Hillary felt the need to return to Scott Base to plan his next move and he took with him Peter Mulgrew, who would be back once the tractors were ready to continue across the Plateau. Ron Balham was also returning but on a permanent basis. He had requested that he only partake in the Scott Base to the Skelton Glacier leg of the overall journey, so he too would be flown out. A couple of days later Murray Ellis sustained a severe back strain and had to be repatriated for medical treatment. Ed Hillary now needed to replace at least one member of his tractor group so that he could proceed with all the vehicles across the plateau to set up the next depot at 480 miles from Scott Base. Although Peter Mulgrew was due to return to the Plateau Depot after a couple of days at Scott Base, Hillary still needed an extra man to take the place of Ron Balham. Two days after Mulgrew had arrived back at the depot, he fell from the roof of the caboose whilst trying to secure an aerial and suffered several cracked ribs, so he too was returned to Scott Base for medical treatment. This just left Jim Bates out of the original drivers, plus Hillary when he returned from his stay at Scott Base.

Ed Hillary could not afford to deplete his team at Scott Base so he would have to request another experienced person from New Zealand and he sent a telegram to Derek Wright, who had been attached to the expedition for the first summer as a film maker and had gained some experience driving the tractors. If he could come, he would also be able to film this next section of the trip. Admiral Dufek, the American commander at McMurdo Sound, was also contacted in the hope that he could bring Derek Wright over from New Zealand aboard one of the supply flights to the American bases. Derek Wright agreed and within a couple of days arrived at the McMurdo Base and was soon winging his way to the Plateau Depot to join the others.

The four teams of dogs and their drivers were eager to move farther south, now that the Plateau Depot had been repositioned and all the stores at the old site had been retrieved and transferred to the new one. The only snag was the absence of most of the tractor team. Two had been repatriated with injuries and Ed Hillary was still at Scott Base. Dr Ron Balham had also returned to base camp to continue his studies on seals. If the dog teams started out to the south, only Jim Bates would be left and it was an expedition policy that nobody should be left on their own in this, the most testing of environments. Frustrating as it was for the sledgers, at least they had been on hand to unload the Beaver each time the plane arrived with more supplies to stock up the depot.

On 8 November the Beaver brought in the final load and the Scott Base's radio operator Ted Gawn to replace the injured Mulgrew. The four sledging teams could get ready to depart. Each sledge had on board supplies for a month weighing about 1,000lbs and it was hoped that they could reach the proposed site of Depot 480, 200 miles farther south. The route would take them westwards across the ice cap away from some major disturbance that had been seen from the plane during a short reconnaissance carried out earlier in the year. Then they would be able to swing their teams onto a southerly course.

The dogs were raring to go, as were the four men, Miller, Marsh, Ayres and Carlyon. What none of the drivers realised was that the surface consisted of ice crystals that had the consistency of sugar – notorious for really heavy going. As mentioned earlier in relation to the Inuit putting mud on their sledge runners, efficient skiing or sledging relies on the pressure of the runner against the ice causing it to melt slightly, allowing a film of water to form – but not so on the day they set out. The mileage says it all, just 6 miles on the first day and not much better in the subsequent two. The decision to depot several cases of supplies would mean that if the tractors did not catch them up, the dogs and men would have to travel on reduced rations until the plane could bring them some extra food. The aneroid barometer they carried indicated that the plateau was still rising and this and the more rarefied atmosphere put extra pressure on the men and dogs' ability to cope.

After such a disappointing start they arrived at the point where the group could at last turn towards the south and, following an appreciable improvement in the surface conditions, the mileage increased to a creditable 16 miles in the first day on the new course. They built a large cairn of snow blocks to indicate to the tractor team where they also needed to turn.

When the dog sledge teams left the previous depot they were equipped with newer and better radio sets that would enable them to keep in touch with the other units and Scott Base over longer distances. In one of the scheduled communiqués on 12 November they learnt that the tractors were now ready to get back on the road. Ed Hillary had persuaded Ted Gawn to try his hand at tractor driving. Ted was in fact the chief radio operator at Scott Base but Mulgrew could cover for him while he convalesced after his fall. The new tractor team was now composed of Hillary, Gawn, Jim

Bates, the mechanic and the new boy recently arrived from New Zealand courtesy of the American Air Force, Derek Wright.

The vehicles, like the dogs before them, were being tested to their limits by the weight of cargo, 11 tons in total. This was mainly the fuel they would need before the plane could resupply them. The surface had not improved since the dogs passed over it a week or so before. The Weasel was coping quite well but the three Fergusons kept struggling and each time they met the softer snow they tended to dig themselves into the surface and have to be hauled out. Their progress was severely retarded for the first four days in addition to which Hillary was suffering from a bout of flu picked up at Scott Base.

They were about 9,000 feet above sea level and at that height the carburettors of the four tractors needed to be adjusted to allow for the lack of oxygen. Most of the adjustments could be achieved by changing the jets in the carburettors but it was fiddly work and with temperatures dropping to as low as -42°F, the engineer's fingers were exposed to the risk of frostbite.

The scenery was changing from day to day. As they continued to gain height the distant peaks of the Trans-Antarctic Range gradually slipped from view reminding the men of how remote they had become from any other human beings. Both teams were by now resigned to the torment of the weather and as this affected the dog teams more than the tractor party, the gap gradually diminished between them. By 28 November both groups were nearly at the site of the depot, which they hoped to establish 480 miles from Scott Base.

The tractors had taken a wider course round some crevasses that the dog teams driven by Miller and his three associates had discovered and as the last few miles were ticked off to the site the two parties found themselves on slightly differing courses. In spite of the detour, the tractors were the first to arrive, despite two of them dropping into unexpected crevasses. On 25 November they turned off their engines, happy in the knowledge that they had arrived at Depot 480. The dog sledges arrived soon afterwards and now the eight men could discuss their experiences during the 210 miles covered since they were last together, and how best to proceed.

A message received by the New Zealanders on 19 November from Bunny confirmed the Weddell Sea men had finally broken through to their advance camp site of South Ice. Bunny was glossing over the fact that this part of their expedition had taken much longer than he had anticipated but he was forever hopeful of making up the lost mileage once they got into their stride when the whole movement from Shackleton to South Ice was repeated in a few days' time. Remember, he had only just reached South Ice on his first foray – it would all have to be done again when he brought forward his three remaining Sno-Cats and the mass of stores. At this early stage Bunny gave an estimated arrival time at Scott Base as late as 9 March 1958. This last bit of information was the last thing Hillary wanted to hear as it could entail some members of the Ross Sea contingent being asked to stop over for another winter.

At about the same time as Bunny's telegram reached Ed Hillary so did another passed on to him from Arthur Helm in New Zealand requesting any further thoughts that Ed might have had relating to his proposed push to the Pole after the last depot had been established. The New Zealand Committee seemed to have had a rethink about their initial cold shoulder to the idea. Even if the New Zealand Committee consented, it would only be with the overriding permission of Bunny and the London Committee, so nothing new here.

When the original depot-laying journeys were being planned, not a lot of credence was given to the possibility of getting the tractors onto the Polar Plateau but now it was a fact, thoughts were turned to the possibility of reallocating the four dog teams to more innovative use.

Miller and Marsh had work to carry out to the west of the last main Depot 700 miles from Scott Base, and would need to rely on their reserve stores being laid down from that depot. Ayres and Carlyon had been allocated the task of exploring an area between the vast Byrd and Nimrod Glaciers so it would be a waste of their time hauling stores all the way to Depot 700. But if a smaller intermediate depot was set up for them, then they would be free earlier to veer away from the main southward thrust and carry out their own expedition sooner rather than later.

After a day's rest the surveyors in the group started taking readings to establish the depot's exact position for the benefit of the Beaver, which was waiting to bring in all the fuel and other stores. The latitude reading for Depot 480 was 79° 52′ South, virtually the same as Mackintosh, Joyce and Wild had reached on 20 February 1915 when they had completed their first season of depot laying. Without the modern aids of tractors, radio and aeroplanes that were available to the TAE expedition, they had accomplished the task in just 27 days and their starting point was from Cape Evans some 20 miles farther north than Scott Base. It had also included the dangerous frozen sea crossing that lay between the two huts.

The leader of the New Zealand party's air squadron John Claydon was waiting at Scott Base ready to fly. In anticipation of the workload he and his fellow flyers would be required to carry out, he came up with an interim plan to help move the stores more efficiently. The Beaver would be required to climb to over 9,000 feet to reach the two new depots and at this altitude her carrying capacity would be reduced. The plan was simple in its conception: an intermediate landing and refuelling location on the Ice Shelf would enable the plane to bring heavier payloads from Scott Base much closer to Depot 480 before tackling the now shortened flight to the new depot. The plane could refuel at this new landing strip for the homeward flight, reducing the weight of fuel required by the plane to complete the return journey. This would enable more stores to be loaded onto the plane at Scott Base for onward shipment to Depot 480, or any other depot set up on the Plateau.

The proposed new base could also act as an emergency landing strip in the event of deteriorating weather. It was to be manned by the two new members of the aircrew who had come out for the second summer season. They were Corporal Peter Tate and Leading Aircraftsman Ian Chapman. The site chosen for this staging post was close to the Darwin Glacier but still on the Ice Shelf.

Flight after flight became the order of the day as the Beaver transported the vast amount of stores up to Depot 480. At this juncture a reshuffle of the men who formed the motorised group took place. Peter Mulgrew rejoined the depot-laying party after his convalescence to replace the radio operator Ted Gawn, who returned to his duties at Scott Base. Murray Ellis, the driver who had hurt his back, was also flown in and another addition was Douglas McKenzie, a freelance journalist who had been appointed to be the official press representative covering the story of the expedition during its second season. The tractor group now totalled six men, the original team plus the two newcomers.

The dog teams had left Depot 480 on 1 December, six days ahead of the tractor convoy. The tractors had received a considerable amount of TLC in the period they were idle. The next leg would enable the New Zealanders to establish two more supply dumps. The final one at 700 miles from Scott Base would be the first one reached by Bunny on his trek from the Pole to the completion of the crossing at McMurdo Sound. The other depot, called Middle Depot, would be placed about halfway to Depot 700 as a backup for the two dog teams under Harry Ayres and Roy Carlyon who were going to explore a region not as far south as Miller and Marsh.

Miller and Marsh were to cover a total of 1,400 miles during the course of that season and consistently achieved mileages of 15 to 20 miles a day. They had a routine of taking it in turns to lead for two or three days at a time and found that the dogs responded well to this pattern of travel. They were in daily contact with the tractor team and in that way could pass on advice about any adverse conditions likely to be encountered. To assist the tractors even more, they continued to build snow cairns to mark where they had changed direction or wanted to make the following group aware of any problems ahead.

The tractors left Depot 480 six days behind Miller and Marsh and with the excellent weather and surfaces they encountered they were achieving in the region of 50 miles a day. But the Weasel began to make some unpleasant engine noises and the mechanics swapped sledges around so that it only had the caboose to pull. Dropping off some fuel drums and dog pemmican at the site chosen for a midway depot lightened the loads. The six drums of tractor fuel were actually of American manufacture and not the usual British Petroleum ones. They had been brought over from New Zealand by an American plane to replace a stock of BP drums that had been swept overboard in a gale that had struck the US freighter being used to ship them to Scott Base for the expedition's use earlier in the season.

The Weasel gave up the ghost with a shattered thrust bearing for which there was no spare available and was dumped, despite a last desperate attempt by the two mechanics, Murray and Bates, to create a spare from other parts they carried with them.

Miller and Marsh had expected to be overhauled some miles before the site of Depot 700 was reached but the troublesome Weasel put an end to that possibility. 13 December was the culmination of a magnificent run of 220 miles for the two men and their dogs. The weather had held for the duration of the run between the two depots and the tractor party pulled into the base site two days later.

John Claydon was already making plans for the first of many journeys to bring in the additional supplies that would be crucial to Bunny's crossing team plus back-up stores for the two dog teams under Miller and Marsh that would soon be off again, this time exploring the Beardmore Glacier complex.

A quick look across the continent to the progress of Bunny's half of the expedition finds him poised for the second time to set about surmounting the obstacle that the men had christened the Ice Wall. South Ice had been established about 300 miles inland from Shackleton Base. It had been stocked up by plane the previous season. Bunny would finally get to South Ice for the second time on 22 December and would set out for the South Pole on the evening of Christmas Day 1957.

From Depot 700 to the South Pole was another 500 miles and the 'gap' had been tempting Ed Hillary ever since he realised that the tractors were doing such a fine job up in the rarefied air of the Plateau. The latitude for the position of this last depot was given as nearly 83° South, this was approximately the same as the depot laid by Shackleton's Ross Sea party who had managed to reach this point with their depleted dog team and the men suffering from the onset of scurvy over 40 years before. Hillary could feel justifiably pleased with his team's progress to date. The weather had been kinder to them than it had to any other expedition in the past and compared to Bunny's progress, they had also been blessed with a forgiving travelling surface.

There were a few problems brewing however, and these were not so easily overcome. The two dog handlers had requested a secondary depot be set up about halfway towards the Queen Alexandra Mountains using the tractors. It was in the vicinity of this range of mountains that Miller and Marsh would carry out what they regarded as their most important work of the whole expedition. Hillary was adamant that he could not spare the fuel required by the tractors to carry out their request and this infuriated both men.

By this time everybody was aware of Hillary's plan to proceed on from Depot 700 to reach the South Pole. He would require a considerable quantity of fuel for the three Fergusons to carry out the journey and did not want to delay his departure waiting for extra fuel supplies to be ferried up from Scott Base. He did offer the exploring party the possibility of the plane landing somewhere in the vicinity of their proposed route and dropping off some stores for them, but could not guarantee this arrangement.

Naturally, the two dog team handlers were just as anxious to get underway as Hillary, and waiting for the plane just added to their sense of frustration. They felt very strongly that Hillary was putting his own agenda before their surveying activity.

Although the weather at Depot 700 was still very good, the plane was being held up by snow storms and low cloud at Scott Base. Even the stock of fuel that John Claydon had thoughtfully laid in at a halfway storage facility between the two Plateau depots could not be accessed.

The waiting was to last until 18 December. Then Claydon could take off and ferry in some much needed stores. Once the unloading was complete at the new depot, Miller and Marsh were given the chance of being flown out over their proposed route and this at least mollified their frustration with Hillary. The flight enabled them to scrutinise their proposed route and it revealed several crevassed areas that they would now be able to circumvent, saving them valuable time. In all, there were to be four flights to complete the stocking up of the last depot before the Pole and the two New Zealand pilots John Claydon and Bill Cranfield shared the burden of the sometimes hazardous flights.

The final arrangement for the two sledgers was that they would receive some extra supplies en route courtesy of the plane tracking them on their outward journey from Depot 700 and landing as close to them as possible to bring in the extra rations.

They set out on 19 December just as some unpleasantly cold wind was bringing with it the ever present threat of drifting snow and reduced visibility. Undeterred, they said their farewells and headed out and in two days had covered nearly 40 miles. As arranged, the plane tracked them down using a SARAH beacon they were carrying and topped up their supplies with extra dog and man rations. This was to be their last supply drop for their entire time away from Scott Base and it meant loads of up to 1,200lbs for the two sledges pulled by the nine dogs that made up each team.

The arrival of Douglas McKenzie and David Wright at Depot 480 was another source of unease for Miller and Marsh. Both the newcomers were allied to the press and it looked to the two scientists as if Ed Hillary had arranged for them to tag along for the express purpose of publicising his next move – which they knew would be the run through to the Pole. Miller and Marsh could not understand the necessity for this extra publicity, when the clear brief that the New Zealand party had been given was to lay down the depots for backing up the crossing party under Bunny Fuchs and then concentrate any spare capacity towards exploration in the Antarctic Zone that New Zealand lay claim to.

In his book, Douglas McKenzie wrote about his experiences with the expedition and this took a more pragmatic look at how he saw the saga relating to the so-called 'Race to the Pole' developing. His observation of the situation as the tractor party arrived at Depot 700 highlights the impatience shown by the two dog sledgers. The two men had been in camp four days by the time the mechanics in the tractor group had recovered sufficiently to start preparing the tractors for what would turn out to be the run to the Pole. All Miller and Marsh were interested in doing was getting underway again towards the mountains, and any delay meant lost mileage to them.

McKenzie had tagged onto the tractor team at Depot 480 and initially hoped to stay with them right through to the South Pole if possible, but at Depot 700 he had a change of heart and asked to be flown back to Scott Base to continue his coverage of the expedition from there. He cited as his main reason that any messages passing through the radio network at Scott could be more easily monitored and he would then be on the spot to send his reports directly to the New Zealand agency dealing with the press releases as they occurred.

Ed Hillary now had five men and three Ferguson tractors to get him where he so dearly wanted to be. He had enough fuel, barring any unforeseen delays, and all his other requisites were catered for.

The run through to the Pole was carried out with almost military precision and the three tractors completed the first mechanised run to the South Pole in history. The New Zealanders arrived at the American Antarctic station at the South Pole on 4 January 1958 having covered 1,250 miles to cross half a continent of ice, snow and crevasses, all the while overcoming blizzards and breakdowns to get there. They had set out from their base on Ross Island on 14 October 1957 with little knowledge of what lay ahead but buoyed up by a great deal of hope and a fair degree of daring, as befits all explorers.

Ed Hillary flew back to Scott Base on 6 January taking with him all his polar party except Peter Mulgrew who remained behind at the Scott/Amundsen Base to act as the communications hub for the New Zealanders at Scott Base. This would enable them to receive messages firsthand from Bunny Fuchs, which were being forwarded through the Americans at their polar station.

Bunny was expected to get to the South Pole within the next two weeks or so and it looked as though the great meeting between the two party leaders would still take place, with Hillary being flown back to the Pole, courtesy of the Admiral Dufek. Ed Hillary left his options open just in case he could not reach the rendezvous in time to meet Bunny but stated that he would definitely be at Depot 700 if all else failed to guide the crossing party down to Scott Base from the plateau. In his view this was what he had been asked to do and he was not going to give anyone an opportunity of criticising him for not doing his job.

South Pole to Scott Base

Following Bunny and his Trans-Antarctic team's arrival at the Pole all the various formalities had to be gone through. This included a series of hand-shakes with Ed Hillary for the benefit of the newspapermen gathered there. Then Bunny carried out a short press conference and calmly answered all the questions posed to him with the authoritative air of one who knows when he has accomplished a difficult task and is master of the situation. One of the key questions was about Ed Hillary's suggestion of dividing the crossing into two halves and returning next year to complete the journey. Bunny was adamant that they would push on and despite being behind schedule there would still be enough time to arrive at Scott Base for the expedition members to sail back to New Zealand as originally planned. After all, Scott did not reach the Pole until 17 January and Bunny reassured them all that he and his party had Sno-Cats to see them through. Having satisfied the questioning pressmen, everybody adjourned to a reception laid on by the Americans.

Admiral Dufek, the American commander of the McMurdo station, then made it known that he and his entourage would be returning by plane to their base; he took with him Ed Hillary, who had promised Bunny that they would meet again at Depot 700.

The weary travellers were invited by the base commander to take full advantage of the facilities they had to offer and to spend the next few days relaxing and re-organising themselves ready for the long journey still in front of them. The two engineers availed themselves of the workshops to carry out timely repairs to the overworked tractor units. The two dog handlers made sure their animals were fed and rested, even though their work was now done. Then there was the luxury of sleeping in beds, eating proper meals at real tables with decent chairs to sit on, showering and shaving and of course, as with all American bases throughout the world and not just here in Antarctica, watching movies. The Americans were interested in listening to all the tales the new arrivals had to tell about the exciting and dangerous times they had encountered on the way from South Ice. Their own daily routine was rather mundane compared to the travails of these bone fide explorers.

Bunny took the opportunity of bringing both London and Wellington in New Zealand up-to-date with all that had transpired over the period when the expedition had been too busy to bother with detailed communiqués.

The crossing party set out north for Depot 700 with four Sno-Cats and one Weasel on 24 January 1958 – 900 miles to the good but still not halfway, with about 1,250 miles still to go. The way ahead had at least been marked out by Ed Hillary's Pole dash and for nearly 800 miles the route was across the Polar Plateau, which would not hold the unknown terrors of the path they had already covered.

Bunny was confident they could travel a lot faster on the Plateau over known ground. The dogs had been airlifted out to Scott Base and he planned to increase the distances between seismic shots to 50 or more miles. There were a lot of imponderables as they set off, the weather and temperature chief amongst them. Other issues that might hold them up were ones that they had grown used to, such as vehicle reliability and the ever-present danger of crevasses. Despite all the pressures heaped on his shoulders Bunny kept his equilibrium and instilled a great deal of confidence in his men, something that had not always been apparent through certain periods of the journey south. The first three days put 100 miles between them and the Pole and that included a seismic shot.

On the fourth day out, David Stratton discovered Geoff Pratt unconscious in one of the Sno-Cats. He had apparently collapsed as the result of carbon monoxide poisoning and the only way to resuscitate him was to administer copious amounts of oxygen to compensate for the lack of it at the high altitude. The ideal solution would be to evacuate the patient down to sea level but, of course, this would only be possible with the help of the Americans and only then if they could find a suitable surface on which to land. The expedition's own planes, the Beaver and the Otter, did not have the range or takeoff capabilities at this altitude. Fortunately, the Americans were able to parachute two large oxygen cylinders to the convoy using one of their Neptune aircraft flown up from McMurdo Sound. Geoff Pratt made a full recovery after about three days of being administered the oxygen.

This was another example of how generous the Americans were with the help that they dispensed to the crossing party. Due to the spontaneous help from McMurdo, Geoff Pratt's life had been saved and this enabled the crossing to continue.

On the last day of January the faithful old Weasel appropriately called 'Wrack and Ruin' succumbed to engine failure and Bunny decided that repairs were not practical, so it was left behind. Although the Sno-Cats were consuming the miles each day, this was not without cost. Most of the pontoon caterpillars were getting slack and eventually one of them slipped off its wheels and brought the Cat to an abrupt halt. This time, they would have to carry out repairs. Upon inspection other pontoon caterpillars were also found to be in need of tensioning.

The altitude readings that were taken every day showed a distinct downhill trend meaning that they were definitely on the homeward run. They were making substantial progress and the mood of the party was noticeably more relaxed. Another positive sign was that the fuel consumption, which had always been a concern, had improved markedly and no more was there a nagging feeling that the depot being 100 miles nearer the Pole that Bunny had requested of Hillary was going to cause a problem.

Having taken a detour to skirt a crevassed area that Hillary had indicated on his provisional map, it was a great relief when the leading Sno-Cat suddenly pulled up just short of a collapsed snow bridge. It appeared that the crevassed area was far more extensive than expected and after a lengthy appraisal of the situation Bunny decided to set up camp, carry out a seismic shot and in the morning before the sun had time to affect the bridges too much, try and find a way through the labyrinth. After probing the way ahead, which took most of the day, the convoy cleared the last of the obstacles and another 25 miles was ticked off.

The promising run slowed when Bunny in the leading Cat felt a lurch and just managed to get the Sno-Cat to climb out onto the other side of a hidden crevasse, bringing the two sledges it was towing successfully behind it. This led to another lengthy delay while several men went ahead on skis, roped together, to reconnoitre a safe path. There appeared to be too many crevasses to be able to find a safe passage so Bunny decided that the best plan would be to run parallel to the new field of hazards and try to pick up Hillary's tracks. They had already taken a diversion some miles earlier to get clear of the original batch of crevasses that the New Zealand party had marked on their outward journey. The skirting ploy failed to bring any results so once more they took the plunge and proceeded to force a way across the chasms. The bridges were definitely stronger and progress was once more resumed. The convoy had split due to some problems with one of the Sno-Cats, but Bunny felt sure that once the breakdown had been sorted out, the back markers would be able to follow in his tracks. He managed to contact them on the two-way radio and they confirmed they were about to resume their journey.

Towards the end of one of the most mentally exhausting days since leaving the Pole, Bunny caught sight of the marker that indicated the depot 700 miles from Scott Base. Contact was soon made with Scott Base to advise Ed Hillary that weather permitting he could now join them for the rest of the journey down off the Plateau through the Skelton Glacier, along the circuitous route that would eventually bring them back to Scott Base and the end of their historic journey. The date was now 7 February 1958 and since leaving the Pole they had averaged nearly 55 miles a day.

Scott Base was experiencing some poor flying weather and Bunny acknowledged this, explaining that once his vehicles were all back together and checked over, they would resume their journey in the hope that Hillary would be able to track them down once he could get into the air and help them through what was probably the most difficult part of the way, getting down the Skelton Glacier. Two days were spent at the depot and just as the convoy was about to get underway to the Midway Depot, John Claydon brought the Beaver into land with Ed Hillary on board.

The route north now led them further across the Plateau and every mile covered brought them lower and lower in altitude. They were down to 7,500 feet by the time they reached the Midway Depot. Now that Ed Hillary was with them, travelling in the leading Sno-Cat, they were pursuing the route he had pioneered on his way south over 10 weeks earlier.

Mechanical problems continually dogged the team and one after the other of the Sno-Cats gave them trouble. Perseverance was the name of the game but at least they were making up the ground that had been lost in the run to the South Pole. They had now been on the (non-existent) road for 25 days and had covered just over 700 miles, or nearly 29 miles per day. A whiteout enshrouded them for three days but still they headed northwards and on 22 February the first mountains marking the edge of the Plateau could be seen on the distant horizon. The next depot came into view as they followed a line of cairns that had been set up by the New Zealand scouting party. To cap a good day's run, the expedition planes flew in to welcome them to the depot. From this depot, Ken Blaiklock and Jon Stephenson would complete the crossing aboard one of the aircraft, to be reunited with their dogs. This came as a relief to the two men as they had been cooped up in the back of the Sno-Cats since leaving the South Pole. Riding in cramped conditions amongst all the impedimenta that formed the necessary baggage which couldn't be stored on the sledges. This had proved to be a stressful experience, especially when compared to the total freedom they had enjoyed driving the dog teams from South Ice.

The descent of the Skelton Glacier began shortly after leaving the Plateau Depot and although a strong Katabatic wind followed them down most of the way, causing the Sno-Cat cabs to become very cold and blocked up with driven snow, it was a problem they endured, knowing that to stop would not help matters. They passed

Mount Huggins, which had been successfully climbed by Richard Brooks and Bernie Gunn on 23 January. The Skelton Glacier took them just three days to negotiate and the depot stores at its base were taken aboard ready for the last leg of 180 miles to Scott Base.

The best day's travel was achieved as the Sno-Cats sped across the Barrier on the last part of their epic voyage, clocking a magnificent 75 miles. They camped on what was to be the last night of the crossing within easy driving distance of Scott Base.

A whole armada of assorted vehicles streamed out of the New Zealand and American bases to welcome them. There was even an impromptu band. Everybody was armed with cameras and the icing on Bunny's cake was a telegram from the Queen bestowing upon him a knighthood.

The prophesied completion time of 100 days was bettered by one day, the difference being the actual date set to arrive at Scott Base; instead of the end of January, they actually completed the crossing on 2 March, about five weeks later than planned. The expedition ship had waited patiently for them. They arrived in New Zealand on 17 March to a tumultuous reception – and that would be repeated all the way back to London.

A few statistics about the travelling times achieved by both halves of the expedition, and a brief comparison to Scott. Scott took 77 days to reach the Pole, all of it on foot. Ed Hillary was on the road for 82 days, 18 of these he was waiting at the various depots for them to be established by the supporting planes. Bunny took a total of 99 days to complete the crossing from Shackleton to Scott Base but only 37 of these days to get from the South Pole to Scott Base.

With hindsight, Scott's achievement stands up well against the New Zealand party's performance – who of course had tracked vehicles – and Roald Amundsen's, who completed his journey from the Bay of Whales to the Pole in 57 days but used dogs and sledges all the way. Amundsen travelled about 60 miles fewer each way than either Scott or Hillary because of his starting point being that much farther south. That geographical advantage had proved the deciding factor in the first 'Race to the Pole'.

New Zealand's Other Target – IGY Exploration

There were to be three main subsidiary expeditions carried out while the New Zealanders were in the Antarctic. Two of the parties consisted of two men and their dog teams and the third one had a four-man contingent, also accompanied by dogs.

The Northern Journey, as it became known, was carried out by Guyon Warren and Bernie Gunn, both geologists, accompanied by Murray Douglas and the leader of the group, Richard Brooke. Brooke was the only English member of the party but he was also the most experienced having spent two years on the Greenland Ice Cap. On 4 October 1957 they set out from Scott Base and travelled northwards along the coastal ice and then found a route inland towards Mount Newall, where at 7,000 feet they established a survey point. The overall plan was to survey an area about 200 miles long by 100 miles wide from the coastal strip up onto the Plateau and then turn south to be picked up from the Skelton Depot that had been established by Hillary at the foot of the Skelton Glacier. They reached the depot on 6 February, four months after setting out from Scott Base the previous October. During this time they had received several supply drops. No major accidents had occurred, although there were several narrow escapes from falls and crevasses. The four men and their faithful dogs had covered more than 1,000 miles and surveyed topologically and geologically nearly 20,000 square miles of unknown territory.

Harry Ayres and Roy Carlyon who had travelled up to Depot 480 teamed up for what became known as the Darwin Journey. To help them with their sledge loads they had an advance depot laid down about 75 miles from their starting point near to Westhaven Nunatak. This would be on their route to the Darwin Glacier, where they were to carry out surveying and taking geological samples. They made excellent time to reach the Nunatak and here they establish a round of angles to start the survey.

The next surveying point was on Mount Longhurst; but before reaching the mountain they had to deal with what was potentially one of the most serious accidents to befall any of the parties throughout the whole expedition. In its own way, it exceeded even the spectacular crevasse incidents that befell Bunny's Sno-Cats. Skiing alongside the leading sledge, Harry Ayres was just quick enough to throw himself forward to land on the lip of an unseen crevasse that had opened up as the dogs and sledge were crossing. Looking back, he saw the whole sledging unit disappear into the yawning gap that had been revealed with the collapse of the snow bridge.

His companion Roy Carlyon was soon on the scene and together they assessed the situation. The loaded sledge had come to rest across the crevasse several metres down and the dogs had fallen farther, restrained by their harnesses. The first priority was to rescue the nine dogs. Their combined weight being in the region of 750lbs, it was an impossible task to pull them all up at once so after securing the sledge against it falling any further Harry was lowered down until he reached the first two dogs. Slipping a rope through each dogs harness in turn and then releasing them from the sledge's trace the dogs were pulled to the surface by Roy.

Harry then descended deeper into the crevasse to where he could retrieve four more of the terrified animals. Each one was hauled out independently. The crevasse narrowed as he went deeper and deeper. With six dogs now saved, he again ventured down into the depths to try and find the three dogs that had fallen out of their traces. Due to the fact that the crevasse did not go straight down but slanted off at an angle Harry was not able to see the top once he had been lowered beneath the bend in the wall. When he reached the bottom, that he estimated was about 70 feet deep, the next two dogs which had survived the fall had to be carried by him one at a time whilst climbing up the rope to the obstruction before they could be hoisted out. Imagine trying to climb up a rope with a wriggling dog that weighed between 70 and 80lbs under one arm. Sadly, the last dog had died as a result of its fall.

This rescue operation had taken a large part of the day and now there was still the sledge and its load to retrieve. By now they were exhausted but could not rest until they had the tent and some food salvaged from the sledge. Finally the tent was released and together with a stove and a few supplies they were able to refresh themselves and get a few hours rest. The next day they carried on unloading the sledge being careful not to drop anything else into the abyss. The relief that they must have felt can only be imagined because they were completely on their own and there was no way they could have called for help, as even the radio was down in the crevasse on the sledge. Having retrieved all their belongings they set about stowing all the essential safety items onto the second sledge, reasoning that the first one was the most likely to be at risk of falling into a crevasse.

The most direct comparison to this event – and sheer bad luck in sensibly keeping essentials out of the leading sledge – happened on an expedition being carried out by the Australian explorer Douglas Mawson. He and two companions were sledging across King George Land in 1912. He was leading on the day in question when suddenly he heard a shout from Mertz, who was second in the group, calling him to come quickly as there was no sign of Ninnis and his sledge, who were the back markers. The events that followed are some of the most tragic in the annals of Antarctic exploration. Briefly, Ninnis had disappeared down an extremely deep crevasse and despite all the efforts of Mawson and Mertz they could not get any response to their calls and apart from an injured dog more than 150 feet below on a ledge, they could see nothing of the sledge or its driver, nor did they have the means of descending the vast chasm to such a depth to attempt a rescue that in their hearts they knew would be abortive. Mawson had reasoned that the first sledge would be the one most at risk and when Ninnis and his team disappeared forever, most of their food, the major part of their camping equipment and other vital supplies went down with it, leaving the two survivors with the task of trying to retrace their steps for over 100 miles to get back to the safety of their hut. Further disasters lay in wait as they turned for home but for these you need to read Douglas Mawson's book *The Home of the Blizzard*.

The remainder of the trip held no further terrors for Carlyon and Ayres, although their sense of apprehension was always heightened as they approached a crevassed area. Various mountains were ascended for the first time to achieve a thorough survey of this portion of the Plateau and its attendant glacier system. One final challenge faced them, the descent of the Darwin Glacier down onto the Ross Ice Shelf. After that it would be the luxury of a flight back to Scott Base. One of the New Zealand pilots, Bill Cranfield, had expressed a wish to accompany Ayres and Carlyon on this last leg down the glacier and the two Darwin men appreciated the help that he and Selwyn Bucknall, who also came along, would be able to give them in getting the dogs and sledges past any of the obstructions such as ice falls that they were likely to encounter. Cranfield and Bucknall were flown in to the top of the glacier using the Beaver and arrived on 14 January. The four men needed to complete the descent in time to be picked up by the plane so that they could get back to Scott Base in time to catch the American ship that was going to leave McMurdo Sound on 25 January. All went well and they arrived three days early. As with the Northern group, they had covered an enormous area and surveyed something like 10,000 square miles in six weeks.

The last remaining pair were Bob Miller and George Marsh who, it will be remembered, had travelled on south ahead of the tractor party to reach Depot 700 on 14 December. The two-man team had to wait for the plane to bring in a top-up of dog pemmican before they could start their final exploration of the year. By 19 December they were itching to get away and with their extra supplies now loaded onto the sledges, they could finally depart. It had been arranged that the Beaver would seek them out in a few days' time to bring additional stores for their trip towards the mountainous kingdom of the Beardmore Glacier. The Beaver with Cranfield at the controls made the pre-arranged rendezvous just two days into the trip towards the glacier and it would stretch to the limit the capacity of both men and their dogs to carry forward such a large load, now nearly a ton. But at least it would give them ample supplies to keep them in the field for a longer period, which is exactly what they wanted.

They celebrated Christmas Day 1957 far away from any other human beings. On the previous evening they had enjoyed a radio transmission aimed especially at all the explorers taking part in this epic expedition. The message had been sent to them from Radio New Zealand. It had made the distance from home seem much shorter than it was.

Boxing Day found the two dog teams again underway headed towards a range of mountains that were named after Queen Elizabeth. Distances to faraway landmarks were regularly underestimated and 5 miles would soon become 15 as they travelled towards their targets. The clarity of the air high up on the plateau played games with them time and again in this respect.

The survey continued at every point they stopped and when the chance came to do some geological work on any exposed rock, it was taken. At one camping site the chance came to set up a survey station but it entailed leaving the dogs in camp and going forward on foot, backpacking all the necessary equipment to carry out the survey and tackling any climbing they might have to do thus encumbered. By the time they arrived back at their tent they had been away for 17 hours and had covered nearly 30 miles on foot. This was typical of the enthusiasm displayed by all the teams. The weather generally speaking had been very good and none of the three groups had lost much time.

Of the three exploring parties out in the field that summer, Miller and Marsh certainly carried out the most comprehensive survey, but on 7 January their freedom was curtailed by a request from Ed Hillary to get back to Depot 700 by 16 January at the latest to help unload some extra drums of fuel that he wanted to put there to assist Bunny when he arrived. The Sno-Cats were using more petrol than at first estimated and the margin for error was becoming rather narrow. This request meant that Miller and Marsh would have to turn back to Depot 700 sooner than they had planned. It entailed a long haul back of over 200 miles. They arrived a day late, which was a magnificent effort. Both the Beaver and the Otter – that had flown over from Shackleton Base on its epic transcontinental flight from South Ice back in December 1957 – brought in the extra fuel drums.

Miller and Marsh were not content to rest on their laurels and decided to retrace their route all the way back to the Skelton Depot, 550 miles north. Even after arriving at this point they disregarded an offer to fly them out and take them back to Scott Base. After a couple of days to recuperate at the Skelton Depot they set off once more, this time heading for Scott Base, where they arrived on 23 February. During this epic sledging trip the two men heard the welcome news that the crossing party had firstly reached Depot 700 and then subsequently arrived at Depot 480.

In all, Bob Miller and George Marsh had covered an estimated 1,700 miles since leaving the depot at the bottom of the Skelton Glacier as far back as the second week of October the previous year. During this period they had been responsible for the reconnoitring of the whole route to Depot 700 and subsequently surveyed the mountainous area situated between the Beardmore Glacier and the Shackleton Inlet for the first time. During this survey the two men were able to position accurately many of the prominent mountainous peaks that had originally been seen by the expeditions of Scott and Shackleton, including the then highest known peak, Mount Markham. They estimated this mountain to be in the region of 4,570 metres high. Mount Kirkpatrick nearby is 4,530 metres and several others in that range can claim to be over 4,000 metres. Not yet discovered at this point was the Vinson Massif, which measured an impressive 4,900 metres and would eventually be located overlooking the Ronne Ice Shelf. Erebus could only claim to be a disappointing 3,795 metres!

Conclusion

The final outcome of the project was an undoubted, essentially bi-national success and credit must be given to all those involved in the planning, administration and most importantly to the men on the ground who carried out the onerous task of overcoming the multitude of obstacles that assailed them.

We have seen how from the very beginning the first task force that went down in the *Theron* had to battle through almost impossible ice conditions and consequently was so late arriving at the base site. This delay had a domino effect on the next phase of erecting the hut at Shackleton, when eight men were left with the body- and soul-destroying work load of putting together a complicated structure whilst being storm-bound for days at a time in their wooden crate and four small tents. Against all the odds and despite losing a large proportion of their stores as the ice shelf broke away, they completed the shell of the hut and even managed to move into it before the relief column arrived nearly 12 months later.

At the start of the second season, one of the most difficult decisions was how to allocate the very limited work force to complete the various tasks in time for a start to be made on the actual crossing. The stationing of three men at South Ice reduced the manning level at the main base camp, Shackleton, to 13. Of these, three were responsible for the flying and maintenance of the two aircraft. As the weather improved it was always hoped that the men who would be the key members of the crossing group could be given some field experience prior to the final departure. This didn't happen to the extent that had been hoped. Apart from a couple of short journeys using the dog teams and the stocking up of South Ice, most of the men were fully employed coping with everyday tasks and keeping a full scientific record. The two engineers in the group grappled manfully with the backlog of work to get the vehicles into some sort of order prior to the exploratory run across the mountainous territory that lay between Shackleton and South Ice. It would often be the case that they found themselves trying to carry out restorative work on the fleet of snow vehicles that should have been carried out back in the UK.

This work was to prove too much and when departure time arrived for the pioneering task force to set out, the first major breakdown occurred only a few miles into the journey when one of the Weasels had to limp back to Shackleton for further repairs. In fact, of the four tractor units that set out, only two eventually arrived at South Ice, although one of the two Weasels was salvaged in time for the main push to the South Pole.

Four men were delegated to carry out some geological field work while the first convoy was reconnoitring through the mountains and this left just six others to complete all the work ready for the final push. They were undermanned. No margin of error seems to have been allowed for and, in reality, the budget was too tight. Only an enterprise such as the one that the Americans were carrying out had the finances and reserves of manpower that enabled them to ride out any trials and tribulations.

One of the factors that had an immeasurably beneficial effect on the Commonwealth's crossing of the continent was the positioning of three American bases that coincidentally found themselves at strategic points along the way. The American presence in the Antarctic at the same time as the TAE took place was because of their participation in the International Geophysical Year. The Americans had six bases altogether on the continent, but the three crucial to the TAE were McMurdo Sound, the terminus of the TAE, the Scott/Amundsen Base at the South Pole and – to a lesser extent – Ellsworth Station, about 40 miles to the West of Shackleton. This was a fortunate situation, which Bunny Fuchs and to a greater extent Ed Hillary were able to avail themselves of – and at no extra cost.

Throughout the narrative there are a number of references to the American's willingness to assist in any way they could. The first offer of help came when the New Zealand Committee needed to send down a team of three men to search out a suitable base site and a possible route up onto the Plateau. The Americans were using New Zealand as a staging post for supplying their station at McMurdo and it was because of the frequent air and naval shuttle service that the three New Zealanders found an easy way to reach Antarctica in 1955. The hosts provided for their every need, flying them to the suggested new base site at Butter Point and taking them firstly to the Ferrar Glacier that had been suggested as the most promising route onto the Plateau and when this proved too difficult, flying Ed Hillary to inspect the Skelton Glacier as an alternative.

The following year when the main group were setting sail in the *Endeavour* they had to rely on the Americans to bring down the stores that their ship could not hold. The assistance did not stop there because when Hillary and his men arrived in Antarctic waters they found the sea ice keeping them from reaching their destination. The Americans despatched their ice breaker to force a passage through towards Butter Point and when this base site and the glacial route proved unsuitable, more help came: first, flying Ed Hillary to check out other areas and second, once the new site had been chosen, using the ice breaker to make a way through for the *Endeavou*r to get to within working distance of Hut Point. Once unloading had started the American cargo ship that had brought down the extra supplies was also guided into place so that she could be unloaded.

More help was made available in the form of several helicopter trips to search out a different glacier for the polar route. The unstinting assistance given by the commander of the American Station, Rear Admiral Dufek, at this early stage of the expedition enabled the New Zealand team to get established early enough to be able to build their hut complex and complete a series of exploratory trips to gain vital experience of their new environment.

As the New Zealand project to lay down depots for Bunny Fuchs came to a conclusion and Ed Hillary had decided that he would push on to the South Pole, it must have occurred to him that he would need help to ferry him and his men back to Scott Base at some stage. He knew that Bunny was still a considerable way short of completing the first leg of the crossing, so waiting at the Pole was not an option. If his tractor party had got into difficulties after they left Depot 700, any assistance was unlikely to come from his own men, who were all away exploring; and the distance from Scott Base was too far for his own planes to retrieve the group. There is no mention of this in Hillary's book, but rescue is a very serious matter especially in the Antarctic, and he probably knew he could always ask the Americans for their help.

Four of the five New Zealanders were flown back to Scott Base after their successful completion of the last 500 miles to the Pole from Depot 700 and the Americans obliged again when they flew Ed Hillary once more to the Pole to meet up with Bunny. Not only that, they then took him back to McMurdo Sound together with the two teams of dogs that had completed their own pathfinder mission from South Ice ahead of Bunny and his Sno-Cats.

Bunny and the crossing party had a four-day break at the Pole Station courtesy of generous American hospitality. This help became a matter of life and death when they resumed their journey and Geoffrey Pratt was overcome by carbon monoxide poisoning some 200 miles north of the South Pole. Getting him down off the Plateau was not a possibility but supplies of oxygen might just save him. The gas cylinders were dropped by parachute as the Americans could not land in the vicinity of the British camp site. Another instance of American generosity came during the attempt to fly the single-engined Otter from South Ice across the continent to Scott Base in one hop. The first attempt was thwarted due to bad weather part the way into the journey but on retracing their flight path and landing back at South Ice, the crew knew the only spare fuel they had was back at Shackleton and to get it would take up most of that supply, rendering the exercise pointless. The Americans stepped in and flew the four crucial barrels of aviation fuel up to South Ice. Several days later as the weather gave them a window of opportunity the four-man crew took to the air and eleven hours later landed the Otter safely at Scott base on the Ross Sea.

Adaptation to changes in circumstances was the key to success and it is worth recalling briefly some of the instances that took place during this epic voyage.

The eight men left to build the base hut at Shackleton surmounted all that the weather could throw at them and despite losing a huge proportion of the stores that had been landed, managed to survive by working as a team under the leadership of Ken Blaiklock who never really received the praise that should have been his by right. The two engineers plugged away at the task of readying all the vehicles working in sub-zero temperatures. They did not have the luxury of heated workshops, as the Americans had at their stations. The ingenuity of all the team out on the trail retrieving Sno-Cats and Weasels from dangerous situations as they came close to losing them in crevasses is best appreciated by viewing some of the photographs that were taken. The two pilots carried out a number of landings in circumstances that required determination and a very steady hand on the controls. They also were responsible for the rescue of two men who had been exploring and were attempting to make their way back to South Ice in atrocious weather conditions, and the retrieval of the doctor and the other pilot when the Auster had to land in an unknown area when engaged on a mercy mission to Halley Bay. The New Zealand party had their share of daring and dangerous crevasse rescues where men, dogs and precious lifesaving equipment could have been lost. Their two pilots carried out an impressive number of flights and they never once lost control of the situations they found themselves in, landing and taking off from some of the remotest spots on earth to bring in the vital stores that the men on the ground required.

Most of the expeditions that had preceded the TAE and the IGY had elements of scientific research built into them, but exploration of a geographic nature prevailed. However after these two great events in the history of Antarctica, the momentum towards scientific research accelerated. Many of the bases that had been set up by the participating countries during the IGY were maintained and other countries contributed to the international effort once the Antarctic Treaty was formulated and subsequently ratified.

All of a sudden there were so many questions. The discovery that the ozone layer, the protective mantle surrounding the Earth against the harmful effects of ultra violet rays, was disintegrating due to the use of aerosol propellant gases and the damaging influence of greenhouse gases such as carbon dioxide contributing towards climate warming has led to numerous international environmental conferences to try and limit the use of fossil fuels. Scientific teams in Antarctica are currently studying the structure of the ice cap and its surrounding ice shelves. Several of these have recently broken away from the continental land mass and the long-term effects of these dramatic occurrences is causing alarm.

The ice itself is a history book containing evidence of what has taken place on Earth over thousands of years. To gain access to this information, engineers have developed drilling machines that can penetrate through the thousands of metres of ice and withdraw ice cores. These cores consist of annual layers of accumulated snow that when cut into thin slices and looked at under special microscopes can reveal fluctuations in the Earth's climate. The closest analogy to this process is dendrology, the examination of tree rings. Captured in the ice as each annual layer accumulates are minute particles of atmospheric dust, pollen and microbiological spores present in the atmosphere when precipitation took place. The snowfall each year becomes compressed and turns into ice. Gradually the air trapped in the snow together with the particles is carried deeper and deeper into the ice cap. The samples obtained from the drilling operations enable the scientists to uncover the story of what has happened to the Earth down through the centuries.

This international co-operation will hopefully be the springboard to a much wider effort on the part of governments to reduce the damage of climate change. If the political will of countries can be channelled towards a mutual goal in preserving our environment, then the lives that have been sacrificed on the altar of exploration will not have been in vain.

Throughout the whole of the TAE not one man and only (but still tragically) a couple of dogs were lost. This alone speaks volumes for the tenacity and bravery of all the men attempting what Sir Ernest Shackleton considered the last great journey in the world.

Appendix I
The Americans in Antarctica

American exploration in Antarctica can be traced back to 1839 when they sent an expedition under the command of Lieutenant Charles Wilkes. The findings of this early foray into the frozen seas that surrounded the mysterious new continent were allowed to gather dust for nearly a century before the next official American expedition set sail. There were, of course, many hundreds of American whaling and sealing trips in between. Exploration was only entered into with a view to exploiting the natural resources of the sea and the beaches that bordered it. In fact, any discoveries that were made were mostly kept under wraps for fear that other captains and their crews would steal a march and make off with the spoil of lucrative cargoes of seal pelts or the valuable oil that could be procured from the whales and sea lions that were so abundant when the industry was at its height.

In 1928 the first flight took place in the Antarctic regions when Hubert Wilkins flew from Deception Isle in the South Shetland archipelago. Then in 1930 Richard Evelyn Byrd led an American expedition down to the Ross Sea and established his base in the Bay of Whales.

Although the expedition was privately funded, it was intended to demonstrate that they wanted a share of the continent in competition with the other countries that had already marked out the ground. America, in the end, never formally annexed any of Antarctica – nor did she recognise any other state's declarations.

Byrd's base was called Little America and was to be followed by at least three other expeditions in subsequent years, all with the same name but with 2, 3 or 4 added as a suffix. This series of expeditions was to take place over the next 27 years and culminate in the American participation in the 1957/58 IGY.

The total money raised for the 1930 expedition was in the order of $800,000 and this was sufficient to send down two ships, three planes, 76 men and 150 dogs for two seasons.

The highlight of the expedition was the first flight to the South Pole and back. Byrd and two others flew a tri-motored Ford monoplane they christened the Floyd Bennett. This was in memory of Byrd's friend and pilot of the plane that flew him over the North Pole in 1927. By reaching the South Pole as well, Byrd became the first man in history to fly over both the geographic Poles. Floyd Bennett had died of pneumonia contracted prior to attempting to fly from Europe to Canada in 1928. He had insisted he felt well enough to tackle the flight. The co-pilot Bernt Balchen took over the controls. This same man was at the controls of the Ford plane that flew Byrd to the South Pole.

In 1933 the Americans were again headed for the Bay of Whales and again their leader was to be Richard Byrd. Two ships ferried them south for another two seasons. On board were three planes and an autogyro. This was the forerunner to the helicopter; as with most of the expeditions that ventured south, Byrd was keen to experiment with new technology. Further evidence of his willingness to experiment was the inclusion of several vehicles, the most successful of which were three Citroen trucks fitted with tracks. They gave a good account of themselves and paved the way for the larger tracked Weasels and Sno-Cats that Bunny Fuchs and others used in subsequent expeditions. Another tractor made by the Cleveland Tractor Company and named the Cletrac was taken down, partly as an experiment but mainly because there just wasn't really a lot of choice. It weighed an impressive six tons and it could carry a load of between three to five tons depending on the cargo. Despite the leaning towards motorised transport, Byrd also took a large number of dogs knowing that without them he would be blocked if conditions did not favour vehicles. Dog teams made trips as far as the extremity of the Ross Ice Shelf, some 400 miles away from base camp and the aircraft were used to explore mainly westward across the mountainous interior of Marie Byrd Land.

About 120 miles directly south of Little America, Byrd decided to set up a weather station to be manned on a permanent basis by two men. Owing to a shortfall of supplies arriving before winter set in, he made the decision that he would stay in the camp alone. His decision nearly resulted in his own death from carbon monoxide poisoning and it was only the prompt action of his fellow explorers that saved his life. They detected that his radio messages were becoming more and more garbled and that led to a rescue mission being mounted. He had been alone from 28 March until the relief column finally managed to get through on 10 August. The rescuers had been trying since mid-July to force a way across the ice shelf but bad luck and the weather hampered all previous attempts. The fumes from the generator were building up in the close confines of the cabin which had been sunk below the snow's surface, gradually poisoning Byrd.

Two members of this expedition were to become prominent in 1957 when the IGY took place. Both men became well known in the world of polar exploration in their own right. Paul Siple became leader of the Scott/Amundsen Base for a while and Finn Ronne commanded the Ellsworth Station.

In 1939 Germany announced its intention of sending an exploratory party down to the Antarctic. This, together with Norway trying to forestall the German's intentions by declaring its own claim to a sector of the continent, focused the attention of the United States on the fact that soon there would not be any of Antarctica left to lay claim to.

During the latter half of 1938 and the early part of 1939 the American president, Roosevelt, directed that various State departments should co-operate in planning an expedition to Antarctica. Soon a task force was being assembled. It would be comprised of two ships. These would carry up to 150 men and even more dogs, plus four planes. The initial budget of one million dollars did not seem to raise many eyebrows.

The middle of January 1940 saw the two ships edging towards the Antarctic coastline. They were once more headed to Byrd's old stamping ground, the Bay of Whales. The intention was to set up an East and West base. The East Base would be as far along the unexplored coast as could be safely reached before winter set in and in fact the ships actually managed to reach Marguerite Bay. It was here that the Australian, John Rymill, who had led the British Graham Land Expedition four years before, had established his southern base. So now the whole coast of Antarctica had been circumnavigated but as yet not fully surveyed. West Base was to occupy the site of both former American expeditions and be built in the Bay of Whales. This time it would become Little America 3.

The success of establishing their base in Marguerite Bay was short-lived. Apart from several flights using the amphibious planes giving the crews tantalising views of unknown territory, the enterprise was swiftly curtailed in the spring of 1941. It had become evident that America had other things to think about.

On the cessation of hostilities America started looking to her northern borders on the Arctic Ocean and realised that any new military threat would probably come from that direction. A start was made to carry out military manoeuvres in the Arctic but it was soon realised that these would be seen as a provocative move by the Russians. Polar warfare could be a reality at some time in the future and a major training programme was seen to be essential for the defence of the country. So the Americans turned to the Antarctic, which would provide an ideal alternative theatre. Operation High Jump took shape.

There were to be three groups forming the task force, Central, Eastern and Western. The newly promoted Rear Admiral Cruzen had command of the Central group. His mission was to penetrate the pack ice of the Ross Sea using an ice breaker and then sail into the same area that the previous expeditions had used, the Bay of Whales. Here he was tasked with the job of establishing Little America 4, where they could construct a landing strip that could accommodate planes launched from the other transport ships. These were two armed merchant ships, an ex-command ship and surprisingly, a submarine. All of them had seen service during the war but none of the captains had ever seen sea ice, with the exception of the captain of the ice breaker.

The Eastern group was led by Captain Richard Dufek, one of Byrd's men from Little America 3 days. His brief was to launch sea planes out over the continental coastal strip that had been observed from the decks of the accompanying ships and from the planes that had been used during the 1940 expedition that had reached Marguerite Bay.

The final squadron sailed further west and they too launched planes towards the stretch of coast that was probably the least-known part of the Antarctic seaboard. They covered about 1,000 miles of coast between the Shackleton Ice Shelf and Adélie Land, venturing about 100 miles inland for photographic reconnaissance.

History tells us that Admiral Byrd returned to Antarctica during this expedition to supervise the photo-mapping of the vast area that surrounded the Ross Ice Shelf, but he probably did more than this. He arrived on the scene at the point where the ice was causing the head of the Central Group to question the viability of keeping men and ships in this increasingly threatening environment. Even with the assistance of the ice breaker, the convoy had been struggling for several weeks even to break though and the thought of being caught in the ice as it refroze in what could be days caused Cruzen to radio that he thought it would be prudent to retreat while they could. This prompted Richard Byrd to intervene and carry out his air survey slightly earlier than planned. As a result the Central Group were encouraged to fulfil their task and with the aid of additional air support finally made it through to establish Little America 4.

Before long however, the Ross Sea would become frozen once more and the ships would have to beat a hasty retreat. Byrd and Cruzen would part company. While Richard Byrd remained with the aircraft and their ground and air crews to carry out a photo survey of the entire region, Richard Crozen would make good his escape using his ships as weather stations for the flying activity once clear of the ice. Nearly 200 men would have to live out the next few weeks in a tent city that had been erected for them, as their relatively short stay did not justify building anything more substantial.

The task for Byrd and his men was, weather permitting, to use the nine planes and fan out to cover as much ground as possible. This was to be the largest air reconnaissance ever undertaken, eclipsing even the German effort just before the war.

A crucial objective was to try and establish whether or not a range of mountains actually spanned the continent. There were currently two schools of thought on this subject. Having considered the positions of the Weddell Sea and its counterpart on the other side of the continent, the Ross Sea, some geographers were of the opinion that the two seas could be linked. This would create two or more huge islands. A continuous range of mountains straddling the central part of the continent would more or less prove that they were wrong and that Antarctica was in fact one vast land mass.

Byrd's planes unfortunately did not have the range to fly across the continent to prove this point and it would eventually fall to the Trans-Antarctic Expedition led by Vivian Fuchs to establish beyond doubt that Antarctica was all one entity .

The full extent of what Byrd and his flyers achieved is beyond the scope of this book but some idea can be gained from the fact that an estimated 36,000 miles were covered in just two weeks of flying. On 23 February 1947 the ice breaker *Burton Island* forced her way through the now frozen Ross Sea and evacuated Byrd and all his men. They were forced to leave behind all the planes, as there was no possibility of them landing back on the decks of the ships they had flown from. Vehicles were also condemned to a frozen future but it was hoped that other expeditions visiting the area might be able to avail themselves of the equipment. In fact, the ice shelf calved and the whole lot disappeared with it, never to be seen again. So ended 'Operation High Jump' which had been the largest and by far the most expensive foray into the Antarctic ever.

There remained just one more expedition by the Americans before the TAE started its operations and that was Operation Deep Freeze. Preliminary work started in 1954 when the ice breaker *Atka* set sail. She arrived at the famous ice cliffs of the Ross Ice Shelf in the middle of January 1955. After some preliminary work near the Bay of Whales where they discovered the loss of the equipment left behind in 1947, the ship set out eastwards to sail halfway round the continent looking for suitable sites on which they could establish landing strips for the aircraft that they later planned to use. They even penetrated into the Weddell Sea but due to damage to one of the ship's two propellers, they did not linger too long for fear of getting trapped by the ice.

The following year another ice breaker, the *Glacier*, with Admiral Dufek on board, completed the circumnavigation of Antarctica, this time sailing westwards from the Bay of Whales. The results of this survey gave the Americans a complete picture of the coastal fringes. From this they were able to position their IGY stations at the most advantageous places for supply and support.

Eventually, six stations would be developed for the IGY. Each one was to have a senior scientist and a naval officer, one of whom would be in charge; but both men were to work as a team where possible to avoid friction. The exception turned out to be Ellsworth station. This was the one nearest to Shackleton and here Finn Ronne would take sole command. The scientists at this station finished up fighting a running battle with him because they felt it was not their job to carry out camp duties and this led to a fractious encampment.

For the Americans, McMurdo Sound was to be pivotal as the main point of entry for stores, men and equipment entering the continent. Compressed snow runways were constructed to take the large cargo planes coming in from New Zealand. Ships could also be unloaded from the edge of the ice shelf. The South Pole Station was built entirely from material ferried by the cargo planes across the icy wastes of the Ross Ice Shelf and on up the route of the Beardmore Glacier to continue their flight across the barren, almost featureless Polar Plateau. Of course no planes could land at the Pole initially and men and supplies had to be parachuted down to begin the task of constructing the essential runway that would allow further supplies to be transported from McMurdo. All this took time, but with the might of the USA behind it the air corridor was soon buzzing with activity and within the few short months of the Antarctic summer the task was complete and ready for IGY to begin in 1957.

Appendix II
Books about the Expedition

Several references to the book by George Lowe, *Because It Is There*, have been made in this narrative but an elaboration on what has already been mentioned is necessary. The book was published in 1959. This could not have pleased the London Committee, which was responsible for the publicity side of the expedition and of course the finances. Any publication that covered the story too soon after the event would be considered as competition to the official book by Fuchs and Hillary and might have contravened that individual's contract with the expedition. The earliest date for publication was three years after 1 March 1958 and anything before that date would be required to pay a percentage of the royalties earned. The money would have to be paid into the Expedition's fund.

The first few chapters cover some of the time he spent with the Everest expedition of 1952 to 1953. However much of the rest of the book deals with his first year's journey down to the Antarctic to establish the advance base and then the author's return for the second season and stay for the duration of the expedition as official photographer all the way to Scott Base in March 1958.

George Lowe wrote about the three leaders with whom he explored. John Hunt, later Sir John, on the Everest expedition, Ed Hillary, later Sir Edmund, and Vivian Fuchs. As the *Theron* made her way back to civilisation he had time to assess the third leader he served under, Bunny Fuchs who received his knighthood after the TAE expedition. George had been watching an arm wrestling bout between Bunny and one of the strongest Norwegian sailors. The ward room was strangely quiet as the two men started and for over a minute they strained against one another to get an advantage and to everyone's amazement, it was Bunny who succeeded. George noticed that Bunny was so competitive in everything he undertook, doing more press-ups than others who liked to keep in trim. At 50 years old, Bunny pushed himself to his limit and so it was with everything to do with the expedition.

Both Bunny and John Hunt were ranking army officers and they tended to deal with problems in a similar way, but whereas Bunny allowed his rank more or less to fade into the background during the expedition, John Hunt still brought a military presence to bear on his way of doing things. The major difference that George Lowe detected was that the other members of the TAE would follow where Bunny led but at times felt resentful that their opinions seemed to be ignored. The Everest team held their leader in great respect and always knew that he could be approached without that feeling of superiority being wielded over them. Ed Hillary had learned a lot from his trip south and when the time came for him to organise his own side of the expedition, he went about it in a very practical way and, where possible, he involved all the other men in the decision-making process. When change was suggested, he took any better ideas forward because he knew that it was teamwork that would get them through.

So in the order mentioned above, Sir John was firm but adaptable, Ed Hillary tried to be flexible and resourceful and Bunny was forceful and decisive. *Because It Is There* reflects on a variety of subjects that most of the other contemporary books about the expedition fail to take into account and as a result the details tend to be more rounded rather than just statements of fact.

Anthea Arnold's book is based on the diaries of Rainer Goldsmith, the expedition's doctor, who travelled down in the *Theron* and stayed with the advance party for the first winter and then returned to England in the *Magga Dan*. The book is appropriately called *Eight Men in a Crate*.

Rainer Goldsmith was born in pre-war Germany of Jewish parents who had fled to England before the war. He had had the benefit of a good education and afterwards attended Cambridge University before qualifying as a doctor at St Bartholemew's

Hospital, where he had studied physiology. Rainer had never been on an expedition when he volunteered but it is a good guess that at his interview Vivian Fuchs saw in him something of himself: German parentage, Cambridge, and the need to prove himself. Perhaps the leader could give this young doctor the same chance he had received from James Wordie all those years before.

Twenty-eight years old when chosen for the expedition, Rainer Goldsmith was one of the younger members but he was observant enough to see that there were things going on he had serious concerns about. He had no expeditionary experience, let alone any in the Antarctic, but as the expedition unfolded he found himself questioning decisions and practices and wondering how so many mistakes could occur. He considered some of the remedies that were applied to be worse than the original errors.

The period spent by the advance party during those fraught and at times dangerous months they were alone has only the diaries of Rainer Goldsmith as a personal record. Anthea Arnold's book is as near to being a contemporary account as possible. Bunny Fuchs had to draw on the advance party's log book, member's diaries and field notes for the chapter in his book that covers this episode of the expedition.

After the landing had taken place and the unloading was in full swing, Goldsmith was astounded at the total chaos that reigned on the ice shelf:

> The lack of organisation caused chaos. Plans changed every minute. No one seemed to be fully in charge. They had been warned of the danger of leaving anything on bay ice, but, despite this by 3pm, when it began to snow and the wind blew harder from the north, there were great piles of stores lying not twenty five yards from the shore.

Goldsmith recalls his first impression of the base site on 6 February:

> How bleak it is ... the only feature an occasional small wave in the snow. In the far distance to the east, a ridge glints golden in the sun, where three bare patches of rock stand out like great scars in the hillside. Everything else is white and flat – not, on the face of it, an ideal spot to make a home.

Rainer's stay lasted just one week short of a year. His summary of the time spent at Shackleton:

> The year in that incomparable, stark, lonely white world has changed me. I don't think I am any longer the brash young doctor who went down there without a thought of his own worth or the worth of others. Whether I am better or worse for this experience I shall probably never know, but I am certainly different.

There are only a few other contemporary books written about the expedition. Bunny Fuchs's *The Crossing of Antarctica*, in which Ed Hillary contributed a couple of sections about the New Zealand component, is the standard work for those interested in the expedition as a whole but does not really bring much personal feeling. It has been well written in the sense that you do not need to be a polar buff to understand the story, but it should be read in conjunction with other books about events as they unfolded. An example of missing information is found at the end of Chapter 6, 'The Return to Shackleton'. Vivian Fuchs covers in a few short paragraphs the reunion of the main party returning to Shackleton Base with the eight men who had battled all winter to build the base hut under such dire conditions. You would think they had only been alone for a month at the most, so casually does the writer refer to the incident. Compare those sparse sentences with the pages devoted to the same event in George Lowe's book. Lowe brings to light the excitement of the eight refugees as they regale him with their stories and he watches them delve into the mail that has been brought to them by the plane ahead of the arrival of the *Magga Dan*.

Hillary's own story, *No Latitude for Error*, was written fairly soon after his return to New Zealand and like the volume by George Lowe it was probably published too soon after the publication of the official book by Fuchs and himself. It contravened the three-year embargo set out in the contract, although there is no record of any action being taken.

His position as leader of the New Zealand group naturally gave him an insight into the machinations in the background and this enabled him to fence off a lot of the criticism and back-seat advice that was being given by well-meaning committee members at home. His leadership was to come under increasing scrutiny as time went by, but overall, the passages in his book that cover any ruptures between him and his fellow expedition members, the New Zealand Committee or for that matter the expedition leader Bunny Fuchs, tend to minimise the frictions and it is only after reading other accounts that the rifts become apparent.

New Zealand had made the decision to incorporate a more scientific approach to the expedition than just laying out depots for the crossing party and Ed Hillary quickly saw the potential that the extra staff he took down with him could bring. Several times in his book he lays out various sets of plans for future exploration to take place using the depot-laying journey.

Once the *Endeavour* had arrived in McMurdo Sound and the original landing site and route onto the Plateau proved to be impractical, he had no qualms about taking up the offers of help that Admiral Dufek presented him with. In fact, throughout the expedition the relationship between the two men was so good that when Bunny Fuchs sought the American's help it was usually through Ed Hillary.

Right at the beginning of the planning stage Ed Hillary was thinking ahead, as shown by the training programme he initiated in the Southern Alps in New Zealand. Bunny placed his faith in taking down men who had previous polar experience and this followed a tradition amongst British exploring parties – but Ed Hillary actually gave most of his men a taste of what they might expect, quite a different thing.

Hillary put into place the modifications that were carried out on the Ferguson tractors. Initially he thought they would be useful carrying and fetching stores around the unloading area and he seems to have never really anticipated using them for the major part of the expedition; reaching and travelling across the Polar Plateau.

Quite naturally, Hillary wanted to write about his and his team's adventures so there are only passing references to the other half of the expedition, just enough to know they are still there. This is a very readable book and gives a detailed account of all that transpired throughout his half of the expedition but it does have to be put into context with what else went on during the four years that it took to complete the epic project.

The volume by A S Helm and J H Miller, is called simply *Antarctica*. This version also deals mainly with the New Zealand participation. Arthur Helm was secretary for the New Zealand organising committee and his co-author Bob Miller was Hillary's deputy.

New Zealand had a twin agenda when they agreed to assist the London Committee with the Ross Sea side of the main expedition. By establishing their base at McMurdo Sound they could implement the secondary side of their plan at the same time. Using the one base station but manning it with two teams of men who would be able to work together, the organising committee in New Zealand put together a very cleverly thought out strategy. Knowing from the start that they would be expected to furnish Bunny with backup depots to within 500 miles of the South Pole, they set about utilising these strategic depots to probe further afield with dog teams and explore a far greater area than would otherwise have been possible if their starting point had been Scott Base on McMurdo Sound.

Arthur Helm and Bob Miller have understandably incorporated all the relevant details for these extra trips into their book but not at the expense of enlarging on the actual crossing side of the expedition carried out by Bunny Fuchs. This part of the expedition had been adequately covered in Bunny Fuchs' book with Ed Hillary's chapters about the New Zealand contribution. Even these had been of a clipped nature to ensure that the book met the publisher's deadlines.

Helm and Miller's version of events is about the only book that incorporates all the exploring activity that took place in the New Zealand sector of Antarctica. Even Ed Hillary's own book skips the finer details of the IGY contingent, which is not surprising because he often found himself at odds with some members of the New Zealand party who were not very sympathetic to his motives for forcing a path through to the South Pole.

There are chapters on the historical background of New Zealand's involvement with not only the Trans-Antarctic Expedition but also the setting up of the International Geographical Year's experiments. Financing both projects became a very time consuming and expensive business and could only be accomplished with the New

Zealand Treasury's substantial help. Before they set out, many of the exploring party were co-opted into fund-raising events and most of the senior members carried out extensive lecturing engagements to help fill the coffers. All in all, Miller and Helm's book represents a comprehensive record of the whole enterprise from conception to completion and with a full evaluation of what took part.

Another volume covering mainly New Zealand's participation, *Opposite Poles*, was written by Douglas McKenzie. As described, he took part in the section of the Plateau journey driving one of the Ferguson tractors from Depot 480 to Depot 700. Noel Barber, the other newspaper correspondent, spent most of his time at the American Base at the South Pole where he could access messages being sent through their radio links with Bunny and Ed Hillary and also at the American's other base at McMurdo Sound. *The Times* newspaper in London had exclusive rights to the expedition's news but both Barber and McKenzie circumvented this by being in situ as events took place and there was little that the organisers in London could do to stop this activity. Noel Barber's book was called *The White Desert*. It would appear that the public were more influenced by these two reporters than by the information emanating from the official source, *The Times*; probably because of the restricted and circumspect data made available by the expedition itself during that crucial stage when Bunny was concentrating on breaking through to South Ice and then grinding his way to the South Pole. At no stage did *The Times* have one of their own journalists accompany the expedition. They relied upon communiqués being passed to them from Bunny or his deputy.

Crevasse Roulette was written by the Australian participant Jon Stephenson who was a young, newly qualified geologist. He went south on the *Magga Dan*, arriving at the base camp on 13 January 1957 and stayed for the rest of the expedition including the actual crossing of the continent until being airlifted out with Ken Blaiklock from the Plateau Depot at the head of the Skelton Glacier. His book was written 50 years after the expedition. It was based on his own notes and diaries written at the time of his involvement. There is ample evidence in his references to other people's work, judging by the extensive bibliography, to show how he carefully compiled the story he tells. This observation is not a criticism, on the contrary, it shows to what lengths he went to ensure memories of his own experiences fitted in with the overall picture that others remembered.

Jon Stephenson was to be the sole Australian member of either component of the expedition, but this did not dismay him as he took to exploring and dog driving like a penguin to water. Once the unloading of the *Magga Dan* was completed and the main base hut built and made fully functional, the next step was to create a satellite station about 300 miles inland for the purposes of reconnoitring further south to try and establish a route for the tractor caravan. He was chosen to be one of the three men to occupy the satellite hut and together with Ken Blaiklock and Hal Lister would remain in residence for the forthcoming winter and on into the next spring and early summer. During suitable breaks in the weather they were free to explore into the unknown area that surrounded them.

Jon Stephenson paints small cameos of his fellow explorers. Once unloading started at Shackleton, Stephenson was given the job of driving the Muskeg tractor. It would appear that he had probably never driven before because he had no idea of how to change gear, but this did not dismay him and soon he had mastered the art, as he would any other task given to him. The inland station of South Ice gave Jon Stephenson a fair degree of independence. The guiding hand of Ken Blaiklock, whom he grew to respect and like very much, would have a lasting effect on his overall impression of the expedition. Having seen distant mountains from the Otter that flew the men into South Ice, the spectacle began to dwell on his imagination and the time could not come soon enough for him to be able to investigate them. Jon and Ken nearly got more than they bargained for, resulting in a rescue operation that because of bad weather could have seen them in dire trouble. He recalls his reaction to being pulled to safety by the timely arrival of the plane as an instance that was bordering on emotional. Although Jon was not part of the New Zealand effort towards the TAE, their activities are recounted in his book and this gives a broader perspective to what was going on throughout the expedition as a whole.

The six months or so spent at South Ice were much more mundane with routine weather readings to take but Stephenson did have a project he could call his own. It involved the study of snow and ice samples taken from cores drilled down into the ice cap, sliced into thin sections and viewed through a microscope to reveal the texture and shape of the snow grains. It was cold work as he had to sit for long periods near the pit that had been dug to obtain the samples. The warmth of the hut would have soon ruined his samples so it was imperative to carry out his observations in the tunnel near his mining activity at below freezing temperatures.

Enforced isolation can play a significant part in the inter-relationships between individuals and this aspect would sooner or later come to the surface during their sojourn together; but the experienced duo of Ken Blaiklock and Hal Lister never allowed any disharmony to reach dangerous levels. Although Stephenson does refer to a period when he withdrew completely for a few days following some minor misunderstanding, the matter resolved itself without any long-lasting ill effects.

When the main thrust to cross the continent began on 24 November 1957 Stephenson was one of the members of the group who set out belatedly from Shackleton Base. The Muskeg tractor was allocated to his care and it was not long before the whole convoy was involved in the first major crevasse rescue. Stephenson has used some superb photographs to illustrate his book and one of the classics is the picture of that leading Sno-Cat perched perilously close to being swallowed by the yawning chasm of the enormous crevasse into which it had fallen.

He goes on to relate that once the crossing party had gathered together for the first time at South Ice, the decision was made that the two dog teams were to be the vanguard of the convoy. For Blaiklock, Stephenson and their faithful teams of dogs, the excitement finished at the South Pole.

Ice – High and Low by Hal Lister, published privately in 2005, devotes one chapter to his North Greenland expedition and another to the TAE. He also spent a number of years exploring through the Middle East, visiting countries such as Turkey, present-day Iran and Pakistan. Scandinavia, Greenland and Iceland also featured in his explorations. His version of events constitutes a first-hand recollection of his participation as a member of the crossing party.

He recalls a number of details that bring to life the experience. How to make a loo: choose a suitable place and start a small fire using some old rag soaked in petrol and paraffin wax. Provided the site has been well chosen, i.e. at the end of a tunnel, then the resultant water vapour will solidify as ice on the roof of the tunnel providing extra strength to the ceiling. Once a suitable depth had been achieved then a convenient couple of pieces of wood surmounted by a toilet seat can be cemented into the top of the pit wall using ice and hey presto, one latrine.

During a short stay back at Shackleton he was rostered for cooking duty. As the men started to eat one of them passed comment about the toughness of the meat and how to improve it by beating it before cooking, evidently the potatoes were not up to this man's standards either and they also came in for some criticism with some supplementary advice on how these should have been cooked. It turned out that the complainant was the best cook at the base and he expected all the others to attain his standard. The advice was given in a way that offence could not be taken.

One of the American's other IGY bases, Ellsworth, was situated only about 40 miles from Shackleton. It was here that they were carrying out scientific work connected to their own IGY programme. Lister recalls that their leader, Captain Finn Ronne, had been flown into Shackleton with several of their scientists who were working on various projects. They had come over for an exchange of information with their TAE counterparts. During a break for some light refreshments the Americans were sitting down at the dining table but the minute Captain Ronne sat down with them Hal Lister could hardly believe his eyes when all the other Americans moved to another table.

It transpired that despite his rank and previous polar experience, having led his own expedition down to the Antarctic a few years before, he was reviled by the scientists in his party. They felt he did not respect their roles at the base, expecting them to do mess duty and other menial jobs when he had command of about 40 enlisted naval personnel who were there to carry out the routine work of keeping the base organised. Ronne managed to antagonise his scientific staff with petty restrictions on their free time such as censoring their messages home or denying them various privileges such as watching the weekly film shows. This was an unknown fact at Shackleton and only really came to light after the expedition was completed and various members of the American party published books about their time spent at Ellsworth.

Hal Lister was given command of South Ice despite his protest that Ken Blaiklock, having run the base camp at Shackleton for the first season of the advance party, should take command. Lister always felt that there should have been four men stationed at South Ice but Bunny turned down both of his requests. He was tasked with the study of snow accumulation and he carried out numerous experiments at South Ice to do with snowfall and the effects of the subsequent drifting that occurred during the winter months.

A book published in 2012 is highly recommended. It is very well researched, as a look at the chapter notes and the bibliography attests. The black and white photos and the maps illustrate the expedition and its outcome in a concise manner. Stephen Haddelsey's *Shackleton's Dream* has been assembled with constant references made to diaries and letters that have been made available to the author by surviving members, of whom there are only a few, and a painstaking search that has revealed documentation held in private hands.

The reader is led through the years of planning that were required to put a viable option on the table and through to its conclusion. This was inevitably followed by sourcing the finance and garnering support from around the Commonwealth to put the expedition on a firm financial footing. Once the alliance was in place recruiting of key personnel could take place and then the process of accumulating all the material resources that would be required to carry out the project.

Stephen Haddelsey looks carefully at the progress of the *Theron* and singles out the smaller episodes of the journey to liven up the narrative by recalling instances from diaries that are not to be found in other accounts. Once the haphazard voyage was back on track after the debacle of the Weddel Sea, space is given over to the sequence of events following the unloading of *Theron* and her rapid departure leaving eight men wondering what had hit them. Two comments at the end of the chapter dealing with the *Theron* sailing for home are not found in any other literature, the first being from the BP cameraman Derek Williams: 'In my opinion the Advance party would have a shockingly bloody winter.' Dr Fuchs also commented in his diary (quoted here but not in his book): 'I'm afraid they have an enormous task ahead of them.'

The drama that unfolded when dealing with the first winter

that the eight men of the advance party spent alone was never published in book form until Anthea Arnold produced her volume based on Rainer Goldsmith's diaries. Stephen Haddelsey has sought out and found other sources of information by getting access to or interviewing some of the other seven members. Once the second year arrived and the crossing group was assembled Haddelsey remains diligent in continuing to glean material from many untapped reservoirs of information to build up a picture of achievement, disappointment, perseverance and attainment.

Climbing the Pole is a short volume written by John Thomson and published in 2010. A New Zealander by birth and a newspaper journalist most of his life, this is his fourth book, and all are related to polar exploration. He researched this latest book using the resources of the famous Alexander Turnbull Library in Wellington. The part played by New Zealand in the project of course features prominently in the narrative. The chapter about the voyage south in the *Theron* spotlights the working relationship between Bunny Fuchs and Ed Hillary. The entrapment of the ship in the ice of the Weddell Sea for over four weeks and the consequent rush to get the Advance party established at the base camp and the chaos that ensued made an indelible impression on Hillary and probably clouded his impressions of Bunny for the remainder of the expedition. John Thompson notes several instances where he finds Bunny short on detail in *The Crossing of Antarctica* and one of these is the flight by John Claydon using the Auster aircraft to try and find a way through the ice floes to help the *Theron* get free and resume a southerly course. This flight virtually saved the the expedition and was described by Bunny in his book, but it would be difficult to say that his narrative actually referred to the pilot as having achieved anything unusual. Ed Hillary states that on John Claydon's return aboard the *Theron* he congratulated him on a 'masterful bit of aerial reconnaissance'.

Thompson's book sums up various stages of the expedition but nearly always from Hillary's point of view or at any rate the New Zealand perspective and considering that in his introduction Thompson states that Hillary did not respond to any of his requests for information, it is telling that Hillary still comes out as a hero!

Appendix III
An Appeal

In the mid-1950s when the TAE took place I was about to leave school and venture into the world of engineering. During my first few years at work I attended Guildford Technical College. In my fourth year I responded to a letter inviting engineering students to apply for a place with a group of Geology undergraduates from Cambridge University who were going to Spitsbergen to carry out field studies for their degree courses.

The trip was to last for about eight weeks and I was one of the lucky four from our college to be picked. We sailed from Newcastle to Bergen and then transferred to a coastal steamer that took us all the way north to Tromsø. From there we transferred again to a supply ship on one of the first visits of the season to Longyearbyen in Spitsbergen. There were 20 or so undergraduates and we four from the college. We were split up into groups of five or six and sent out in small boats equipped with outboard motors, dispersing to various locations across a large area of the main island. (The Svalbard archipelago consists of many islands and Spitsbergen is the largest.)

Our group spent two days travelling up Isfjord camping along the way until we reached a suitable place to start our series of field trips. After two weeks we moved on and crossed the fjord using our boats and set off up a nearby glacier pulling a sledge with all our food and equipment for the next three weeks.

Camping for the night on the side of the glacier, on the following day we split up into two groups and headed up into the adjacent mountains to start the geology fieldwork and mapping we had come to do. My two companions were David Mercer and Stephen Prower. As there was continuous daylight there was plenty of time to complete a round of angles from several stations and collect some rock samples before setting off on a leisurely tramp back to our camp. The scree slopes we encountered on the way up always made for a hard climb and for me a very tiring one as I carried the Theodolite and its tripod. To make light work of the descent we picked out a suitable gulley filled with snow and glissaded downwards. This was to be my undoing. I slipped into some loose, deep snow and before I could climb out found myself sliding down on my back, head first. I cascaded down several hundred feet to the bottom, injuring myself badly. I broke my left thigh and ankle and colliding with a rock smashed my left cheek bone. This impact knocked me out for some time. When I came round it was to find Stephen sitting on me so that I did not move because he was afraid I might have a spinal injury.

David had already gone for help. He rendezvoused with the other trio and then set off on his own to get assistance. Of course there were no GPS or mobile phones in those days and we did not have radio. David was one of fittest members of our party and what a good job that was, as he had many miles to travel across rough ground to reach a Norwegian encampment set up a few hundred yards from our previous camp. David knew that they had a helicopter for their survey work. It was this lucky chance that enabled my rescue.

The helicopter flew back to Longyearbyen where the Norwegians had a small hospital that served the needs of their coal mine. I have no recollection of time but the whole rescue must have taken at least two days before I was delivered into the hospital's care. I have abbreviated my story as it obviously has little relevance to this book – but it does form part of the jigsaw that saw me embark on the writing of it.

As I researched the story of the TAE I realised that any illustrations I might like to use would be copyright. One of the foremost photographers on the expedition was George Lowe. He was a great friend of Sir Edmund Hillary and they had also been together on the Everest Expedition. Sadly George Lowe passed away several years ago but I managed to get in touch with his widow Mary and we corresponded with a view to getting permission to use some of the expedition photos. Finally, we met up at her house where she very kindly showed me some cine film that her husband had made of the TAE. During the conversation we got round to talking about her husband's part in the Everest Expedition and how he and Hillary had set up a fund to support the Nepalese Sherpas and their families. Mary Lowe has been the secretary of the UK side of that fund for many years. The proceeds of the fund go towards all sorts of practical ways to help these very poor people. Here is Mary's description of the the Himalayan Trust UK that she has very kindly written for inclusion here:

In October 1960, at a makeshift camp whilst crossing the 5,800m Tashi Laptsa pass with climbers and Sherpas, Sir Edmund Hillary conceived the idea of schools and a hospital to help the local people. Crowded under tarpaulins, talk turned to the Sherpas and their future. Sir Edmund asked his Sirdar "If there was one thing, Urkien, we could do for your village, what would it be? Sir Ed had thought the answer might be a small hospital as there was neither medical help nor schooling at this time. Urkien's answer was, 'We would like a school for our children. We have eyes but we cannot see, we have ears but we cannot hear'. What Urkien meant was that they knew there was a big world out there. Now that Everest had been climbed foreigners would want to come to their beautiful area to climb and to trek and they needed education to make sense of it all.

The Himalayan Trust NZ was formed and before long Sir Edmund's friends had set up supporting organisations in the USA, Canada, UK, Australia, Germany and France. The Himalayan Trust UK still supports work in the Everest region but also works in 30 schools in Taplejung District in the east near Kangchenjunga, the 3rd highest mountain but largely off the tourist trekking areas. A focus has now begun on helping three struggling village health clinics and donations are urgently needed. Following the earthquake devastation in 2015 the Trusts in NZ/Australia/UK have a combined programme to 'Build Back Better', so that hundreds of students can resume their education.

Working with a team of Nepalese Teacher Trainers, the HTUK supports annual training courses involving teachers, improvement of schools and scholarships at 16+ for the highest achievers with a developing programme of medical facilities in remote areas. Help to local people has continued every year since Sir Edmund's work began in 1961. All projects are approved by the government and much work is carried out by local labour, which helps the village economies, plus many foreign volunteers. Apart from education and health, one of the most successful projects has been the work based at three forest nurseries and the planting of over 2 million indigenous trees.

All donations should be sent to Treasurer, HTUK at 54 Winchester Road, Chandlers Ford, Hants, SO53 2GN or by credit card at himalayantrust.co.uk or just giving/himalayantrust/donate. UK taxpayers can indicate if Gift Aid is to apply.

Looking back on my experience in Spitsbergen I can see now how important it was for me to have the support of so many people trained to carry out my rescue. My friends on the mountain, the Norwegian helicopter pilot, the doctor and his two nurses at the hospital and all the care and attention I received in Bodø Hospital after I was ferried back to Norway to complete my convalescence.

When I heard about the Trust I determined that I should try and repay my debt to all those who helped me in my hour of need, so at least half of any proceeds that I earn from this book will be donated to the Himalayan Trust, in the knowledge that one day it might help the family of a Sherpa.

Bibliography

Arnold, Anthea. *Eight Men in a Crate* (Norwich: Erskine Press, 2007)

Barber, Noel. *The White Desert* (London: Hodder & Stoughton, 1958)

Behrendt. John, *Innocents on the Ice* (Colorado: Colorado University Press, 1998)

Burke, David. *Moments of Terror* (London: Robert Hale, 1994)

Darlington, J. *My Antarctic Honeymoon* (London: Muller, 1957)

Fiennes, Ranulph. *To the Ends of the Earth* (London: Hodder & Stoughton, 1983)

Fiennes, Ranulph. *Mind Over Matter* (U.K: Sinclair-Stevens, 1993)

Fisher, M, & Fisher, J. *Shackleton* (London: James Barrie, 1957)

Fuchs, Vivian. *Antarctic Adventure* (London: Cassell & Co., 1959)

Fuchs, Vivian. *Of Ice and Men* (Shropshire: Anthony Nelson, 1995)

Fuchs, Vivian. *A Time to Speak* (Shropshire: Anthony Nelson, 1990)

Fuchs, V. & Hilary, E. *The Crossing of Antarctica* (London: Cassell & Co., 1958)

Giaver, John. *The White Desert* (London: Chatto & Windus, 1954)

Griffiths, Tom. *Slicing the Silence* (Cambridge, Mass,: Harvard University Press, 2007)

Haddesley, Stephen. *Shackleton's Dream* (Stroud: The History Press, 2012)

Helm A. S. & Miller J. *Antarctica* (Wellington NZ: R. E. Owen, 1964)

Hillary, Edmund. *No Latitude for Error* (London: Hodder & Stoughton, 1961)

Lansing, Alfred. *Endurance* (New York: McGraw-Hill, 1959)

Lister, Hal. *Ice – High & Low* (Self published: 2005)

Lowe, George. *Because It Is There* (London: Cassell & Co, 1959)

McElrea, R. & Harrowfield, D. *Polar Castaways* (Canterbury, NZ: Canterbury University Press, 2004)

McKenzie, Douglas. *Opposite Poles* (London: Robert Hale, 1963)

Messner, Rheinhold. *Crossing Antarctica* (Marlborough: Crowood Press, 1991)

Ronne, Finn. *Antarctic Conquest* (New York: Putnams, 1949)

Shackleton, Ernest. *South* (London: Heinemann, 1919)

Simpson, C. J. W. *North Ice* (London: Hodder & Stoughton, 1957)

Steger, Will. *Crossing Antarctica* (New York: Alfred Knopf, 1992)

Stephenson, Jon. *Crevasse Roulette* (Australia: Rosenberg Publishing, 2009)

Stroud, Michael. *Shadows on a Waste Land* (London: Jonathan Cape, 1993)

Walton, Kevin. *Two Years in Antarctica* (London: Lutterworth Press, 1955)

Illustration Credits

Index